W9-AXF-513

WITHDRAWN
No longer the property of the
Boston Public Library.
Sale of this material benefited the Library

SPEED KINGS

SPEED KINGS

THE 1932 WINTER OLYMPICS
AND THE FASTEST MEN IN THE WORLD

ANDY BULL

AVERY

AN IMPRINT OF PENGUIN RANDOM HOUSE

NEW YORK

An imprint of Penguin Random House LLC
375 Hudson Street
New York, New York 10014

Copyright © 2015 by Andy Bull
Penguin supports copyright. Copyright fuels creativity, encourages diverse voices, promotes free speech, and creates a vibrant culture. Thank you for buying an authorized edition of this book and for complying with copyright laws by not reproducing, scanning, or distributing any part of it in any form without permission. You are supporting writers and allowing Penguin to continue to publish books for every reader.

Photos on pages 96, 144, and 160 courtesy of the Lake Placid Olympic Museum. The image of the painting on page 242 is courtesy of the artist, Ronald Wong.

Most Avery books are available at special quantity discounts for bulk purchase for sales promotions, premiums, fund-raising, and educational needs. Special books or book excerpts also can be created to fit specific needs. For details, write SpecialMarkets@penguinrandomhouse.com.

Library of Congress Cataloging-in-Publication Data
Bull, Andy.
Speed kings : the 1932 Winter Olympics and the fastest men in the world / Andy Bull.
p.   cm.
ISBN 978-1-59240-909-9
1. Bobsledding—United States—History—20th century.   2. Olympic Winter Games (3rd : 1932 :
Lake Placid, N.Y.)   3. Bobsledders—United States—Biography.   I. Title.
GV856.B85   2015   2015025173
796.9'52—dc23

Printed in the United States of America
1   3   5   7   9   10   8   6   4   2

Book design Elke Sigal

FOR MY MOTHER,
CATHERINE BULL,
1950–2010

CONTENTS

PROLOGUE   IX

PART ONE

CHAPTER 1   THE KID   3
CHAPTER 2   A NEW SPORT   15
CHAPTER 3   THE PLAYBOY   29
CHAPTER 4   A CALL FOR VOLUNTEERS   51
CHAPTER 5   THE MUSICIAN?   63
CHAPTER 6   THE RACE   81

PART TWO

CHAPTER 7   A MAN WITH A MISSION   97
CHAPTER 8   THE BOXER   119
CHAPTER 9   THE NEW US TEAM   145
CHAPTER 10   THE SUICIDE CLUB   161
CHAPTER 11   THE FINAL   173

PART THREE

CHAPTER 12   THE NEXT BIG THING   195
CHAPTER 13   THE WAR BEGINS   225
CHAPTER 14   THE LAST FLIGHT OF BILLY FISKE   243
                 EPILOGUE   265
                 AUTHOR'S NOTE   275
                 ACKNOWLEDGMENTS   281
                 INDEX   283

PROLOGUE

The lunch van arrived at a quarter to one. And about time too. Bill Little-more's stomach was starting to growl. They had been up before dawn again, fitting and rigging the fighters, loading the bullets, checking the repairs, running the engines. That was the job, so there was no sense complaining. Which never stopped them from doing exactly that.

Bill volunteered to run over to the van for his fellow mechanics. He could already see the queue starting to form as he trotted across the grass. He quickened his pace. Started to sweat a little. It was hot now. The early morning haze was long gone. This was the first bit of blue sky they'd had all week. He looked up. The pilots were up there somewhere, but he couldn't see them. They must be out over the Isle of Wight. He said a quick prayer to himself, asking God to send them home safe. He often did that when they were in the air, and he didn't mind admitting it.

He'd already eaten half his bun by the time he got back to the dispersal hut. He had to duck his mouth down to it because his hands were full and he didn't want to spill the tea on his uniform. The lads were all idling around, waiting for news from Control. The squadron had taken off half an hour ago, when the radar stations had picked up a formation coming out of Cherbourg and heading across the Channel. By now they'd either be in the thick of it or already on their way back home.

"Any news?" he asked as he put the three teas down. He already knew the answer. No one was moving, so there was nothing doing.

He passed the buns around, one apiece for each of the two Jocks, Tyrrell and McKinley. They were firm pals, flight mechanics, like Bill, with 43 Squadron, the "Fighting Cocks." And just then, they heard the distant hum of the engines.

"That sounds like them now," said Tyrrell. "That's the Cocks returning."

Bill put his ear to the wind, paused. And he knew, he just knew, that it wasn't them. The pitch was off.

"They're not ours," he said. "They sound like bloody Jerry, don't they?"

The loudspeakers burst into life. "Attention! Attention! Take cover! Take cover!" It wasn't the first time they'd heard that today. But the announcer sounded a little more urgent this time.

Bill heard the words, but somehow they didn't register. They'd done so many drills—he just couldn't believe this was the real thing. Then the air-raid alarms began to wail. He stepped out of the hut and threw his hand up above his brow to block out the sun. And he saw it straightaway. A Stuka. Gull wings, fixed undercarriage, large glass canopy. The silhouette was utterly unmistakable. He watched as the plane turned its nose down toward the earth and swept into a steep dive, down toward No. 1 Hangar. He could hear the howl of the siren from across the field. When the dive reached two thousand feet, a small black orb fell away from the Stuka's belly and carried on down toward the earth while the plane itself pulled up and away back into the sky. And then a pillar of fire and smoke filled the sky, followed, so quick you couldn't tell which had come first, by the thump of the explosion. The bomb fell right by the van, at the exact spot where Bill had been standing a few minutes earlier.

There is no single, definitive account of what happened at RAF Tangmere on August 16, 1940. There are dozens of versions, one for every person who was there. Their memories of the raid don't always add up. Often they contradict each other. Some say they heard the sirens earlier, that the Tannoy warned them sooner, that the first bomb fell in another spot. They are all right. Everyone made sense of the chaos in his own way. This is the story of the raid as told by Bill Littlemore, Leading Aircraftman, 43 Squadron, as he remembered it forty years later.

"From that moment on all hell broke loose, with bombs exploding, the noise of the Stukas strafing us as they dived and pulled skywards, and our ground defenses putting up a barrage of metal which must have made the Hun feel that he was not welcome," Bill wrote. "For many of us at Tangmere that day it was our first baptism of fire, something I shall always remember as a very unpleasant experience when one considers we had no arms to hit back with except the tools in our tool boxes. And I can assure you these felt very inadequate when set against the bombs and cannon fire that was to be aimed at us by the Stuka 87s when they suddenly pounced on the airfield.

"For those of us on the flights, and I am sure I express their feelings as well as mine, we were shaken to say the least, and as per our orders for such a situation the only sensible thing to do was seek the protection of our air raid shelter which lay just to the rear of 'B' Flight dispersal hut. All sprint records were I am sure broken in our haste to reach the safety of the shelter and it is said that fear lends wings to those who need them. I grew a pair very quickly."

Bill wasn't thinking anymore. It was blind panic. He sprinted toward the bomb shelter, and safety. He was almost there when, through the machine-gun fire and the bomb blasts and the sirens and the engines, he heard, loud and clear, what he described as the "stentorian shout" of his boss, Flight Sergeant Savage.

"Stand by!" Savage barked. "Our aircraft are approaching!"

Bill stopped running. All those hours of drills, of unthinking obedience to orders, had their effect. Another instinct kicked in, one even keener than self-preservation: duty. The shout, Bill wrote, "had the immediate effect of doing away with all the panic and bringing us back to awareness that we had a job to do." The Fighting Cocks were returning to base. The planes would need refueling and rearming. It didn't matter that the raid was still going on around them. In fact, it made the work more important than ever, since the pilots might need to get right back up into the air.

"With the disappearance of panic came the opportunity to take stock and look around us," Bill continued. "And it was then I became aware for the first time of burning hangars and the buildings, and a great pall of smoke hanging over the whole scene." For those brief moments, Bill Littlemore stood still, feet rooted to the ground, while the fires raged around him. He was looking upward, scanning the skies for the returning British fighters. He saw four, though at first he couldn't tell whether they were with 43 or one of the other squadrons flying out of Tangmere. "I have etched on my memory the picture of four Hurricanes flying in what could only be described as loose, strung-out formation approaching the aerodrome at about 2,000 feet from the south, and who were to be the first to land on the aerodrome while the three-minute raid was still in progress. Yes three minutes, and yet to most of us who witnessed it, it seemed more like half an hour."

The fighters were in silhouette. "About 8 of us on 'B' Flight were watching the approach of these aircraft when to our horror we observed that one had begun to leave behind it a trail of white smoke." This, Bill knew, was bad news. White smoke could only mean that the engine was leaking ethylene glycol, which burns with an invisible flame. The pilot wouldn't be able to see the fire leaping up through the floor of the cockpit and lapping around his legs. And the smoke was even more dangerous. In those quantities glycol fumes cause, first, involuntary rapid eye movements, then short losses of consciousness. For a pilot, that was fatal. "The white smoke was the forerunner of things to come. For the pilot must very soon make a decision to bail out, otherwise he would be overcome by fumes leaking back into the cockpit, and oblivion would take over."

Bill was transfixed. He started to scream: "Get out! Get out for Christ's sake!"

The Hurricane continued its approach. The white smoke turned black. Flames started to burst up from the engine. It was so close now, right over the hedgerows at the distant side of the field. It was too late to jump. Perhaps the pilot had already lost consciousness. He was done for. Suddenly, the plane broke into a steep dive. The undercarriage was up. It was going to crash. "I felt that this could only be the start of that inevitable plunge toward earth, culminating in that awful crump and plume of smoke that would climb into the sky, marking the spot where yet another of our chaps had plowed into the ground and made his own burial site."

And then, "at the moment when it seemed that this could be the only outcome," the plane pulled up, and the pilot, "struggling to maintain control, leveled out only feet above the ground." The plane landed flat on its belly, bounced up and down, and shot into a skid. A shower of sparks spurted out behind it as it swept across the runway, trailing a wake of great coils of thick black smoke. When it finally came to a standstill, the flames, held in check for so long, burst out into the sky. Two men ran across the turf toward the wreck.

That was the last thing Bill saw. Instinct kicked in again. He came out of the trance, remembered where he was and what he was supposed to be doing. The sky was full of vapor and smoke. Aircraft were coming in from every point of the compass. It was chaos up there. But down below, a kind of calm had fallen. The raid was over. "From that moment my immediate concern had to be looking for my own pilots."

The day passed. The battle passed. The war passed. But that one image of the burning Hurricane making its belly landing always stayed in Bill Littlemore's mind. It froze there, so crystal clear that he could still see, forty years later, the precise position he was standing in, the exact course the plane was flying, and even the specific spot where it finally came to a stop. The one thing he didn't know was who had been flying the plane. Perhaps that was why he never stopped thinking about it. He even commissioned a local artist to paint the scene for him, just as he remembered it.

Some of the veterans preferred not to talk or even think about the war. They shut their memories away and sealed them off. They didn't want to remember. Bill Littlemore wasn't like that. He stayed in touch with his old colleagues, took the newsletters, bought the books, attended the annual meet-ups. And as he read and heard all those other accounts and memories of the raid, he slowly pieced it all together, until he realized, at last, that he had seen the final moments of one of the most remarkable stories of the war.

"It was," Bill wrote, "the last landing of Billy Fiske."

PART ONE

Speed, it seems to me, provides the one genuinely modern pleasure. True, men have always enjoyed speed; but their enjoyment has been limited, until very recent times, by the capacities of the horse, whose maximum velocity is not much more than thirty miles an hour. Now thirty miles an hour on a horse feels very much faster than sixty miles an hour in a train or a hundred in an airplane. The train is too large and steady, the airplane too remote from stationary surroundings, to give the passengers a very intense sensation of speed. The automobile is sufficiently small and sufficiently near the ground to be able to compete, as an intoxicating speed-purveyor, with the galloping horse. The inebriating effects of speed are noticeable, on horseback, at about twenty miles an hour, in a car at about sixty. When the car has passed seventy-two, or thereabouts, one begins to feel an unprecedented sensation—a sensation which no man in the days of horses ever felt. It grows intenser with every increase of velocity. I myself have never traveled at much more than eighty miles an hour in a car; but those who have drunk a stronger brewage of this strange intoxicant tell me that new marvels await any one who has the opportunity of passing the hundred mark.

> —from "Wanted, a New Pleasure," in
> *Music at Night and Other Essays*, by Aldous Huxley,
> written on the French Riviera in 1931

Billy Fiske, Lake Placid, 1932.

CHAPTER 1

THE KID

September 1930. Afternoon on the Riviera. In Cannes, outside the Carlton Hotel, a small crowd of people have gathered on La Croisette. They're standing around a brand-new, racing green Bentley "Blower," exceptionally pretty and extraordinarily fast. Bentley had made only fifty or so of the cars, and this one was especially rare. It was a road model built to racing specifications. The hood was a little longer, the tank a little larger, the dash a little sleeker than was standard. It was fourteen feet long and weighed almost a ton and a half. A good chunk of that came from the silver supercharger mounted at the front, which gave the car its unusual name. The car was so big that the boy in the driver's seat seemed a little lost inside it. The steering wheel was too broad for his chest and too thick for his fingers to wrap around. He was nineteen and he looked it. His mouth was spread out in a broad grin, which puckered up little dimples in his smooth cheeks. He wore his sandy hair swept back beneath a cap, peak turned up so that the wind wouldn't pluck it off his head.

He tugged on the magneto switches, sent a pulse of current into the engine, slipped his hand across the dash to flick the Bakelite switch that controlled the fuel pump, and then pressed the starter button. The crowd stepped back as the engine exploded into life, and the long, square panels of the hood rattled underneath the restraining straps. Dust rushed up off the road and coated their clothes. They had to shout to be heard above the roar.

"Good luck, Billy!"

He watched the dial. He had to wait ten seconds while the oil pressure rose. Oh, and one more thing. He reached across to the little clock on the far side of the dash. There was a stopwatch set into it, three little dials inside a small square window. He'd paid an extra shilling to have it installed. He twisted the cog that flipped the counters back to zero. Immediately, the cylinders began to roll back around again, counting upward. He took a last glance at the St. Christopher's medal strapped to the dash. Then he put his foot down and slipped the car into gear. He had forty miles to travel on a winding road, and sixty minutes to do it. Make that a second under sixty minutes, since he didn't just want to beat the record, he wanted to be the first man to break the hour barrier.

The French authorities had recently scrapped their speed limit, which had been set at just over 12 miles per hour in built-up areas. Billy passed that before he was even a little way down La Croisette, with the sunlight flickering off the silver fittings as the car accelerated out toward the coast road. The new regulations insisted only that vehicles must be driven at "moderate speed." This, Billy felt, was a subjective sort of stipulation, one that entirely depended on what you understood "moderate" to mean. His conception of moderation was a little different from that of the men who had written the rule. But then they had said, too, that "the driver must remain in total control of the speed at all times." And he always was, even as he shot out of Cannes onto the road to Antibes, where he pushed the car so hard that the needle on the rev counter shot up past the red line and the supercharger kicked in. At around 80 mph, it started firing compressed air into the engine, with a high-pitched whine that cut right across the low growl of the engine, which was why they called it a "blower." The car kicked on again, as though it had been booted up the trunk. Up above 100 mph, and faster still, to 110 mph, 115 mph, where the needle held and started to flicker up and down.

As he came into Antibes, Billy reined the car in again. It had a crash gearbox, a bugger to work. Billy pressed the clutch, came out of gear into neutral, revved the engine till it was in synch with the cogs, and slipped back into a lower gear. A double de-clutch. He did it unthinkingly. His foot danced on the pedals, and his practiced hand worked the stick down by his right side, moving, as his friend Henry Longhurst put it, "as smooth as butter." Of course, Longhurst said, "if you got it wrong, you could break your wrist, let alone your gearbox." But Billy was in rhythm with the car. He worked it as a good drummer does his instrument, hands, feet, and thoughts all moving together in time.

Skirting Nice, Billy had to dodge between the traffic, which was moving so slowly in comparison with his car that it may as well have been standing still. There was no point stopping for it at this speed. Billy's maxim was "Don't brake, avoid." Which he did. In, out, and around, his mind working overtime to find the ideal line, making a series of quick calculations, like a man running downhill over rough terrain—his thoughts moving as fast as his feet as he figures out a safe path across the rocks. The car shot on along the Basse Corniche, the sea on one side, the cliffs on the other.

The Bentley's beam axle made it a bumpy ride, and with the big silver supercharger weighing down the front, Billy's model was particularly prone to understeer. On the turns, it spat up gravel as it pulled out wide, away from the road. On the tight horseshoe at Villefranche, he pushed the throttle down farther, forcing more torque into the back wheels, making the cross-ply tires bite in an attempt to balance out the drift. It was a double-or-quits move. And it worked. A bit more throttle. A bit more, and then the back of the car tucked in and the whole thing snapped back into line as they entered the straight road.

He was into the last stretch, across the border into Monaco, and really screaming. The stopwatch ticked onward, fifty-two minutes, fifty-three minutes, up toward the hour mark. He sped on, past Beaulieu and Cap Ferrat, Eze, Cap-d'Ail, through the outskirts of Monte Carlo, that "sunny place for shady people," as Somerset Maugham called it. Past the port and on to Avenue d'Ostende. And there it was, the Hotel de Paris. Billy eased the car back down, changing down the gears as the pace slackened off. He pulled to a stop, for the first time since setting off, just outside the front doors of the hotel. He glanced down at the dash, punched the button on the stopwatch. Fifty-eight minutes. Made it. And with almost two minutes to spare.

Everyone who knew Billy Fiske, however well, agreed on one thing: he loved speed; seemed, even, to live for it. In the 1980s, when the actor Douglas Fairbanks Jr. was asked what he remembered about his friendship with Billy, the first thing that popped into his mind was that "he was famous for setting the speed record between London and Cambridge." Henry Longhurst, Billy's friend from his days at Cambridge University, said that Billy had "an uncanny eye for speed." Like all Billy's friends, Longhurst had a fund of stories about his journeys in the passenger seat of that big green Bentley. Longhurst was a golfer, a good one, and he and Billy used to make the run from Cambridge to the Royal Worlington Course at Mildenhall, a twenty-one-mile stretch. "Sometimes the time would be around 19 minutes," Longhurst wrote in his memoirs. "And without a tremor of apprehension to public or passenger. Day after day, sitting on Fiske's left, I would notice my own front wheel passing within an inch or so of its track the day before. The supercharger came in with a shrill whine at about 80, generally at the beginning of the long straight where the Cambridge road goes eventually uphill through the beechwood to join the London road short of the racecourse at Newmarket. Soon the needle would creep up into the red, staying for a while between 110 and 120 mph, till at precisely the same spot just short of the slope, Fiske would change down to third at exactly 86, and every time the gear would go through like butter."

The brothers Bobby and Charles Sweeny rode shotgun with Billy when he was making all those runs around the south of France, breaking records that weren't set down in books but were swapped back and forth between members of the set—the fifty-eight-minute run from Cannes to Monte Carlo, the seventeen-minute run from Nice to Cannes. "As far as I know," Charles Sweeny said much later, "that second record still stands." There were no prizes to be won for these races, no cups or trophies, only bragging rights. Billy drove quick for the hell of it. Speed was his drug.

Billy was too fast too young to have spent much time learning to drive that quick. His was a natural talent. He was blessed with an intuitive understanding of how to handle vehicles at speed. It didn't matter whether he was in a car, a motorboat, a bobsled, or an airplane. He just relished racing, and always had, right from the first time he got behind a wheel. When he was fifteen, he pinched his father's red Bugatti and took his sister, Peggy, out to race in a hill climb. It was a time trial, up a short, steep slope. He won, with plenty of time to spare. Peggy remembered how he had turned to her and said, "Don't you dare tell Father about this." Billy's dad always hated the idea of his young son competing in track races. He thought they were just too dangerous. When he was still eighteen, Billy was asked to race a Stutz Bearcat in the Le Mans 24-Hour endurance race. But as Bobby Sweeny recalled, "his father soon put a stop to that." Years later, the facts were forgotten, and the story of his race at Le Mans became one of many myths about him, passed on from one newspaper or magazine article to another, mentioned time and again in the various TV documentaries made about his life. He was someone people loved to tell stories about, whether they were true or not.

Racing wasn't in Billy's blood, but he inherited plenty of other things from his father. His name, for one. In full, it was William Meade Lindsley Fiske III, following on from his father, W.M.L. Fiske II, and his grandfather, W.M.L.

Fiske I. But everyone called him Billy, and those who knew him best of all often stuck at plain Bill. The Fiskes were an old American family. They could trace the tree right back to Phineas Fiske, who came over to the United States from England in 1636, just sixteen years after the arrival of the *Mayflower*, and settled in Wenham, Massachusetts. The "William Meade Lindsley" part was picked out by Billy's great-grandfather, who gave the name to his son as a tribute to a close friend.

Billy's father was a banker. He studied at the Polytechnic Institute of Brooklyn and then at Columbia. After he graduated in 1900, he took a trip around Europe for the kind of education you can't get in a lecture hall. While he was there, he fell in love with France and developed a fluency in the language that would serve him well later in life. When Fiske Sr. returned to the United States, he started work at the small Wall Street firm Vermilye & Co., which sent him out to its new branch in Chicago. "By then the passport to Wall Street's investment banking elite was attendance at fashionable preparatory schools and Ivy League colleges," notes the authorized history of the firm. "More often than not individuals with the proper social cachet would call upon a fellow fraternity member who through familial connections had obtained a post and, drawing on past favors and old friendships, have the door opened for him." A couple of Fiske's superiors at Vermilye had attended the Polytechnic Institute of Brooklyn, including William Read, the top earner in the firm.

It was in Chicago that Fiske met and married Beulah Bexford. That was in 1906. They took a house in Winnetka, up on the North Shore. It was a good time. Twelve months earlier there had been a schism in the ranks of Vermilye. Sensing that there would be more opportunities in the new firm, Fiske left to work for the new breakaway company run by Read. He was right. In 1905, Read made Fiske the bank's head of operations in Chicago. Business was good. They had a small staff, but that didn't stop them from expanding into Canada, Britain, and South America. And in 1909, Read made Fiske a full partner in the firm. By then he was a father. His daughter, named Beulah, just like her mother, but known to all as Peggy, had been born in 1907. Billy followed four years later, on June 4, 1911.

Two years later, another new arrival made an even bigger impression on the Fiske family. In 1913, Read sent a young man down from New York to start work underneath him in the Chicago office. His name was Clarence Lapowski, though the world would come to know him as Clarence Dillon. He would become, in short time, one of the most influential men on Wall Street.

Lapowski was the son of a Polish Jew, a dry goods merchant. He was educated at Worcester Academy in Massachusetts and then Harvard, though he failed the Latin portion of his entrance exam three times over. While there, he lost the Lapowski and adopted his mother's maiden name of Dillon. Despite the switch, his friends said that Dillon never tried to deny his Jewish heritage. Certainly, enough people knew to ensure that he was blackballed from plenty of members' clubs in New York—which explains why he felt he should hide it in the first place. At Harvard, anyhow, his classmates knew him by the nickname "Baron," given in recognition, he said, of his love of gambling, poker, and horse racing. Much as he enjoyed money, Baron Dillon never planned to work in high finance. The story goes that he bumped into a college friend out on a walk in Manhattan, and the friend asked him, "What are you doing nowadays?" Not much, was Dillon's answer. "You should get into the banking business. Come on over and meet William Read. He is a man worth knowing." So they strolled on over to Read's offices. "I never had less intention of becoming a banker than on that day," Dillon remembered. "But Mr. Read seemed well disposed." Read was no less impressed. He asked Dillon to take a desk in the office and decide for himself whether he wanted to be a banker. Dillon replied that he would have to talk it over with his wife, since she would be reluctant to leave their home in the Midwest. So Read offered to fix him up with a job in Chicago on a starting salary of $250 a month.

In Chicago, working as a bond salesman under Fiske, Dillon made a name for himself when he convinced the millionaire William Horlick, president of the malted milk company, to let the firm handle his investment portfolio. That was just the start of it. Dillon said he found the banking business "more fascinating than a game of no-limit stud poker," and he went on to make a series of remarkable deals, most notably when he set up a chemical firm to produce phenol, needed for the manufacture of TNT—a shrewd move given how great demand would be once war broke out. It made him the best part of his eight-million-dollar fortune. By then Read had summoned him to New York.

By 1916 Dillon had been made a partner at Read & Co., just three years after he started working at the firm. He was thirty-three and already, as the company history puts it, "considered not only the critical banker there but one of the brightest and most promising individuals in financial history." William Read died of pneumonia the very next month, leaving each of the partners—including Fiske—twenty-five thousand dollars, but the company without a head. Dillon, despite being the junior partner, took over from him. He'd always said that he was reluctant to take on the job. But according to the Wall Street gossip of the time, the partners had been discussing the succession when Dillon simply stood up, walked into Read's vacant corner office, and took his seat. Which sounds about right. Certainly when he decided to rename the firm Dillon, Read & Co. in 1920, the first Fiske and the other partners heard of it was when Dillon told them, "Gentlemen, I have bought in 85 percent of the business here. Those who do not like it can withdraw."

Dillon was infamously ruthless, "hard and inhuman" according to his associate Hugh Bullock. "The stories about Dillon being a mean, tight-fisted bastard were true," he said. "I have never met a man that was as tough and hard-boiled." And the economist Eliot Janeway memorably described Dillon as "nothing but a money guy" who "wouldn't have bought God with a whorehouse attached if it wasn't a bargain." Long before Jordan Belfort borrowed the title for his book, or Martin Scorsese used it for his movie, Dillon was known as "the Wolf of Wall Street," a name he was given by his employee James Forrestal. But Dillon was well known, too, for the fierce loyalty he showed to his old friends. He personally bailed out a bunch of his old partners and associates during the Wall Street crash a decade later. And he never forgot the debt of thanks, and friendship, he owed Fiske from their early days in Chicago, when Dillon got his start in the industry as a bond salesman. He liked Fiske—saw in him qualities he admired, even desired. As Dillon's grandson put it, "My grandfather had brains but he always wanted to be socially acceptable . . . It was the one thing he didn't have himself. So I think he was conscious about doing things for himself and for his children and grandchildren to make them socially acceptable." William Meade Lindsley Fiske II, worldly, well-spoken, from old blue-blood stock, could teach Dillon a thing or two, even, while working alongside him, lend him a little of his social standing. So long as Dillon was in charge, Fiske had a job for life. And so did his family. Dillon employed Fiske's nephew, Dean Mathey, right out of college. There was always a job waiting for Billy, too, whenever he wanted it.

Back in Chicago, Fiske and his family thrived. They had a house on East Chestnut, just a couple of blocks up from the lakefront. They lived there with three female staff: a cook, a servant, and a nurse. They had a couple of dogs too: a dachshund they called Riley Grogan and a border terrier, Billy's, who went by the name of Cuddly Demon. In 1919 they traveled up to Canada for a vacation in Banff National Park, a trip Peggy documented assiduously in her scrapbooks. Happy days, these. Billy was eight. It was here, up in the Canadian Rockies, that he got his first taste of life in the mountains, as a small blond boy scurrying around the hiking trails on Big Beehive and around Lake Louise. Their father was a keen horse rider, swimmer, and golfer, and he encouraged a love of the outdoor life in his children. Billy, Peggy remembered, "was always interested in keeping fit." He used to prop his feet up on the top edge of the large freestanding tub in the bathroom and do push-ups. She was a bit of a tomboy herself, who wore her hair cut short, and the two of them would rough-and-tumble together, wrestle.

For much of their childhood, Billy and Peggy were taught by private tutors, which meant that their parents also took on a lot of the responsibility for their education. Their father, in particular, tried to inculcate a strong set of values in his children. He was a Presbyterian, a staunch Republican, and had a furious work ethic, but instead of forcing them to adopt his beliefs wholesale, he urged them to develop inquiring, independent minds. Their father used to instigate debates at the dinner table. He'd ask one child to explain why it had been a good day and get the other to explain why, on the contrary, it had been a bad one. The next night they would swap roles. "Bill got his tremendous curiosity and drive from his father," Peggy said. "They both wanted to learn about everything."

The twist of fate that would shape Billy's life wasn't brought about by his father, however, but by the work of his father's boss, Dillon. At the very same time the Fiskes were up in Banff, Dillon's work with the War Industries Board had taken him to France for the signing of the Treaty of Versailles. While there, he fixed on the idea of expanding his bank's business into continental Europe. He settled on Germany. It was a bold decision, and one that would ultimately have horrendous consequences for both Dillon's firm and the Fiske family. But in 1921, all Dillon saw was opportunity.

The Germans made a first war reparations payment of $250 million in 1921 but were unable to make the second, of another $250 million, let alone the $500 million that was due in 1922. The economy collapsed, the currency with it, and so many new notes were printed that the German mark was soon worth less than the paper it was made of. By November 1923 you could get five million marks to the dollar. Brigadier Charles Dawes, director of the US Bureau of the Budget, concocted a repayment plan under which Germany would start paying annual reparations of $250 million, rising to $625 million within four years. The country would also get a new currency, the reichsmark, and a new German central bank, which would have a fifty-year monopoly on the issuance of paper money. Crucially, there would also be a foreign loan of $200 million to the German government. This was where the American banks, Dillon Read among them, stepped in. The loan was floated in Britain and the United States by a syndicate led by US banks J. P. Morgan and Dillon, Read & Co. For Dillon himself, this was just the opportunity he had been looking for. The loan was a preliminary step that would enable him to begin serious business in the German market. "Our opportunity lies in industrial Europe," he told the *New York Times*. "The railroad and public utility financing that is to be done in Europe is tremendous . . . and lucrative."

Dillon, then, needed a man to head up his new European operation, which was to be based in Paris. He had hired Colonel James A. Logan, who had been involved with the Reparations Committee, because he felt Logan had excellent connections in France and Britain. But Logan was, in the words of Dillon's biographer, "aggressive, and crude, and lacked the diplomacy needed." Dillon required someone with finesse who was familiar with French culture and had a good grasp of the language. He chose William Meade Lindsley Fiske II. So, in 1924, the Fiske family moved to France. They sailed on the SS *Belgenland* in April, stayed for a time at the Hyde Park Hotel in London, then went on to Paris. They bought a house on the Avenue Bugeaud, and a little later a château in the south, just outside Biarritz.

Billy's father wasn't exactly engaged in banking work as we understand it today. Dillon, Read & Co. were busy funding loans to Belgium, Italy, and Poland as well as to Germany, and much of his time was spent schmoozing with European aristocrats and diplomats. In the summer of 1924 he traveled with Dillon to Warsaw to negotiate with the Polish government over a $35 million loan. They were given use of their own personal train to travel to Lancut, in Galicia, where a man named Prince Alfred Potocki met them. Potocki walked them down a red carpet, then drove them to his castle "through streets lined with peasants, heads bowed in supplication." Potocki was still living in nineteenth-century splendor. His wife and daughters apparently sent their lingerie to Paris by coach so that they wouldn't have to suffer the indignity of knowing the local laundresses had touched their underwear.

Years later, the son of one of Fiske's colleagues, Ferdinand Eberstadt, recalled his father's stories about the visits to Potocki's castle: "When they arrived a sumptuous ball was under way with scores of beautiful women, lavishly dressed, footmen carrying champagne and great heaps of caviar and other exotic food on silver trays, all accompanied by music from wandering minstrel groups and string orchestras playing waltzes. Everyone was dancing, eating and drinking and having a fine old time which continued to dawn . . . The following day the men mounted their horses and went off to hunt wild boar for exercise and to rid themselves of their hangovers from the night before. The following evening another gala took place; revelry appeared to be the normal state of life in the castle—contrasting sharply with the austere peasant surroundings outside the castle grounds. The Polish cavaliers rode out early each morning, eager for sport, in spite of night after night of drinking and wenching."

This, then, was the kind of company the Fiskes were keeping. Even Dillon seemed a little overwhelmed by their high living. Billy's father was entirely at ease in their company. The Polish government rewarded him with a medal, the Commander's Cross of the Order of Polonia Restituta, "for furthering good relations between Poland and the United States." He was in his element.

While his father was swanning about Europe, and his mother was making a home in Paris, Billy was packed off to boarding school in England. He was thirteen when he arrived in the village of Sutton Courtenay, just outside Oxford, to study at what he called "a somewhat unorthodox school." The boys were allowed to keep pets, and he got himself a little Welsh terrier. Billy wasn't there long, but these teenage years shaped him. At Sutton Courtenay, he began to grow into a man with the kind of independent mind that his father had always encouraged him to have. Billy came to settle down there, saying, "Altogether my roots are almost stronger here than any place I know." He thought of it as home, perhaps because it was during the school holidays that he first started to travel on his own.

When Billy turned fifteen, his father arranged for him to go to South America to spend a summer working on a sheep farm in the countryside outside Buenos Aires. He sailed in May, with a chaperone, and spent the summer with family friends his father had made through his work in the region with Dillon, Read & Co. "My first real trip by myself was when I went to South America," Billy later said. "And I have commuted between continents ever since." He did it, he explained, "just to see what it was like." He didn't seem to learn much about sheep farming, but he did feel the first stirrings of the wanderlust that would later lead him to travel around the world. He came back from Argentina through Rio, a city that made such an impression on him that he was idolizing it a decade later. When he first saw Sydney, he wrote that the harbor there "vies with Rio de Janeiro for the honor of being the most beautiful in the world. Any Australian will tell you Sydney is by far the winner whether he has seen Rio or not. But in spite of this I think Rio comes in a fairly easy first. Sydney Harbor seems to have more little 'high-ways' and 'by-ways' than Rio, but it has not got the marvelous sugar-loaf mountain or the background of high mountains. Its promontories and islands seem too well-covered by cheap houses, and somehow flat and squalid by comparison. After all I had heard about the beauties of Sydney Harbor I was just a bit disappointed. But perhaps I had been spoiled by seeing Rio first."

Billy was blessed with the means to indulge his appetite for adventure and to satisfy his inquiring mind. Later, he would write in his journal a couple of lines that served as a personal creed: "The two great characteristics to develop in any child are *courage* and *justice*. Broadly speaking, with these well-developed a person can face the world and be successful." He came, over time, to be irritated by his father's conservative streak and the way he put his banking work before his family, but he would never forget the pains his father had taken to teach him those very qualities, courage and justice. And whatever measures of them he possessed, he owed to his father. And, while he never would have said it about himself, everyone who knew him agreed that Billy had plenty of both. Years later, when Billy's name was on the front pages of the papers and the tongues of American high society, "a young San Francisco society matron," who had known him when she was a little girl in the south of France, told one reporter that "when he was 14 years old, Billy saved a man's life at Biarritz—a drowning swimmer. The surf was too rough for the rescue boats, but not for Billy. He went out and got him." There's no way of knowing now whether her scanty story, like that of Billy racing in the Le Mans 24, is one of the many myths that grew up around him as the years went by. Whether the details are correct or not, the spirit of it is in keeping with what we know. Billy, just back from his travels in South America, was a brave young man in a hurry to "face the world." And if he didn't have any idea where he was heading in the long run, he at least knew where he was going to make his first stop: Switzerland, and St. Moritz.

Billy Fiske and crew on the run, St. Moritz, 1928.

CHAPTER 2

A NEW SPORT

To understand why St. Moritz came to hold such a fix on Billy Fiske's mind, we need to turn back the best part of a century. The town, high in the Engadine valley, was once a sleepy sort of place. Tourists came for its mineral springs, which had been famous since the early sixteenth century, when Pope Leo X promised to grant absolution to anyone who took the waters. As late as the 1850s there were only two hundred year-round residents, their ranks swollen each summer by the tourists who came to soak their bones in the waters. The locals were perplexed that so few of their visitors stayed on once the summer was gone, since the sunshine carried on right through the winter, and were vexed by the fact that their trade fluctuated so wildly from one season to the next.

Johannes Badrutt, the son of a local craftsman, bought a hotel in St. Moritz, the Pension Faller, in 1856. And like everyone else in the town, he soon found himself despairing about the seasonal slump in business. So, in the summer of 1864, he decided to make a wager with four of his British guests. They were deeply skeptical about the idea that the town would be a pleasant place to stay in the winter. He told them that if they returned to St. Moritz later that year and found that the weather wasn't better than what they got in London—a low bar, that—then he would pay all the expenses for their trip. They took him up on it, and they arrived by horse-drawn sleigh that December "perspiring and nearly blinded by the sun." Badrutt met them on the terrace of his hotel, in his shirtsleeves. He was so delighted to have won his bet that he paid their expenses anyway.

Badrutt's gamble worked. Word spread, and by the 1870s winter tourism was beginning to grow in St. Moritz. Badrutt, certainly, was doing well enough to find several thousand Swiss francs to spend on a rudimentary electric lighting system that he spotted at the Paris World's Fair in 1878. By that Christmas, the grand dining room of his hotel was illuminated by electric lights, the first of their kind in Switzerland. They burned for only ninety minutes, and once they were on, you couldn't turn them off again, but Badrutt wagered that the novelty and glamor of it would bring in extra customers. And he was right. The trouble was that once his guests had admired the lights, the lavish views, and had a long dinner or two, there wasn't much else for them to do. A lot of his guests were invalids who came because they had been told the dry mountain air would be good for their tuberculosis. But, as one observer put it at the time, "the real disease that the people suffered from in St. Moritz was boredom."

With so much time on their hands, and so little to do, Badrutt's British guests took to racing each other on little toboggans around the winding streets of the town. This was the start of the famous Cresta Run, a course that involved a head-first trip downhill on a one-man sled, known today as a skeleton. The Cresta would become the most iconic winter sports venue in the world, but in its early years it infuriated the locals, who took to calling the riders the "English devils"— or at least so the Brits liked to think. It seems just as likely that they were saying "to hell with the English" and something got lost in the translation. The British riders set about organizing this new sport. They developed sleds with metal runners to increase the speed, and primitive steering mechanisms so they could exert at least a measure of control. Still, though, there were so many complaints from the imperiled locals that Badrutt felt compelled to have his staff carve out a couple of toboggan tracks down the slope that ran from the front of the Kulm Hotel, just to keep his guests off the roads. And it was there, in December 1888, that an Englishman named Wilson Smith found the best cure yet for the St. Moritz ennui. Smith had the lunatic idea of lashing together two of the toboggans and a plank of wood. He invited three of his friends to hop on with him, and they all took a run down the mountain together. Just like that, he invented the sport of bobsledding. The name comes from the way the riders had to rock back and forth to build up their momentum, just as a child rocks to gain height on a swing. Once going, the new bobsleds were by far the fastest thing on the slopes.

Or so the story goes. Like many origin myths, this one is likely to have gained a little and lost a lot in the telling. The sleds certainly existed before Wilson Smith came along. In Canada and New England, bobsledding dates back to at least the middle of the nineteenth century. In 1887 the *New York Times* reported that the playwright Denman Thompson included a bobsledding scene in a production of his play *The Old Homestead*. When the producer suggested they use a toboggan instead, Thompson told him, "New Englanders don't use toboggans, they use bobsleds." So there was already a tradition of bobsledding in parts of North America. Earlier in that same decade, the sport had started to spread across to Europe. In February 1881, the British weekly newspaper the *Graphic* had run a story about "a new and most enjoyable pastime, namely, riding on a bob-sleigh" being practiced at Harrow School. "The fun consists in seven or eight people going downhill on a sleigh at a rate of 35 to 40 miles per hour." The bob itself was made of "two cutters, or small sleighs, and between these a plank is laid about nine feet long, and fastened to the hind cutter by two bolts, thus rendering it stationary, and to the front one by one bolt, which enables this one to turn around on a pivot." The pilot steered the sled by holding the front runners and pulling them to the left or right. "Though new to England," the *Graphic* noted, "this 'coasting' is one of the favorite winter amusements in Canada, where it is alike popular with ladies and gentlemen, young and old." This, then, seems to have been exactly the kind of contraption Smith was riding in St. Moritz nearly eight years later. And so the Wilson Smith story can be consigned to the "good if it's true" pile, along with that of Abner Doubleday inventing baseball, and William Webb Ellis creating rugby by picking up the ball during a school soccer match.

It is clear that in the early years there were two separate schools of bobsledding: one in Canada and the United States, where it was seen as a hobby; and another in Switzerland and St. Moritz, where it soon become a sport. One early historian of the sport described it as "a pastime characterized by perfect liberty and constant variety of incident and scene." You simply "gathered your crew, set out in any direction you wished, and returned when Providence of the weather or good pleasure decreed." You just made sure to "avoid the precipices, if you could, and trust to luck to meet no other vehicles in the darkness." A far more perilous business, this, then he makes it sound. In the United States, the bobsledding craze led to a spate of deaths. Between 1892 and 1906 the *New York Times* alone carried reports of twelve deaths in bobbing accidents, as sleds, sometimes laden with as many as sixteen riders, hurtled around busy streets, weaving in between—or as often as not colliding with—cars, trains, trams, horses, milk wagons, and pedestrians. The casualty list in that period ran into the hundreds. It's one long litany of broken arms, smashed legs, fractured skulls, twisted ankles, crushed hands, gouged eyes, and gashed scalps. In the winter of 1908 there were so many crashes in the small town of Montclair, New Jersey, that the police banned bobsledding. "Public sentiment," the *Times* reported after the latest smash-up between a bob and a trolley car, "will probably lead to an ordinance being adopted by the town council which will permanently abolish coasting on the streets of Montclair."

Back in Europe, the British were also looking to impose some kind of order on the fledgling sport. In 1897 the St. Moritz Bobsleigh Club was formed; the cost of subscription was ten Swiss francs per person per season, worth around two U.S. dollars at the time. At first the preferred run was down the Cresta Road, along the very same route used by the tobogganers, not to mention all the other traffic through the town. Rule six in the SMBC's book stated that "as far as is possible traffic will be directed to give each bob a clear course, but no allowance can be made for the fact that a bob has been delayed by meeting a sleigh." The SMBC soon realized that it needed to build a dedicated bobsled run.

By now St. Moritz had become a busy place. Business had been so good for the Badrutt family that in 1892 they'd purchased a second hotel in the town, the Beau Rivage. Johannes's son, Caspar, ran it. He traveled to Zurich to hire the leading Swiss architectural firm of Chiodera & Tschudy to convert it into the Palace Hotel. It took a team of five hundred Italian workmen four years to finish it. When they were done, the Badrutts were the owners of two of the very finest hotels in Europe.

With so many idle rich around town each winter, the SMBC soon found a few wealthy sportsmen willing to stump up 20,000 Swiss francs to help pay for the construction of a dedicated bobsled track, the world's first. The backers were a cosmopolitan and aristocratic bunch. There were 200 francs from a German prince, 500 from a fellow count. An Irish marquess and an English army captain provided another 500 each. Finally, Count Larisch contributed 650 francs. His wife, Countess Marie Larisch, was a niece and confidante of Empress Elisabeth of Austria. Later Marie Larisch's descriptions of sledding in the Alps so enchanted the poet T. S. Eliot that he used them as inspiration for these apt lines from *The Waste Land*:

> And when we were children, staying at the archduke's,
> My cousin's, he took me out on a sled,
> And I was frightened. He said, Marie,
> Marie, hold on tight. And down we went.
> In the mountains, there you feel free.

The new course opened in 1902. It started at the top of the hill, in what was now known as Badrutt's Park, up by the Kulm Hotel. From there it wound down through avenues of pine trees into the valley below, until it made a sudden turn to dip down beneath an arch of the railway bridge, and then ran onto the finish by Cresta village. Now that St. Moritz had a specialist bob track, it meant that most of the people who crashed—and plenty did—were unlikely to suffer anything much worse than "a sudden nose-rubbing in the snow," as one observer put it. Crowds gathered around the key corners, named Devil's Dyke, Sunny, and Horseshoe, where the bob would swing round in about twice its own length, hoping to catch a glimpse of a crash so they could enjoy a "Roman holiday," their schadenfreude made all the sweeter by the fact that the sled's occupants "would usually be seen within a few seconds completing their journey with great cheerfulness."

The development of a dedicated course and a few rudimentary safety measures meant that the sport was a lot less dangerous than the ad hoc version they were practicing in the United States at this time. In St. Moritz, during this brief period after the move off public roads and before it became too fast for anyone but the brave to try, bobsledding was a sport that almost anyone could have a go at. And almost everyone did. The Cresta Run, which used single-seater toboggans, may have been more thrilling, but that didn't necessarily mean it was more fun. Bobsledding was altogether more sociable. In fact, it was a perfect sport for flirts. In the early days, the SMBC had a rule stipulating that every bob should contain at least one woman. "She is not permitted to steer or brake, man-made law debarring her from her natural functions," reported an especially wry "Special Correspondent" in the *Times* in 1909, "but in an early Victorian way she adds to the amenities of the bobbing life. The sleighs which pull the bobs back hold only two, and it is hers to decide which of the crew shall drive with her up the hill. She attends to the crew's apparel, and decorates it further with the badge of the bob. Further she likes bobbing, and the bobbers like her; as the heroine of 'Josephine vendue par ses soeurs' said to her sister when suggesting that she should marry the guardian of the hareem, 'There is not much to do, and after all it is a position.'" A turn on Badrutt's bobsleigh run was now the key attraction in the burgeoning winter resort of St. Moritz. "The track is the meeting place of the whole population, regardless of age, rank, or nationality," the *Times* reported. There, the tourists would often wager with one another on the races.

Some felt that the specialist course was a step too far, a perversion, almost, of the amateur spirit of the sport. "The fact is," ran a 1904 editorial in the *Alpine-Post*, "that the expert, record-breaking, almost professional element has laid its hands on bobsleighing." The *Times* agreed: "There can be little doubt that the true sport of bobbing is best enjoyed on a road, but there can be none that a public road is the most unsuitable place for a bob race." It bemoaned, too, "the almost excessive number of cups and prizes to be won" since, while "it is an easy matter for well-to-do people taking a holiday in Switzerland to offer some prize, and it is a form of spending that offers obvious attractions," it "engendered a spirit of pot-hunting," which the paper considered altogether too vulgar. Bob-sledding, only a few years old, was already starting to become a serious sport. The British press began to carry regular reports on the races in St. Moritz. A timing mechanism was introduced. Threads were strung across the start and finish lines. When the sled broke the first, the clock started, and when it snapped the second, the clock stopped.

It was true that this caused some to start taking the competition a little too seriously. In 1906, the SMBC ran trials of a new sled fitted with a squirt that sprayed a stream of powdered graphite out in front of the runners, the better to speed their passage over the ice. This was all part of the drive to make the sleds faster. There were amateur races in the United States in this era, too, down rough tracks rather than specially cut courses like the one they were using in St. Moritz. In Caldwell, New Jersey, the locals were amazed when, in 1909, "a richly appointed German" brought a "de luxe sled" to the town's annual bobsled race. It was fitted with an electric searchlight, an automobile's steering wheel, and rubber-coated runners. It weighed three hundred pounds, cost three hundred dollars, "and created a sensation among the racers."

In St. Moritz, such sleds were becoming increasingly common. In those years the course was five yards shy of a mile long, and between 1902 and 1912 the record time for covering it dropped a full thirteen seconds: from 1:46 to 1:33. That meant the sleds were traveling at an average speed of between 30 and 40 mph, which seems slow by the standards the riders were to reach in the 1930s, but at the time, it was still quicker than the vast majority of people could travel without boarding a train. It was as fast as the finest thoroughbred racing horse could run, and matched the speed records set by the earliest automobiles. The first car land-speed record was 39 mph, achieved in 1898, only a few years earlier. That particular mark was broken seven times before 1910, and by the end of the decade stood at 125 mph. The bobsledders couldn't match those kinds of advances, but they, too, were driving one another on, faster and faster, toward the limits of what the sport would allow.

Crew sizes had been fixed, by then, at five riders per sled—one to drive, one to work the brake, and three in between to make the weight. The basic body of the bobs stayed the same. They had a long flat iron frame supported by tubular runners, two long bars down either side to hold on to, and a series of shorter bars running across to lean on. At the back, the brake was essentially a metal comb attached to two bars, which the last man in the sled would pull on to make the teeth bite into the ice. But the steering technology was still evolving, with rival sledders using different mechanisms. Some preferred steering wheels, others bars that were attached to the runners. And the techniques were advancing too.

At first most rode sitting up. Then they started to lie on their backs, heads laid flat on the chests of the riders behind. In 1912, an Englishman named Lord Carbery won a series of races in St. Moritz with a crew riding flat on their fronts, with the driver up at the front and the torso of each rider overlapping the legs of the person in front of him. The style became known as ventre à terre, and was adopted by anyone who reckoned himself a serious racer in that era. It was, according to the official history of the SMBC, "a pernicious habit, which drove many a would-be female bobber from the run." Someone spread around the odd idea that it caused breast cancer. Still, it was, indisputably, fast. Carbery won his races by four seconds and more over the teams using the older methods.

As the sleds got faster, the risks increased. In the winter of 1911–12, three men died on the St. Moritz bob run in the space of a month. A German engineer was killed when his sled "capsized" on a corner and the metal frame smashed into his head. Four weeks later, two riders were killed, and two more seriously injured, when their sled swerved to avoid a patch of rutted ice and shot off a bank into a tree. There were three more serious accidents the following season, and another death in 1914, when a rider crashed into the railway bridge. For any but the brave, bobsledding at St. Moritz was starting to become a sport to watch rather than one to participate in. "There is arising a new winter sport, 'Spectatorism,'" reported the *Times*. "It flourishes in St. Moritz." The reporter railed in particular against the ranks of "plump, bronzed, and jovial" Germans. In a large puff piece in 1914, the *New York Herald* gushed, "Who, on arriving at one of the many mountain villages frequented by tourists from almost every corner of the world, has not watched enviously those crews of bright-eyed, merry-faced men and women dashing madly down steep, snowy slopes, yelling from sheer exhil-aration and healthy animal spirits as their long, low bob whizzes around a sharp banked bend!" And it was true: envious watching was now all most felt able to do. The brief heyday of popular bobsledding was over. It was about to become an elite activity, a sport for daredevils.

Of course that very same year, 1914, the members of the SMBC had rather more pressing threats to attend to. During the First World War "the club tem-porarily ceased to exist," as the official history quaintly puts it, "and the majority of its members were engaged in a more dangerous, more unpleasant, form of winter sport." But Switzerland was neutral territory, and in the mountains there the ill feeling engendered by the brutal conflict didn't intrude on the convivial relations enjoyed by the cosmopolitan bobsledding crowd. This was well illus-trated by the reception afforded to Crown Prince Wilhelm of Germany, eldest son of the kaiser, when he returned to the resort for the first time after the Ar-mistice.

Wilhelm had been a keen bobsledder before the war, riding a sled he named Red Eagle. The SMBC, described by its secretary Hubert Martineau as having "always retained its British feeling and organization," had made the German prince an honorary life president in 1913. It was in St. Moritz, in fact, that he was given the nickname "Little Willie"—a handle the British tabloids delighted in using whenever they regaled their readers with lurid accounts of his frequent infidelities and affairs. The man was a well-known womanizer and, during the war, public enemy number two, second only to his father. In 1918 effigies of Wilhelm were strung up from the scaffold gallows in towns up and down En-gland. And yet Martineau, now the SMBC's president, recalled meeting Prince Wilhelm outside the Kulm Hotel in St. Moritz in the early years after the war.

"Hullo Martineau, how are you?"

"Very well, sir."

"I suppose after all the vices which the Daily Mail has laid at my door, you've kicked me out as honorary president?"

"No, sir, we have no politics in the bobsleigh club."

The prince went off delighted, murmuring, "Good, good, good! I must come to the run."

And so, once the Swiss government had relaxed its wartime restrictions on foreign visitors—"terrifying formalities," in the words of the Times—life at St. Moritz simply carried on. In fact a new passenger air service between Zurich and St. Moritz made it easier than ever before for the rich to get away there for the winter. The town was soon busier than it ever had been before the war. It was starting to swing.

This was the beginning of the golden era of bobsledding in St. Moritz—"the gay old days," as Martineau called them in his memoirs, the age when "gifted amateur socialites went down the run, partly for fun, partly because he or she had a lot of guts, partly because he or she was bent on trying anything going." But the idea that bobsledding was a sport for everybody was long gone; it was now for those rich enough to afford it and bold enough to brave it. "Far more than the weather or the run," Martineau wrote, "it is the people who count: they make the season. Everything was taken light-heartedly. All the bobbers stayed at the Palace Hotel. At 2pm they were all out on the run, and at 2am they were all out on the town." Downhill skiing wouldn't become popular until the tail end of the 1930s. Bobsledding was the fashionable thing. The roll calls run in the British papers listing who was in St. Moritz for the season began to read like a European who's who. One week's entry, entirely typical, included the following names: Prince Odescalchi, Princess Lowenstein, the Marchioness Curzon of Kedleston, the Earl of Northesk, the Baron and Baronne Napoleon Gourgaud, Comte Philippe de Marnix, and Sir Philip Sassoon. Only the young and brave would be out on the run to take part in the big races, but everyone would gather at the Kulm and the Palace in the evenings for the balls, dances, and dinners.

As president of the SMBC, Martineau had two things to do. The first was to try to raise the funds to keep the club running, through auctions, raffles, sweepstakes, and generally by twisting the arm of any rich visitors who came his way. It cost $1,500 a season to rebuild and maintain the run. The second was to try to keep the members in line. This was by far the harder job. In the winter of 1924 a mysterious newcomer arrived at the club, a pretty young Russian lady with "auburn hair, vermilion cheeks, and scarlet lips." She went by the name of Mademoiselle Krasnowski. "She was, unfortunately, quite unable to talk or understand a word of any language except Russian," but she insisted on racing in the Boblet Cup, a competition for two-seater sleds. "As the race proceeded it was evident from the accounts given by her partner, and from her time when steering, that she was no novice at the game; and it was soon seen that very good times would have to be done to beat her and her partner. These times were not forthcoming, and her boblet was declared the winner." The problems started on the way back to the hotel, when Martineau was "waylaid by a horde of indignant wives" who accused Mlle Krasnowski, as she drove from the bottom to the top of the run, "of deliberately (to use a vulgarism) 'giving the glad eye to their husbands,' a statement which we are bound to confess was reluctantly corroborated by the lady's partner." It got ugly at the prize ceremony. When Krasnowski was called up to receive the cup, she was accosted by a hot-blooded Argentine, Arturo Gramajo, who grew so incensed at the way the rest of the company was shouting him down that he dashed forward and grabbed her hair "before he could be dragged from his murderous assault." Those in the audience "were stricken with horror, a horror which changed to consternation a few seconds later" when, as Gramajo reeled back triumphantly with two curls of auburn hair in his hands, there stood revealed, with painted cheeks and lips, a man.

Then there were the crashes. In 1925 Martineau oversaw extensive renovations of the twelve-foot-tall bank at Horseshoe Corner to make it safer for the riders. "But unfortunately," he wrote, "the work came to nothing when a bob drove right through it." The following season a sled went over the top at Sunny Corner and flew into the crowd, scattering the spectators. Three were injured, one of them a German high court judge "who had several ribs broken." The local authorities took a dim view of it all. They decided that the president of the SMBC should be held accountable. They collared Martineau. He was compelled to report to the police station twice a day for several days until the club's insurers coughed up. "The idea of impounding all my wife's jewelry, which was at the back of their minds, was thus, fortunately, frustrated." Martineau was gratified when he was called down to the lobby of the Palace one morning to be met by the local mayor in full fig, bowler hat, and chain of office, who duly apologized and asked for his forgiveness. "The SMBC is British, and we do not receive much co-operation from the Swiss," he wrote. "They regard us as odd-men out, with a certain amount of suspicion. The suspicion is, however, tempered with respect."

It was Martineau's job, too, to smooth over some of the bust-ups that happened off the course—like mollifying the nameless businessman who was hoodwinked into playing dice on the billiards table at the Kulm by three con men who fleeced him of large sums and then cut out of town. Tricks like this seemed to happen quite a lot, though Martineau was too diplomatic, even years later, to share names. "An American who competed in one of the races asked a lady friend of mine to dine with him," he wrote in his memoirs. "He did the thing in slap-up style, with caviar and champagne, and they both had a most enjoyable evening. Next morning, when she came down, she was presented with the bill for the two of them. The American had disappeared and was never seen again."

Then there was the case of "Andrew," "Susan," and "Paul," none of them their real names: "Andrew was in St. Moritz with a very beautiful girlfriend, Susan, on whom he lavished all his time and a great deal of money. A generous chap, he did not grudge any of the expenditure till he found her in bed with a rather good-looking bobber, Paul. Even then he was civilized about the whole thing, and quite prepared to retire gracefully as long as Paul was prepared to recoup him for his capital outlay—£1,000 for a mink coat, £500 for clothes and another £500 for a bracelet: in other words for £2,000 Andrew was willing to relinquish the flaxen-haired Susan to Paul and there would be no hard feelings. Paul rapturously agreed. That afternoon Paul went down the Bob run, watched possessively by Susan, while Andrew hovered in the background waiting to collect his check. Paul returned to the start for a second run, and again, for a third, but he did not return for a fourth. His last descent had been nicely calculated to connect with the train at Celerina station, and by that time Andrew realized he had lost his £2,000 and Susan realized that she had lost her lover! He was well on his way back to England."

So, in St. Moritz in the early 1920s, anything went. Just so long as you had the cash. And even if you were broke, there was a chance that the Badrutts would put you up for free in the Palace if they took a shine to you. "It was easy for any man—especially if he was single and a good sportsman—to become quickly accepted by the sporting and social crowd which then flocked to St. Moritz," wrote Martineau. Just don't try it without that elusive extra quality "sportsmanship." Bad manners didn't wear. Martineau banned one man from the bob run for five years after he'd overheard him complaining that he had been cheated out of a victory by the race officials, whom he reckoned had fiddled the timing. "You think you can do this to me just because I'm a German," he told Martineau, who took great satisfaction in noting that the man had gone on to become an officer in the Waffen SS in World War Two.

The social mix was enriched by Americans who came over from the French Riviera, among them the extraordinary Helen Kelly, known at the time as the Princess Vlora because the third of her ex-husbands was an Albanian prince. She was also the widow of Ralph Hill Thomas, ex-president of the American Sugar Refining Company. And before that she had been Mrs. Frank Jay Gould, wife of one of the richest hoteliers on the Riviera. She divorced him because of his insatiable jealousy of "the homage paid her by other men." At least that was what they said in the smart papers; the yellow press reckoned it had more to do with the fact Gould felt there was "too much mother-in-law" in the marriage and so started an affair with an English actress. Helen Kelly had a fortune of her own, inherited from her father. What she wanted, though, was something money couldn't buy: social rank. That's why she settled on Prince Nourredin Vlora. "She soon learned to her sorrow that being an Albanian Princess is far from the advantageous thing she thought it was when she was being wooed," one journalist wrote. "Albania is a mere tenth-rate principality, with no great standing in the courts of Europe." So they, too, were divorced. By 1926 she was on her fourth husband, the soap manufacturer Oscar Burke. Martineau didn't give a damn about any of that. Princess Vlora loved to watch the bobsledding, and she was wealthy, so he welcomed her onto the committee of the SMBC. She presented the club with the Gold Cup, one of the grandest of the many trophies the bobbers would compete for over the course of the season.

The Dolly sisters, Rosie and Jenny, according to Martineau, "managed to make most of the European capitals hum when they passed through them." They were identical twins, born in Budapest but brought up on Broadway, where they had both been dance girls. They were a hard-living, high-rolling pair, neither ever seen out and about without some rich, smitten man for company. In 1925 they were both supposed to be having an affair with Harry Gordon Selfridge, the man behind the department store, who was said to be bankrolling their gambling habits.

And then there were the three Heaton brothers, John (known as Jack), Jennison, and Trowbridge, and their sister, Ninette, from a New England family who had made their fortune in the clipper trade. "The boys—Trowbridge, Jennison, and Jack—were all well-known in winter sport and motor-racing circles," Martineau wrote. "Fairly quiet and withdrawn in the daytime, except on the run, they were as gay and carefree as anyone when they had glasses in their hands at night." The Heatons were three of the finest riders the run had seen yet. Remember them, because we'll be seeing them again.

And of course there was that charming family from Chicago by way of Paris, the Fiskes: William Lindsley Meade II, wife Beulah, daughter Peggy, and young son Billy, "blessed with all this world's goods" and "beloved by all who knew them."

Every galaxy needs a star. And at the center of this little American ex-pat scene in St. Moritz was a man described by the journalist Odd McIntyre as "a good-looking fellow with a soft southern drawl, the life of the party, at which he seems to be the perpetual host." Martineau found him "a very affable and good-looking young man about town" and took a shine to him from the first, picking him to serve along with Princess Vlora on the SMBC's committee almost as soon as he first popped up in St. Moritz, in 1926. And Martineau's great friend Harry Hays Morgan remembered him as "a very popular American," an "excellent overall sportsman." That wasn't the half of it. He's the second of our heroes: the infamous, and extraordinary, James Jay O'Brien.

The USA's No. 1 crew in St. Moritz, 1928. Jay O'Brien is far left.

CHAPTER 3

THE PLAYBOY

Jay didn't have to look back—he could feel them coming. He cracked his whip hard into his horse's flank. "Come on, Kersey!" The water jump was up ahead, and the chasing pack was strung out behind. They were gaining. The brown mare, Simper, was first among them, and almost up level now. The water came and went. Then Liverpool, the stiffest fence on the course. After that they would be into the homestretch. If he could just hold his lead. In the corner of his eye he caught glimpses of the crowd flashing by on the far side. He could hear their cheers over the pounding of the hooves. Virginia Vanderbilt herself was there somewhere, along with the rest of the Great Neck smart set. And his mind turned, just for a moment, to the thought of all the glory that would soon be his. The silver cup. The kisses on the cheek and the claps on the back.

And that was when it happened. C. H. Bell, riding Gold Van, bolted up the inside and beat him to the fence. The two horses clashed as they landed on the other side, and Kersey was forced wide. He swerved way off the racing line—off, in fact, across the course. The shouts of encouragement became screams of panic. Jay tried to rein back, but it was too late. He had lost control. The close-packed crowd scattered as his horse burst through the row of flags that marked the edge of the track. Gowns billowing, hats flying, they raced for the safety of the traps and carriages arrayed around the outfield.

Jay forced Kersey back onto the track and whipped the horse hard into a hot finish. But he was way back when Gold Van broke the tape. Jay was still seething at the presentation ceremony. He cursed under his breath as he watched Bell receive the trophy, and again out loud when one of the patrol judges hurried up to tell him he was officially disqualified. A few kind words from Virginia Vanderbilt soothed his wounded pride. She said that the race was "the most sensational of the day," and the sweet smile she shot him as he spoke almost made it all seem worthwhile. Jay's friends always said that few things mattered to him more than winning. Pretty women were one of them.

Jay O'Brien grew up rich. He was born in New York on February 22, 1883, and enjoyed all the privileges his father had worked so hard to earn for his family. Miles O'Brien had emigrated from Ireland in the 1860s. His parents had wanted him to take a career in law, but instead he traveled, alone, to New York. He got a job as a clerk at H. B. Claflin & Co., a wholesale dry goods retailer in downtown Manhattan. But Miles was bound for better things. He worked his way up to the top of the company, and on the way he became a leader of the Fenian society Clan na Gael and an active member of the Irish Parliamentary Fund Association, which supported the campaign for home rule. An enlightened, compassionate man and a prominent independent Democrat, he moved into public service. When his friend William Russell Grace became the first Irish-born mayor of New York, he brought O'Brien up with him. He appointed him to the city's board of education. There, Miles campaigned against overcrowding in classrooms and called for the introduction of school baths and free lectures for adults. He became president of the board in 1900.

If that all sounds a little too clean for a man who successfully negotiated his way through the cut-throat world of Irish-American politics in late-nineteenth-century New York, there are hints of shadows in Miles's story too. He certainly had his tangles in Tammany Hall, the Democratic society that controlled politics in New York City and State from the 1790s on. Tammany relied on support from the Irish immigrant community, and Miles was one of many men the society helped gain a foothold in American politics. By his time, it was infamous throughout the city for its corruption, graft, and internecine squabbling. In 1883, Miles was accused of being one of the organizers of the Fenian dynamite plot. He denied all involvement and told the *Boston Herald* that he was opposed to dynamite—that he believed "constitutional agitation" was the way to overthrow British power in Ireland. Then, in 1889, he was caught up in a minor scandal when two friends of his fell out over dinner and one challenged the other to a duel. They kept that out of the papers, but Miles was exposed twelve years later when his son Thomas, Jay's younger brother, was arrested for disorderly conduct. The boy was released without charge the next day, but the matter was muddied when the arresting officer reported that Miles had threatened him outside the courthouse. "Can I do anything for you?" the policeman had asked. "No," O'Brien had replied. "But I will do something for you. I'll cause you to lose a good deal of sleep over this matter. You'll not stay at the 100th Street station very long, you'll be transferred." O'Brien insisted that the story was "made out of cloth," an "utter fabrication." The precinct's commanding officer agreed with Miles, but that didn't necessarily do much to dispel the idea that he had the local police in his pocket. O'Brien owned an entire block of the Bronx, and by the time he died in 1910, he was president of the Bank of New Amsterdam. No doubt he drew a lot of water.

Jay was raised in his father's image. He had a quick temper and contempt for authority. He was used to getting his own way. He'd first learned to ride during his summers in Long Branch, New Jersey, on a horse his father bought for him. He was strictly amateur. Did it for the fun and the glory. At first the courses he rode were all up in Long Island. The race that had so thrilled Virginia Vanderbilt took place at Gracefield, the private estate of the former mayor and an old friend of his father's, William Grace. The news reports of the races in the papers paid more attention to the people than the horses and always included long lists of the luminaries who had been in attendance. Despite what happened that day at Gracefield, Jay was an excellent jockey. In November 1906 he won four races in a single afternoon at Huntington, two on the flat and two over the jumps. He would have won the fifth, too, if he hadn't fallen head over heels as he came over the first jump on the second lap; he leaped up, remounted, and made for the finish, but came in fourth. "A small but select group" was there to see him do it. In 1907 he moved up a notch: he started to enter races at the great tracks of Saratoga and Belmont, where crowds of more than ten thousand filled the grandstands. He didn't fare well. He took a bad fall at Saratoga while urging the nag he was saddled with over the steepest jump on the course, and was whisked away to hospital in an ambulance. He fell again while riding the favorite at Sheepshead later that summer, breaking a bone in his leg.

After that he began to get a reputation as an unlucky jockey. Truth was, he was taking too many risks. But that was more than half the fun. If there was nothing at stake, Jay lost interest. At Baltimore he gave up when well beaten. He was easing toward the finish when he was overtaken by a horse he had thought was far behind him. The stewards suspended him because of his "carelessness," suspecting he had thrown the race for second place. Characteristically, Jay protested the decision to the National Steeplechase and Hunt Association, which not only upheld the decision but also stripped him of his license to ride as an amateur jockey. Piqued, he drifted away from racing. He gave it up altogether when a horse he owned, but wasn't riding, fell during a race at Saratoga. It landed on a rival jockey and crushed him to death.

Not for the first time, Jay left one passion behind him and pounced on another. He had studied law at Princeton, and he dabbled in stocks and bonds for H. L. Horton. But honest work didn't interest him much. All the time he had spent at the track had given him a taste for gambling. His game was baccarat, though, in the words of his first wife, "he would bet on anything under the sun." In 1913 he took a holiday in England. He sailed back to New York on the *Mauretania*, the largest, fastest ocean liner in the world. Jay spent the voyage holed up in the smoking room, playing cards. By the time the ship docked in New York, he had won twenty-five thousand dollars, almost half of which was made in the final twenty minutes of the voyage as his desperate opponents tried to win back what they had lost in a frantic final game. Word spread around the ship that something extraordinary was afoot in the smoking room, which was soon filled with spectators. They were keener to watch the cards than they were to take in the sight of the city from the deck. It was worth it; Jay won five thousand dollars on the turn of a single card. This caused whispers. Someone muttered the phrase "card-sharping" to the press, but nothing came of it.

Jay had another narrow escape later that same year. He and his friend Al Davis had hired a bachelor pad above Murray's Roman Gardens, the most famous of the ritzy "lobster palaces" that popped up on the Gay White Way of 42nd Street. Downstairs at Murray's they had a rotating dance floor, which turned lazy circles underneath a ceiling filled with electric stars. Showgirls flitted in between the statues and fountains and took turns dancing tangos with the clientele. And if any of the guests found all that to be insufficient entertainment, well, the showgirls would show them upstairs to Jay and Al's apartment, where there was what one journalist called "a wonderfully circumspect roulette wheel" ready and waiting for anyone who was rich, drunk, or dumb enough to take the chance. Until they made the mistake of taking twenty-five thousand dollars off a staff member of the Russian consulate. He woke the next morning with a thick head and a slim wallet. Incensed, he reported Jay and Al to the police. He said he had been fleeced.

And so he had. They called the con "shearing the lamb." The showgirls, who took a cut of the profits, were paid to spot victims, liquor them up, and lead them to the suite. Then they lured the mark into splashing his cash on the crooked roulette wheel. Astonishing sums were lost at that little gaming table. Angier Duke, who was then a trustee of Duke University, was forced to issue a public denial that he had dropped eighty thousand dollars there. He admitted, a little coyly, that he had met Jay in Murray's, but insisted that he was "just very fond of music and dancing" and had dropped in at the club to "tango away a little time." Snaring and shearing a foreign diplomat, though, was just asking for trouble. Unlike Angy Duke, he wasn't about to let them off easy.

Deputy Commissioner of Police Newburger led the raid himself. He and his men hustled into Murray's and busted down the door to the suite. But Jay had been tipped off. The room was empty, except for one little roulette table. They picked it up and carried it away, past the replica of Cleopatra's barge, the thirty-foot marble fountain, and out through the restaurant. "Tumult reigned among the gay throngs clustered in horrified bewilderment," read one report. "Certain attractive girls professed to have no idea what it was all about. Others nudged their companions and winked significantly." It took Newburger a couple of days to track down Jay and Al. They turned up in "another Broadway trottery" and were brought in for questioning, then charged with gambling. Jay insisted it was a "frame-up" and that the police were being used by two men who owed him money. The charges were eventually dismissed. But then, Jay had some low friends in high places. His thousand-dollar bail was paid by Arnold "Ace" Rothstein, one of the biggest racketeers in the city.

They called Rothstein "the Big Bankroll." He would become the biggest bootlegger in New York, but back then he was making his money fixing horse races. Which is how Jay came to know him. So, you see, if Jay wasn't deep in the underworld, he certainly got his feet wet flitting around its shores. He and Rothstein remained friends and business partners. In 1923 Rothstein was called to testify in the bankruptcy hearing of an associate, E. M. Fuller, during which he was made to reveal that he had recently loaned Jay twenty thousand dollars.

Jay's pal Al Davis certainly had a reputation on Broadway as a "sharp-shooter," as one paper put it, a man able to make a living "through his wits in a score of ways." One of which, it turned out, was convincing a wealthy young woman named Eugenia Kelly, the "first flapper of Broadway," that he was a man worth marrying. The two of them burned through twenty thousand dollars of her million-dollar fortune in the space of nine months. Her mother called Davis a "tango pirate." She was so disgusted by their affair that she tried to have her daughter arrested on the grounds that she was an "incorrigible person." She took her to court, just so she could expose the mess Davis had made of her inheritance. Eugenia's sister was Helen Kelly, better known as Princess Vlora, whom we met in the last chapter. She was a lifelong friend of Jay's from their days running around Broadway. The Eugenia Kelly case caused real outrage and prompted a group of the more upstanding members of New York society to launch a "moral crusade" against the "social gangsters" who frequented the Broadway dancing palaces.

Again, then, Jay had to find another way to get his kicks. In 1914 he started betting on professional sport. He won $10,000 on the World Series that year by backing the Boston Braves against the Philadelphia Athletics. He was offering bets around town, staking $1,200 on the Braves to $2,000 against the Phillies at first, then more still at odds of 2–1. He won a large chunk off Rothstein, through the bookmaker Sport Sullivan. Rothstein and Sullivan would go on to fix the 1918 series between the White Sox and the Cincinnati Reds. There were suspicions that the 1914 series was crooked, too, especially as Sullivan took so many bets on Boston. They had been at the bottom of the National League as late as July 4 but ended up winning the series that October in a clean sweep, 4–0. Nothing was ever proved, though. Instead, Jay's win was put down to his pluck. And perhaps that was right. "The man who studied the form, the scientific bettor, placed his money on the Athletics," said the *Day* newspaper. "The man with the hunch was the one who cashed in." Jay, they said, was a "daring bettor and operator in the market."

Let's move in for a close-up. In the spring of 1915, Jay was spending his evenings at the San Souci club, in the basement of the Heidelberg building on 42nd Street. The star attraction there was a young dancer named Mae Murray, a short blonde with heavy eyelids and a thick, full mouth. She was soon to become famous throughout the world as the "girl with the bee-stung lips," the brightest star at MGM. Back then she was, she insisted, an innocent little ingenue, trying to break out from the chorus lines on Broadway. Her chance came when Irving Berlin asked her to fill in for Irene Castle, the female lead in his production of *Watch Your Step*, which had opened a few weeks earlier and was still playing to full houses. "You've got to go on," Berlin told her. "Irene is very ill. The doctors won't allow her out of bed. You've got to help me." He didn't need to twist her arm. Murray was about to go on stage, but she cut out of the San Souci and skipped down to the New Amsterdam Theatre. She had four hours to get ready, time enough to get a costume fitted and rehearse a few steps with Irene's husband and dancing partner, Vernon Castle, while Berlin accompanied them on a piano.

She was a sensation. The *New York Times* reported that she made "a decided hit and received round after round of applause." Vernon Castle told her, "It's all for you, Butterfly," and dragged her out on stage to take a bow. "Vernon and I formed an unbreakable bond during that exciting, hectic, never-to-be-forgotten night," Mae recalled. "It was the bond of rhythm lovers." (Irene Castle, it has to be said, never really warmed to Mae. Not that Mae minded.) She took a cold shower and a quick supper, then raced back to the San Souci so she could perform there. After her number she received her second standing ovation of the night, the applause ringing on long after her encore. She slipped backstage to change into a long white gown, then stepped out into the club. She accepted a white gardenia, refused a glass of champagne, and fell into conversation with a man named Jack de Saulles.

De Saulles was thirty-seven, a real estate broker. He had been a star quarterback at Yale back in 1901, and was named that year in the *New York Post*'s All-American Team. He swept his arm around Mae's shoulders.

And then she saw him, walking toward her from across the room. "A striking man, about 36, with dark, svelte hair, dark eyes, very well-groomed. He looked as if he had just been released by his valet. His white dress shirt gleamed with pink pearl studs." Jay O'Brien. Mae couldn't take her eyes off him.

Jay explained that he had been at the New Amsterdam Theatre that night and had watched her dance with Vernon Castle. And though she thought him fresh, she found she was "strangely grateful" for his praise. At that moment, she said, it felt "as though there were only two of us in the room." De Saulles, understandably, seemed displeased with the interruption. Mae, who could surely have made a living writing penny romances if she hadn't been blessed with so many other talents, remembered that she looked into Jay's eyes and thought how "lustrous and dark they were," then wondered to herself, "What is he like behind that white-white shirt, behind those pearls?"

De Saulles moved to turn her toward the dance floor, but Jay took de Saulles's arm, lifted it from her shoulders, and slipped his own around her waist. "I bet I would dance with her tonight," he told de Saulles as he led her out into the crowd. She assumed he was joking. He wasn't. Later de Saulles, whose young Chilean wife was also there that evening, tried to persuade Mae to let him take her home. She refused, and he explained to her, "Look, Jay and I have a bet on. He's already won once from me tonight. Now you help me win over him." He and Jay were pals; but then, as he commented to Mae a little later, "no men are friends where a woman is concerned."

Jay was, Mae said, a glorious mover. "Our timing was so perfect that I could not speak," she gushed. "I closed my eyes and wondered if all this night had been a dream." Some of it might have been. "I looked up into his immobile, finely chiseled face and saw it registered no expression. It had the perfect proportions and even features of a statue. The only difference, I thought, was that I could see a muscle throb in his right jaw." She gasped. Her heart skipped a beat. "Although this man was many years older than me"—all of two years, to be precise—"the attraction was undeniable." As they turned across the floor, stepping together in time to the band, Jay, one eye on his bet with de Saulles, told her, "Don't go away from me, because I tell you I am going to take you home."

It wouldn't quite be right to say that Mae fell for Jay that night. She said she found herself both repelled by and attracted to him. She thought he was typical of "the wealthy play crowd, who lived on inheritance," and part of her "wanted to get away from these people whose lives seemed to be made up of betting, of intrigues, of matching wits." Best to take that with a little pinch of salt. She also insisted that she kept asking herself, "What do these men want from me?" Was it "her charm, her natural sweetness?" Was it her newfound "success and acclaim?" Or was it something else altogether? Well, quite.

Before the week was over, Jay had inveigled himself into Mae's life. He declared, after sneaking into her taxi and accompanying her home, that he was in love and intended to marry her. She balked at that. Jay, wrote Mae's biographer Jane Ardmore, "had a high-flown way of talking that shocked her with its excessive ardor. It made her feel like a schoolgirl." She mustered the courage to turn him down, though, telling him, "I want to be free." Until de Saulles returned, that is. He invited her to a party at his apartment. His studio, she remembered, "was so ornate and extravagant and luxurious," and it seemed to her that "every celebrity on Broadway sat around the table." They ate "pheasant and wild rice from silver platters, and drank champagne from crystal glasses." A little too much champagne. De Saulles began to paw at her, pleading for a dance. "I want to hold you in my arms," he said. And then he leaned in for a kiss.

That was when Jay arrived, which was impeccable timing on his part, or perhaps that of Mae's imagination.

"Jay!" I cried, my hand going guilty to my wet, kiss-smeared cheek.

"Hello party crasher!" said de Saulles.

"So you've won, you skunk!" Jay shot back. "You said you'd get her to your apartment, all right, and you have. But before I pay you, I've got something else for you."

At which point, of course, he clobbered him. He knocked him onto the dining table, spilling rice and champagne and silver and crystal all across the floor. Then, as Mae remembered it, Jay seized her by the elbows, lifted her from the floor, and . . . well, again, it's best to let her take over:

"Why did you come here?" he asked me.

"Jay! You're mad!"

"Why did you come?" he asked. "I don't want you here."

"You're hurting me. Let me down I tell you!"

"Answer me first!"

"I've told you before. I don't belong to you or anyone. I want to be free."

"I told you that you couldn't be free."

"Then I did something that broke the tension. I laughed."

So did everyone else. Apart from Jay. He blanched, started to shake, and then wrapped his fingers around her throat. Mae, always the heroine of her memoirs, said she told him, "Go on. You'll justify all my doubts and answer every question I had about you." Mae thought that it was her words that made Jay let go. It may also have had something to do with the two waiters who grabbed him by the arms.

She left with de Saulles. She admitted that she didn't have much choice about it, since he threw her over his shoulder and carried her out to his car. They drove out into the city, far from the San Souci, where Mae was meant to be appearing on stage that evening. De Saulles had an "evil smile on his face," Mae said, "as if he were enjoying my upset night." He cautioned her against seeing Jay again, though you'd think that after what had just happened, she would hardly have needed the warning. But then when she returned to her flat that night, she found that her bedroom was filled with red roses. Her maid brought her a note, from Jay, begging her forgiveness, pledging his love. But as Mae told de Saulles, "I don't want to be 'a woman' in your and Jay's lives, I want to dance, to make my own living and live my own life."

She was doing exactly that. The great impresario Florenz Ziegfeld—"Ziggie" to Mae—had just signed her up to perform in his famous Follies, "a salad of sex and art," as one of his biographers put it; the front-row seats sold for one hundred dollars each. And Adolph Zukor, who had just founded Paramount, was trying to persuade her to move to Hollywood. Jay was beside himself, "tortured and jealous, in a constant state of depression." He couldn't stand having all these rivals for her affection.

Enter Rudolph Valentino. He was only twenty then and still using his real surname, Guglielmi. "He was a magnificent specimen of humanity, and had a disposition which matched his physical beauty," Mae said. "Just to see his expressive hand lying on the back of a chair was art." She was utterly smitten. As was everyone else. Which explains why she was so ready to admit, "We were attracted to each other from that first afternoon. Call it sex, if you will, but I call it a dancing friendship."

As enraptured by Valentino as Mae was, she was beginning to realize that she was still obsessed with Jay. She noticed that he didn't come to her opening night at the Follies. Her big number was an "oriental love dance" in the Elysium scene, set in a Persian harem. Each night she looked out into the crowd, hoping to catch a glimpse of him. Each night she tore open the envelopes bearing notes from her admirers, hoping to find one signed by him. He never came, and never wrote. Heartbroken, Mae ended her affair with Valentino—who promptly fell in love with Jack de Saulles's long-suffering wife, Blanca.

We shall step back here, just for a moment. Mae's memoirs, which were serialized by the Hearst Corporation, were considered sensational, in more than one sense, when they were first published in 1942. Her friend Anita Loos called them "one long Valentine." Even then people wondered how reliable they were. Years later, we can be sure that she twisted the truth for the sake of the tale and her sales. Jay's own version of their affair, you suspect, would have read very differently had he ever written it. If, however, her account sometimes seems unbelievable, we should remember that Mae's life was an incredible one, and her world was extraordinary. Nothing better illustrates that than this little side story.

Blanca de Saulles, now in love with Valentino, was, understandably, desperate to get a divorce from her husband. Valentino agreed to testify that Jack de Saulles had had an affair with his dancing partner so that Blanca could secure her divorce and keep custody of her child. Jack, in turn, arranged to have Valentino arrested on vice charges by falsely alleging that the actor had been having an affair with a brothel madam. "This," Mae wrote of the way de Saulles had Valentino arrested, "was a terrible and vicious thing to do, and Jack was to pay, for Rudy never deserved such treatment." Soon after the de Saulleses' divorce was finalized, Blanca drove to their country house in Westbury and demanded that Jack give her custody of their son, as the court had stipulated. When he refused, she drew a gun and pointed it at his head. When he tried to disarm her, she shot him dead. She was acquitted of murder, essentially on the grounds that de Saulles deserved it. It was, the *New York Times* said, "a popular verdict," but one that had "no justification" other than the "emotional" one that she was a young, comely mother and he had been "dissolute, led an evil life, and had wasted her estate."

So the truth was sometimes even stranger than Mae made it seem. Remember that, as we move on to the most extraordinary chapter of her story.

By the time of Valentino's arrest, Mae had already quit New York for Hollywood, lured there by Zukor's promise that he would arrange a red-carpet reception for her, with a brass band, when she got off the train. When she arrived, she was disappointed to find that Zukor had sent instead a fat man with a bunch of flowers. Mae saw Jay twice before she left the city. The first time was at a party, when he had ignored her as he offered his congratulations to all her co-stars in the Follies. "He never said one word that I might take personally! NOT ONE WORD! I felt the full cruelty of his blow then." She flounced out. Jay's somewhat transparent ploy seemed to be working. "His name rushed out and roared and tingled in my ears after every performance . . . and beat there cruelly in my heart when I was alone, disturbing me as I tried to rest." The final time was when she bumped into him on Fifth Avenue. It was then she told him that she was moving to the West Coast.

"I am a dancer and an actress," she said. "I want to believe that I am, and with you I can't believe anything. Not even that you love me."

"You seem to think it is what you want that counts," Jay said. "It's what you are. You are just a precious baby who belongs to me, not to Broadway, not to Hollywood. Dancing and acting and running away from me and doing the things I don't want you to do—they don't count! You're still my baby. Don't you understand that by now?"

And with that, he bundled her into the back of a cab, pressed his lips against hers, and then began to sob into her hair. Mae said, "I was more puzzled than ever about the strange bond between Jay and me"; he "was in torture because of me and I had been unhappy because of him. It did not seem right. His influence on my emotional life had not ended."

"All right, all right," she said, out of pity as much as love. "I will marry you."

Jay and Mae agreed that she would go to Hollywood to work on her first picture—*To Have and to Hold*, co-starring "the screen's most perfect lover" Wallace Reid—and then return to New York for the wedding. They parted the next day, with Jay telling her, "I intend to hold you to your promise, baby, about coming back after one picture and marrying me. Remember, if you don't come back, I'll come out and get you." She did come back to New York, but only so she could break off the engagement. She was working for Cecil B. DeMille now and had fallen in love with her director on *A Mormon Maid*, Bob Leonard. Jay, just as he said he would, went out to Hollywood to persuade her to change her mind.

Another of Mae's biographers, Michael Ankerich, says that she changed her story about what happened next almost as often as she did the year of her birth. In her preferred version, Jay promised to leave her to Leonard if she would just come to the train station to say goodbye before he got on the train to New York. When she arrived, she was met by Jay and his friends "Pud" Sickle and his wife.

"Jay's train doesn't leave for an hour," Pud said. "We're going out in my car. We have a little surprise."

They drove until they reached a large white house. She assumed it was the Sickles', but then they had to ring the door to get in. As they sat in the sitting room, Mae asked Jay, "Who lives here?" And he replied, "The judge who is going to marry us." He put one arm around her and pulled her close, then slipped his other hand into his pocket.

"You can't do this, Jay!" she said

"Yes, I can. It is all arranged. What do you think I have been doing in town all day?"

Mae felt the coat pocket press into her side. "And I knew what I felt was a gun."

She looked around for Pud and his wife, but they had left the room.

"You can't do this, Jay," she insisted. "I'll tell the judge I don't want to marry you and that you have got a gun in your pocket."

"You can take your choice," Jay said. "I could kill you but I couldn't have you then. I could kill your red-headed boyfriend and you couldn't have him, and you couldn't have your career either. Know why? The publicity of having a director killed over a movie star would fix everything for you with your public."

"I couldn't scream or even try to get away from him any longer. He had thought of everything. Everything. For the first time in my life I knew fear, and that's why the situation slipped from my control."

Pud Sickle and his wife came back into the room with the man who owned the house.

"Judge," Jay said. "This is the future Mrs. O'Brien."

"The gun punched into my ribs," wrote Mae. "I felt my face stretch into a smile. I heard my voice say 'Yes, yes.' I was so frightened I couldn't think of anything else to say. Then, with Jay's arm locked through mine, with his gun still jammed painfully in my side, we went through with the marriage ceremony."

In her memoirs, Mae said the couple then headed back to the Alexandria Hotel. During dinner she slipped out the bathroom window and caught a taxi back to the studio, where she was reunited with Bob Leonard. Certainly she and Jay quarreled at their wedding supper. Anita Loos remembered the couple had come to the Hollywood Hotel, rather than the Alexandria. "We all stopped dancing to applaud the glowing bride as she made her way toward the broad staircase on the arm of Hollywood's first socialite bridegroom. But it is dismal to report that a brief two hours later the bridegroom booted the bride down the same staircase, out into the night. What happened between those honeymooners in the bridal suite is a mystery still."

What few facts can we extract from all that? Jay and Mae were certainly married by a justice of the peace on December 18, 1916. The witnesses were, indeed, one "Mr. and Mrs. J. Harrington Sickle." Both the bride and groom lied about their ages. And they were divorced on August 30, 1918. Mae testified in court that between the wedding night and the court date she had seen Jay only once, when he had "choked her and thrown her across a room." She left the courthouse in tears.

We have to leave Mae behind now. If it seems a sudden separation, it is no sharper than the break between the two of them. While they were separated but still married, they were once seen out at the same restaurant, each eating with someone else and refusing even to acknowledge the other. A fortnight after the divorce, Mae and Bob Leonard announced that they were engaged to be married. Her haste made Jay seem almost reserved: he waited almost an entire a year before he got engaged again.

His second wife was Irene Fenwick, a star like Mae, but brunette rather than blonde, and a real actress rather than a dancer and showgirl. She had dabbled with the movies but was best known for her work in the theater. They were married on June 14, 1919. This time the marriage lasted beyond the wedding night, but not all that much longer. By the summer of 1922 the papers were full of rumors that Fenwick was in love with her costar in *The Claw*, Lionel Barrymore. When Barrymore divorced his wife in the winter of 1922, Irene decided to publicly deny the affair. She and Jay were "happily married." This was a lie. It was common knowledge that the two of them had drifted apart, but Jay was refusing to grant her the divorce she wanted. Soon enough, the decision was taken out of his hands.

Irene and Jay had separate charge accounts at the same Fifth Avenue jewelry store, which they had once used to buy each other surprise gifts. The bookkeeper there mistakenly billed her for "a number of expensive trinkets and baubles" that she hadn't bought. When Irene questioned the salesman at the store, he soon spilled the story that Jay had been there buying jewelry. This would have been little more than embarrassing if Jay had ever given Irene those same "trinkets and baubles." But whoever they were for, it wasn't her. So Irene hired a private detective, Val O'Farrell, to tail Jay. O'Farrell followed him to the McAplin Hotel and watched him dine with a "28-year-old girl in a Hudson seal coat and hat." After dinner they went to an apartment on West 144th Street. A short but judicious wait later, O'Farrell kicked the door down and caught the two of them "en déshabillé." The divorce process started soon after. It was discreetly done, with all references to Irene's profession and stage name omitted from the papers and proceedings. Jay had been entirely outwitted by his wife—and, you suspect, by Lionel Barrymore. He and Irene were married in Rome on July 14, 1923, four days after her divorce from Jay was made absolute.

You'd think going through two divorces in the space of five years might change a man, or at least teach him a thing or two. Not Jay. The only real differences between the man who married Mae and the one who was divorced by Irene were his pastimes, and the company he kept while he was at them. He still bet big money on baseball. In 1922 he lost at least $2,700 to Rothstein backing the Yankees against the Giants (Rothstein always backed the Giants). But Jay played golf now, not cards, and had taken up polo instead of horse racing. So he was in more rarefied air, at a remove from the seedy New York scene he had been in.

In the summer of 1923, he had to step back from it after getting caught up in the "Fuller-McGee mess," a bankruptcy case that had spun out into a high-profile fraud scandal. Rothstein was called to testify and was grilled about a mysterious entry in his books called "Account No. 600," which the lawyers were convinced would provide evidence of his complicity in fixing the 1919 World Series. There were two names on the account. One was Rothstein's, the other was Jay's. So he quit town for a time, headed down to Miami to play a little golf. And then, when the heat had died down, he traveled up to Sands Point, on the North Shore of Long Island, to take part in a polo tournament at the Lindens, a grand country pile owned by a man named Julius Fleischmann.

Jay and his friends were wealthy, but Fleischmann was in a different bracket altogether. His father had created the United States' first commercially produced yeast, and, cannily enough, set up a distillery to make gin from the alcohol that was left over from the process. His factories supplied the yeast that allowed people to bake warm, fresh bread, and his distilleries turned the by-product into the booze they used in their martinis. That formula made him a millionaire many times over. Julius, his eldest son, was worth at least sixty million dollars, even though he had to share the family fortune with three siblings. And he had political power. He had been mayor of Cincinnati, the youngest ever at the age of twenty-eight, and he had served as William McKinley's aide when he was state governor. He had a stake in almost every major commercial interest in the city, from the Market National Bank right down to the Cincinnati Reds baseball team, which he co-owned with his brother.

Fleischmann, born in 1871, was a great philanthropist and an even better bon vivant, in his pomp a prototype Gatsby. His house in Cincinnati sat in the middle of two square miles of land. Great glass doors opened from the indoor pool out onto the lawn, where a fountain ran down to the moat encircling the house. Alongside the pool was a ballroom, and beneath that, a wine cellar. If he wasn't there, Fleischmann was as often as not on his steam-powered yacht the *Hiawatha*, at 138 feet long one of the largest privately owned vessels in the world. Or he was in Kentucky, where he kept a stable of thirty thoroughbred steeple-chasers. Or he was at his house on Long Island, the Lindens. He played polo, poorly, but loved it so much that in 1922 he had built his own ground at the Lindens, with a six-room stable for twenty-four ponies, alongside a kennel that housed a pack of fifty Sealyham terriers. People came for the sport and stayed for the parties, where, as F. Scott Fitzgerald would put it in *The Great Gatsby*, "floating rounds of cocktails permeate the garden outside, until the air is alive with chatter and laughter, and casual innuendo and introductions forgotten on the spot," and the women were accompanied by "men said to be their husbands."

It was during just such a party that Jay fell in love for the third time, with a lady named Laura Hylan Heminway. Everyone called her Dolly. She was twenty-nine, younger than both Mae and Irene. She wore her brunette hair up, piled in curls around her ears, and had eyes that came brilliantly alive when her lips, one a perfect cupid's bow, spread into a smile. Jay was absolutely enchanted by her. The problem was that Dolly was Julius Fleischmann's wife.

They had always seemed an odd sort of couple. The ceremony had taken place two days after Fleischmann had finalized his divorce from his first wife, Lilly. He had been with Lilly for twenty-three years, through his two terms as mayor, and had three children with her. Until in 1920, in his late forties, he fell head over heels for Dolly. She was two decades younger than him and had two children of her own from her first marriage. The split from Lilly cost Fleischmann a one-off payment of two million dollars, a summerhouse in Connecticut, and another twenty-five thousand dollars every year in alimony. He didn't regret a cent. He said Dolly was "the most beautiful woman [he] ever met." Fleischmann promised her that once they married, neither she, nor they, would ever want for money. He was almost twice her age, married, bald, beetle-browed, and needed a cane to walk. But for a single woman with two boys to support, his appeal was obvious, and irresistible. Especially since Dolly's first husband had lost the money he made manufacturing silk and was now working as a cashier at a movie theater.

Dolly, wrote a friend of hers in 1942, was a woman who had "always known what she wanted," and if it didn't come to her, "she went after it, delighting whoever she met with her charm, wit, honesty, and her perennial youth and beauty." There is no doubt she went after Fleischmann. It took her a year or two to persuade him to separate from Lilly, who cited their affair in her testimony during their divorce proceedings.

They said Julius was so smitten with his young wife that he never refused her anything—"a policy," one paper put it, "that cost him a million dollars a year." But it wasn't enough. Rumors about the affair between Dolly and Jay ran around North Shore, and those "casual innuendos" were starting to spread to the gossip columns. Julius tried to protect her, and himself, by paying hush money to some of the grubbier papers—he handed over five hundred dollars to the "noxious periodical" *Broadway Brevities*. It didn't work. Jay, the story went, had seduced Dolly over the course of his visits to the Lindens that summer of 1923. He was a decade younger than Julius, but the difference between them was so much more pronounced than even that gap suggested. When the scandal broke, several papers printed pictures of the two rivals side by side. Julius was shown in a heavy suit and hat, looking squat, short, and stoop-shouldered; Jay was pictured in his bathing costume, black hair swept back, a wry grin breaking out underneath his clipped mustache.

The marriage broke that summer. Julius discovered that Dolly had given Jay twenty thousand dollars, money that, she said, he "had invested for her on Wall Street." He snapped at that, astonished that she was willing to entrust her heart and his money to such a man. In public, at least, he was still warm toward Dolly, but he was icily disdainful toward her lover, whom he considered a playboy with a two-bit fortune. "What is he?" he asked. "He is just one of those strange figures on horseback who appear on the fringes of wealth and society and whose only means of support appears to be the four legs of a horse."

Dolly was insistent. "I don't care who he is or what he is or how poor he is," she said. "He alone understands me. He is the only person in all the world who ever did. I would gladly starve with him."

No one ever fell for Jay in a little way. We may wonder, especially after Mae's account of her marriage to Jay, just what it was about him that was so irresistible. Jay, a friend explained, "possessed that curious and indefinable quality: charm. Call it the personal salt that makes an individual beloved by nearly everyone with whom he comes into contact." Whenever he came up in conversation—which, as we've seen, happened rather a lot—"someone is sure to refer to him as 'that perfect dancer.' Or perhaps it is 'the perfect rider.' Or the man who makes 'a perfect cocktail.'"

The newspapers nicknamed Jay "the King of Hearts," and "the Romeo of the Sporting World." As far away as Utah, the *Ogden Standard Examiner* was asking, "Is the dashing polo player, so well-known in the gay life of New York's Broadway and Paris' boulevards, about to add a third famous beauty to the collection of women who have called themselves Mrs. Jay O'Brien?"

The *Standard Examiner*'s readers didn't have long to wait for an answer. Dolly had tried to leave Julius four times, and on each occasion he had persuaded her to stay. In June 1924 she sailed for Paris, ostensibly to visit her mother. Paris just happened to be the divorce mill of Europe. Jay headed out after her on the very next ship. The two of them were alone together for two weeks before Julius finally caught up with them. He tracked them to an apartment on the Rue Spontini in the 16th arrondissement. He did not stop there long. After a short conversation, he realized that he had lost Dolly. The divorce was rushed through the French courts. Julius's legal counsel insisted that the decision was prompted only by the couple's "incompatibility," that they had, in fact, already been separated for the best part of a year. In a sense that was true, but only because she had been having an affair with Jay, which the counsel strenuously denied. "No scandalous allegations were discussed," he said. "Any statement that any third person was the cause of these proceedings is untrue." He also scotched the widespread reports that Julius was going to give Dolly a five-million-dollar fortune as a final settlement. No one believed that either. Instead, Julius Fleischmann was made out to be a man who had martyred himself for love, a man so magnanimous he'd refused to stand in the way of her happiness. His generosity to her, it was said, had ultimately extended to granting her the divorce she wanted, and on the grounds that he had abandoned her.

The Fleischmann scandal was one of the single biggest news stories in the United States that summer. It spread from Boston to Dallas to Miami, Chicago to San Diego to Seattle. The bare bones were laid out underneath bold headlines on the front pages, and the details picked over in long, lurid features inside. Jay was the "prince of poloists, the most graceful of Manhattan's masculine dancers, wielding his allurement over throbbing feminine hearts." He was "a Greek god on a prancing steed," the "Adonis of the polo field."

Julius Fleischmann returned to New York, alone, on the RMS *Berengaria*. He retreated to the Lindens. On July 12, he faced the press, who had been hounding him ever since his return. He met with a pack of hacks as he came off the tennis court. As they fired questions at him, he listened in silence, idly brushed a little dust from his trousers, then started to speak. "The idea seems to be that I am a hero. I have no desire to be such a hero. Just because my wife is divorcing from me in Paris and I'm not contesting it, someone is trying to picture me as the injured person. That isn't fair—to the woman. Whatever my wife may do, she is my friend, and she is the loveliest woman I have met." The divorce, he insisted, had come about simply because "a man and a woman may be devoted to one another and not be able to live together as man and wife, you know." The story that he was going to give her five million dollars was, he said, "absolute bosh," though "of course she has never lacked for anything, and she never will."

Was it true, someone asked, that he knew Jay O'Brien, that Jay had been a guest here at the Lindens?

Julius smiled wistfully and leaned down to stroke the Sealyham terrier that was nagging at his feet. "Yes, it is true that he has been my guest here. He is a good player, and has played polo on my field. But it is foolish to suggest he is my friend."

Who introduced Mrs. Fleischmann to Jay O'Brien? Was it yourself?

"Now, now, I am rather tired of hearing about Mr. O'Brien. Suppose we just forget about him." And with that, he walked off, turning back only to urge the journalists to "have a glass of lemonade and a look around the stables."

Just over a fortnight later, on July 29, Dolly and Jay announced their engagement. They traveled around France, to Deauville, Biarritz, and Monte Carlo, "in a style that seemed to show no reduction from her old one-million-dollar-a-year style." They were married in Paris on October 20, in a small ceremony at a hall in the 16th arrondissement. Again, the only guests were the two witnesses, but this time there were no reports that Jay had to use a gun to get his bride down the aisle.

As for Julius, he spent the rest of the summer with Edward, the Prince of Wales, who was first in line to the British throne and who had come over with the British polo team to play the United States for the International Cup. Fleischmann put them all up at the Lindens. No one mentioned that the mistress of the house was missing—because, as one paper put it, "a sportsman never would." So it seemed at last, as summer eased into autumn, that life was starting to settle down. But there was still one final twist to come.

On February 5, 1925, Julius was in Miami, where he had just ordered the construction of a new winter house on the beachfront. He and his old friend Carl Fisher were supposed to play polo that afternoon at the Nautilus club, but Julius was unsure about whether he was up to it. Fisher talked him round over a long lunch. After fifteen minutes of the game, Julius was flagging. He took a break to catch his wind, then returned to the field with his teammates. He was laughing. He had just asked them all to join him for dinner on board his yacht that evening. Moments later Julius pulled up and dismounted. He sat on the grass while play went on around him. A friend came over. Julius asked him for a glass of water. Then he lay down flat on his back, put his hand over his chest, and died.

Julius was fifty-three. His heart attack, it was said, had been brought on by "the excitement and strenuousness of the match." His death was the lead story in the *New York Times* and almost every other paper in the United States the next day. Inside, the *Times* ran a long article on the mood in Cincinnati, "a city in mourning." Exhaustive reports related his philanthropic deeds, his political accomplishments, his achievements in business, and his glories in sport. And then, as soon as his funeral was over, the papers began to address the question that everyone was asking: What was going to happen to his sixty-million-dollar fortune?

The will was opened and read on February 12, and this, too, was front-page news. It was just a little more than seven months after Dolly and Julius had agreed to their divorce, and a little less than four since she had married Jay. A short time, to be sure, but more than enough for Julius to have had it completely rewritten. In it, he explained that he had intended to bequeath the near entirety of his fortune to her, but since she had left him, most of the money would instead be split between his two children. Almost everyone got a cut: the captain of his yacht, his valet, his chauffeur, his stable hands. His factory employees got twenty thousand shares in his company, valued at $82 each, to split between them, and there was $200,000 for whichever Cincinnati charities his executors thought fit for it. Dolly got nothing. The date alongside his signature was August 29, 1924—nearly two months after their divorce.

Jay wasn't the romantic hero anymore. He was the man who had cost his wife something between a $35 million and a $50 million fortune, depending on who you listened to. Either way, it would have made her one of the richest women in the world. "Thirty-five million dollars!" exclaimed the *Seattle Daily Times*. "Divide that by the 200 pounds Mr. O'Brien weighs and you get the rate at which it now turns out the former Mrs. Fleischmann paid for him—$175,000 a pound. If she really thinks she got a bargain, she can truthfully say he is worth his weight in gold." If only "she had resisted his impassioned beseeching a few months more," she could have "had Jay O'Brien and the great fortune Mr. Fleischmann planned for her to have."

"If only they had waited another six months!" agreed the *Pittsburgh Post*. "The interest on this sum at 6% is $8,000 per day," it noted. "Every time Mrs. O'Brien gazes at her husband at the breakfast table, it must be apparent to her that within the next 24 hours he must deliver $8,000 worth of tenderness, gallantry, wit, sympathy, attention, amusement, or satisfaction of some sort, or she has made a bad bargain. Can he possibly be worth it?"

The answer, it seemed, was yes, he could. Jay and Dolly stayed out on the French Riviera, far away from the brouhaha. When one particularly persistent reporter finally found them, in Nice, Dolly simply told him, "I have heard all about it and I don't propose to do a thing. I am happy. And that is all that matters."

Jay may not have been guilty of the crimes Mae Murray accused him of, but there was no doubt he was a rogue, a fast-living, freewheeling rake with a violent temper. But he had finally met his match. As his friend Park Benjamin said in 1926, "You never can tell about re-marriages. The beautiful Dolly and her dashing swain were, last I heard, living abroad in permanent and luxurious peace. They seem to have made a go of matrimony after all. It was a love match, pure and simple." Dolly, said her friend Suzy Knickerbocker, "was very happy to be the ultimate female. Her beauty, her chic, her wit, her charm, her radiant sex appeal, her marvelous sense of humor, and, most importantly, her kindness to others."

Jay had always been, as Julius said, "on the fringes of society." Now he was down in the gossip columns as "a perpetual host" on the south coast of France, fast friends with the Prince of Wales—a situation that, one reporter wrote, "must cause the Queen of England to stay awake many a night worrying about her son." In those days Prince Edward was, his assistant private secretary wrote, engaged in "an unbridled pursuit of wine and women, and of whatever selfish whim occupied him." That same secretary thought he was "going rapidly to the devil" and "would soon become no fit wearer of the British Crown." His friendship with Jay and Dolly—the three of them were often seen out playing golf together—did nothing to assuage these worries. What tainted the prince in British papers, though, only burnished Jay and Dolly in US ones. Now that they were friends with royalty, their only appearances in the American papers were in the reports of what the fashionable set was wearing in Europe. Here was Dolly "on the beach at Lido, Venice, garbed in an up to the minute beach costume," or at "a social function for the Florida Club in Paris wearing a cornflower blue lace gown."

"Love," Knickerbocker wrote, "was the most important thing in the world to Dolly. And she and Jay, beautiful creatures, were dazzling and brilliant and golden. And very much in love and very happy." They were "soon the toasts of Paris and London and the darlings of the south of France." And, of course, of St. Moritz, which was, after all, where everyone who was anyone on the Riviera went to play in the winter.

Billy's new crew in their Satan kit, St. Moritz, 1928.

CHAPTER 4

A CALL FOR VOLUNTEERS

B illy Fiske arrived in St. Moritz for the first time in January 1927. He was still a boy, only fifteen, but his puppyish face had filled out a little, making him more handsome, and his slim, wiry body was hidden beneath the thick white polo-necks and cricket sweaters he wore to keep out the cold. His solo trip to South America had toughened him up, which was apparent in his gait. He walked with his shoulders back and his head up. But he was still too young to make much of an impression on the social scene in the grand ballrooms and great dining halls of the Palace and the Kulm. He left that to his parents and his sister, Peggy.

At that age Billy didn't drink or smoke. His father had offered both his children a thousand dollars each if they would refrain from either vice until they were twenty-one. Peggy decided she'd rather look "sophisticated and grown-up" than rich, so she took up both, but Billy collected the money. All that really meant, though, was that he did a good job of hiding his vices from his family. Peggy said that Billy could be "just as happy on orange juice at parties" when everyone else was drinking champagne. And he never smoked. But while he didn't depend on drink or drugs for a good time, he certainly wasn't averse to a binge, especially when he had something to celebrate. He just liked to measure them out against spells of clean living. He was reckless with other pleasures: he always loved to gamble, and he would, in time, become an insatiable womanizer. But all that was a few years away. At this stage of his life, speed was the thing.

St. Moritz provided him with plenty of opportunities to slake that thirst, even at the age of fifteen. Billy took his first trip down the St. Moritz bob run in January 1927, driving a little two-seater known as a boblet. The course started up by the Kulm. It ran into "the Snake," a chicane that buffeted the sled from side to side—"a horrible piece of architecture," as one of the riders called it. From there it went on into Sunny Corner, a twelve-foot-high bank. This was where the spectators gathered. There was a telephone station here, and the times for the sled were shouted out through a megaphone as it shot past. Tom Webster, a journalist who rode the course once for a feature article, reckoned, "If nobody goes over the top here then the spectators rush to the railway company and ask for their money back." They had come, after all, to see a crash. Then came Horseshoe. "All (except the spectators) shut their eyes here. At Horseshoe, a good driver needed to turn late, to gain height as easily and effortlessly as is possible. You need to be brave enough to let the sled run right up to the lip before pulling it back down out of the bend." From there, the sled went into Devil's Dyke. "I don't remember going through that," Webster wrote. "Think we leaped it." Then it was on into the straight, under the railway bridge. "This," Webster continued, "is supposed to last five seconds but not one member of the crew would be surprised if he found himself in a different climate" by the time it was over. Officially, Webster noted, the course was just under a mile. "But I thought it was never going to finish."

Billy was a natural. On January 11 he completed a boblet run in 1:47.5, the single fastest time of the season. He loved the sport so much that when Martineau purchased five new bobsleds for the club from a manufacturer in Davos, Billy persuaded his father to buy one for him. He was lucky: "In the gay old days," Martineau wrote, "few people could afford to buy their own bobs." Back then the bobs all had their own names. In fact, they would be listed first in the results; the steerer's name came second, out of courtesy, so it seemed as though it was the bob that won the race. "Every bob thereby acquired a character of its own," Martineau wrote. "They became personalized. And when it changed hands, one had the impression of a race-horse being bought-and-sold." Billy called his "Satan." His good friend Jennison Heaton bought another and named it "Hell." The names led one Englishman, often beaten by both of them, to wonder how "any one was expected to beat such a diabolical combination as that."

You would scarcely recognize Satan as a sled today. It looked a little like a camp bed with a steering wheel where the pillow ought to be. It was a long, flat frame spanned by a series of metal bars with two long rails on either side and metal runners underneath. There was a brake at the back, though it was considered a sin to use it during the run, since its metal teeth cut up the ice. And at the front, flat down, parallel to the ground, was the little wheel. Back then they were still bobbing in the ventre à terre style: the pilot got on first and lay along the sled, his feet pointing toward the brake; the second rider lay between the pilot's legs, his chest overlapping with the pilot's back; the third was flat on top of the second, a little farther back; and so on, right back to the brake. Only the steerer saw the course; the crew behind him buried their faces in the backs of the person in front and weren't supposed to glance left or right for even a fraction of a second during the run. They were, in effect, a deadweight, remaining motionless until the steerer called out "Left!" or "Right!"—when they would all lean over to that side. The only exception was the brake, who was allowed to get up on his knees before the corners and bob back and forth to help the sled build up speed. Leaning meant that the sled took the corner without any loss of speed, and made it easier to steer. And good bobbing, that back-and-forth motion, made a real difference to the speed of the sled. Ventre à terre was pretty much foolproof in that while a bad or rookie crew wouldn't help the sled speed along, they couldn't cause it to crash so long as they made sure to just stay still. This meant that the onus was entirely on the steerer and, to a much lesser extent, the brakeman.

That first year, the logbook of the St. Moritz Bobsleigh Club singled out two qualities in Billy's driving: "W. Fiske," as they called him then, was an "intrepid" and "hard-working" steerer. And here we get the first two clues about what made him such a great driver.

Every bob course in the world is different. Each has its own personality. There aren't really any hard-and-fast rules about, for instance, how to handle a corner, because each corner on each track is different from every other one. Some demand that you take the sled in low, some that you take it in high, some that you hold the line around the bend, some that you snap out of it before you've finished the corner. At the elite level—the level Billy was working at—the driver can control the position of the sled to within a margin of around three inches. And those three inches matter. Because every bob course has a perfect line. Steve Holcomb, the 2010 Olympic gold medalist in the four-man bob and the greatest pilot in the United States today, explains: "You could draw a line on the track. Follow it, and that would be the absolute fastest way down. And if you hit it the entire way, with a good push, you would destroy the track record. The catch is that you are never on that line; you are always changing. You can go into the first corner, the second, the third, maybe even six, seven, and still be on that perfect line. But to hit it the entire way down? That happens once, twice, in your entire career. I can think of runs where I was like, 'Man, that was it.' But, always, you can go back over it in your mind and be like, 'Ah, I missed these little points.' That perfect line is what everybody strives for."

The more familiar a pilot is with the course, the better he knows that line. So when Billy is described as "hard-working," what that means is that he spent a lot of time learning the ins, outs, and twists of the course, calculating, to the nearest inch, where the sled needed to be at any one particular moment on the track. For an amateur, he practiced a lot. And that work ethic and quest for precision would come to characterize his racing. Billy's friends recalled that later in his life, when he was racing a skeleton sled on the Cresta Run, he had a little party trick that proved how well he knew the course. He would stand, blind-folded, in the bar at the Palace Hotel, with a stopwatch. He would call "Start!" and click the watch, then count off the corners one by one, describing his run down the course yard by yard. And when he called "Finish!" and stopped the watch, the times for his imaginary runs would invariably be within a few tenths of his real ones.

Hard work wasn't the half of it. The second quality Billy had is captured in that word "intrepid." Remember, a company of men who rode bobsleds for kicks singled him out for being particularly brave. They had all done the run themselves—all had their own scrapes and crashes. They were all brave. But the best were braver still. As Steve Holcomb explains: "There are a number of drivers who are great drivers, they are passionate, they love the sport, they know what they are doing. But they don't want to take that risk. They don't want to push it. I raced with a guy who was a phenomenal driver, but he was more worried about going over the edge than he was about winning. He would rather get down safely and successfully than actually push the speed of the sled. And you really have to push the speed. Because you know that somebody else out there—the guys you are racing against—has the guts to push it hard. So to be the best, you don't just need the skill to drive the sled; you need to be prepared to take the risks. And that's tough." When Holcomb talks about "pushing it," what he means is having the patience to wait, to let the sled run right up to the top of the bank before you steer it back; to let it veer right over on to its side, to the very point when it could be about to tip over, before you pull it around. All part of that never-ending quest to find the perfect line.

Of course Billy wasn't the only talented pilot in town. There were the Hea-

ton brothers, for a start, especially the younger pair, his good friends Jack and
Jennison. The three of them would run around town together, along with Billy's
sister, Peggy. She and Jennison were falling in love. Then there were the British,
the best of them Martineau's young son Henry, and Cecil Pim, a captain in the
Scots Guards. The Belgian Ernest Casimir-Lambert, whom everyone called
"Henri," was so brave they thought him a fool. "He was always a source of tremendous danger to the other riders," remembered Martineau. He recalled the
day when Lambert arrived, "late as usual," for a competition on the Cresta Run
sled track. The organizer, Frank Curzon, was so angry that as Lambert set off
on his run, he shouted out, "You ought to go down on your knees!" Lambert
didn't realize it was a figure of speech and set off crouching on his sled. "Frank
was in a terrible state," Martineau wrote. "He was calling out, 'He's going to kill
himself! He's going to kill himself!'" And then there was the "hot-blooded
Argentine" Arturo Gramajo, the man who had unmasked Mademoiselle Krasnowski at that SMBC prize ceremony. "[He was] one of a number of Argentin-
ians who frequented Paris and St. Moritz during those years," said Martineau.
"They were all good sportsmen, as well as having the necessary cash; conse-
quently they were popular wherever they went."

The blue riband race of the season, the one they all wanted to win, was the
Bobsleigh Derby Cup. The prize was a silver cup that had been presented to
the club by John Jacob Astor back in 1899—a gift from one of the richest men
in the world, thirteen years before he went down with the *Titanic*. It went to
whoever could put together the four fastest runs over two days of competition.
Few gave Billy, the new boy, much of a chance. But he was confident. He had
five yellow polo-neck sweaters made up for his team, each with "Satan" stitched
across the front. His father had faith too. The club used to run what they called
a "Calcutta auction," with bidders competing to buy the rights to the racers in a
sweepstake. Billy's father paid 550 francs to get his son's ticket for the derby.

And he collected on it. Billy didn't just win the Derby Cup; he took another
prize, too, the Olavegoya Cup, for the single fastest run over the course of the
two days. And two days later he won more silverware, the St. Leger Trophy. So
in his very first few weeks as a bobsledder, the fifteen-year-old Billy Fiske won
three trophies, one of them the single most prestigious pot on offer in St. Moritz.

Billy's victories barely made the papers in either Britain or the United
States, which seems surprising: you'd think that even by the more reserved
standards of the day, a fifteen-year-old winning the biggest bobsled race of the
season in St. Moritz might have merited more than a passing mention. But Billy

didn't make much of a fuss about his age. In fact, few of his fellow racers knew just how young he was. And besides, by then St. Moritz was only one of a series of Swiss bobsled tracks, and while the races there may have been more prestigious than some of the others simply by dint of their history, the papers now took reports from the rival runs at Davos and Interlaken. The SMBC was particularly worried about the development of a run in nearby Celerina, "which, as far as one can see, will sound the death knell of the SMBC." Martineau considered it "an ominous black cloud in the sky which, if it bursts, will mean the flooding and disappearance of the SMBC run." The St. Moritz run was aging, and seemed a little slow and decrepit in comparison with some of these newer courses at rival resorts, which were thought to provide better sport. St. Moritz needed a major event, a race that would fix the world's focus on the town, give the SMBC the opportunity to reestablish its course as the premier bob run in Switzerland and its sledders the opportunity to prove themselves the best in the world.

"And then," noted the club log at the end of 1927, "floating out of the sky, came the Winter Olympics."

I f it seems odd that the club and its community could be caught short by an event the size of the Winter Olympics, understand that in the 1920s it was a far smaller and less significant competition than the one we know today. Baron Pierre de Coubertin, the founder of the International Olympic Committee, was never keen on the idea of the Winter Olympics. Figure skating had been included in the summer Olympic program in 1908, and again in 1920, when it was joined by ice hockey, but de Coubertin was skeptical about whether winter sports were worth including. "Modern industry has managed to create artificial ice," he wrote in 1909, "but it is hardly reasonable to expect that the time will come when a perfected form of chemistry will be able to place durable, long-lasting snow on hillsides. Thus skating is the only one of the three great winter sports that might be included within the Olympic enclosure if necessary. It would be better to adopt a solution in which these special sports are grouped together in winter, under the title 'Northern Games.'" Which is what had happened: the Nordic Games for winter sports were founded in 1901. Though nominally international, the Nordic Games were always hosted in Stockholm, with the exception of a single edition in Oslo, and were contested largely by Scandinavian athletes. The upshot was that Norway, Sweden, and Finland, three of the leading winter sports nations, were, like de Coubertin, never keen on the idea of a Winter Olympics, since they felt it would be trespassing on their turf.

Despite de Coubertin's objections, the IOC did decide to stage a winter sports week in 1924 at Chamonix, in France. The proposal had been made by the Marquis de Polignac, a French IOC member; he was supported by the Swiss, Italian, and Canadian delegations. It was held as a precursor to that year's summer Olympics in Paris. It wasn't a separate competition, and it certainly wasn't billed as a Winter Olympics. It was called, instead, the "International Week of Winter Sports." Only five sports were contested, and just sixteen countries represented. So it was a thoroughly low-key affair at which, one journalist wrote, "everyone knew each other, at least by sight, because no team was composed of more than 30 or 40 competitors." It was a success, however, so the IOC decided to recognize the event retrospectively as the first Winter Olympic Games, and to stage another in 1928.

Ideally the second Winter Olympics (but the first to go by that name from the outset) would be held in the Netherlands, as the Summer Games were due to be held in Amsterdam, but Holland isn't overly blessed with mountains. Instead, they were awarded to St. Moritz. The town had only a couple of years to get ready, and soon started gearing up. A new ski jump, the tallest in the world, was built, and new stands were put up around the ice rink. A deluxe train service was laid on from the port of Calais to the Swiss border, and plans were made to open up the hotels around the spa, which were typically closed outside summer months, to house the extra visitors.

Otherwise, life went on much as it always did in winter. In fact the organizers were especially keen to stress that the Games wouldn't impose on the tourist season. "Ordinary visitors must not imagine that preparations for the much-talked-of Olympiad will in any way interfere with their convenience or curtail their activities," read a report in the UK *Times*. "Far otherwise. The rinks and runs will be used as always up to the second week in February, and all the usual competitions and sporting events will be organized. Olympic teams and competitors will arrive in January."

For the Bobsled Club, the Games promised a season of "great sport, since men with bobs from every country will be represented there, practically for the whole season." The members relished the chance to compete against the best bobsledders from around the world. There would be twenty-five nations at the Games, with Holland, Romania, Germany, Latvia, Argentina, Japan, and Mexico all taking part for the first time. The bobsledding competition included twenty-three teams from fifteen nations—115 athletes in all, since they were riding five-man sleds. That made it the largest bobsledding competition in the sport's short history.

One thing that wasn't clear at first was whether the United States would be a part of it. Bobsledding had been invented in the United States, but it had been perfected in Europe. There wasn't a single course in North America, and the United States Olympic Committee wasn't at all sure it wanted to foot the cost of sending over to Europe the few drivers who did feel able to compete. In fact it wasn't even clear whether the USOC wanted to send a team to the Games at all. As late as April 8, 1927, they were still discussing whether or not the United States would be represented in St. Moritz. They decided to delay the decision until the committee could "ascertain just how much support the winter sport governing bodies in the country would lend the project."

The USOC needed to corral together a disparate group of governing bodies and amateur sports organizations from across all Olympic disciplines. The new president of the USOC, Major General Douglas MacArthur, had been appointed to the job in 1927 on the strength of the reforms he'd made to the athletics program at West Point military academy. Years before George Orwell first coined the phrase, MacArthur was a firm believer that sport was war minus the shooting. He had these words engraved in the stone outside the West Point gym:

UPON THE FIELDS OF FRIENDLY STRIFE

ARE SOWN THE SEEDS

THAT, UPON OTHER FIELDS, ON OTHER DAYS,

WILL BEAR THE FRUITS OF VICTORY.

MacArthur's speech to the US Olympic team in Amsterdam that summer of 1928 included the famous line "We have not come so far just to lose gracefully, but rather to win, and win decisively." He wasn't interested in the idea of fielding a Winter Olympic team for its own sake, or in paying the traveling and accommodation costs of athletes who had little chance of winning. Under MacArthur, the USOC decided that it would provide guarantees only for the figure and speed skaters; competitors in other sports would have to prove their worth, or pay their own way to Europe.

The USOC appointed a man named Gustavus T. Kirby to be its delegate to the Winter Olympics. Kirby was a New York attorney, "tall, distinguished, and of brisk bearing," as his obituary in the *New York Times* had it. He was a troubleshooter, with a "particular facility for placating dissident groups" (the *Times* again) in the world of sports administration. It fell to him to whip the United States' Winter Olympics team into some kind of shape. Kirby knew plenty of people. He had played tennis and golf, been a yachtsman and a horse rider. He was a familiar figure on the New York steeplechasing scene. He hosted a prestigious horse show at his ranch in Westchester, and even invented a camera timer for photo-finishes in close races. So of course he was friends with Jay O'Brien.

By 1927, Jay was the keystone of St. Moritz high society. He had charmed the British members of the SMBC with his easy manner and apparent sportsmanship. Hubert Martineau had appointed him to the SMBC's committee in 1926. It helped that O'Brien had bought the club a cup, the Boblet Grand Prix, as a prize for one of its races. He was beginning to make plans, too, for a new ski club in St. Moritz. His partners in this scheme were all European aristocrats: the Duke of Alba, the Duke of Sangro, Prince Boncompagni, and the Marquis de Polignac. It would, in time, become the prestigious Corviglia ski club. And he was at ease among the Americans, of course. Jay knew the Heatons and the Fiskes; he knew everyone who was anyone, whatever station of life they were in. One story goes that at the Cresta Ball in St. Moritz early in the winter of 1928, the guests were puzzled by three empty tables in a choice corner. The room was overflowing with people but the prime seats were reserved. Eyebrows were cocked upward, quizzically. They lowered again when Jay arrived, fashionably late, with the former Crown Prince Wilhelm, son of the kaiser, on one side, and Gene Tunney, heavyweight boxing champion of the world, on the other.

Gustavus Kirby approached Jay, and the two of them hatched a plan for the US bobsled squad. They decided that Jay would be put in charge and he would recruit a team of American ex-pats from the club in St. Moritz, and find a few willing men to fill out the ranks. They would all be in town already, and wealthy enough to pay their own way, something Jay was particularly proud of. "The men whom I selected were fine types of amateur sportsmen, brought together by me from throughout Europe," Jay later wrote to MacArthur. "I think it is only justified that I call attention to the fact that the training and participation of these teams did not cost the Olympic Committee one penny in way of expense." There were a few likely bob drivers in St. Moritz, but Jay still needed to find ten men to make up the two crews, with a couple left over for reserves in case of injury. He could take one seat himself, having picked up a little bobsledding experience; friends of his from St. Moritz, like his pal the old soldier Dick Parke, could fill a few of the other slots. But Jay was still short of a full squad. And then he had a bright idea: he would put out an advert calling for recruits.

Jay traveled to Paris to meet up with an old friend of his, Sparrow Robert-son. Sparrow was a sportswriter on the Paris edition of the *Herald Tribune*. He was a sinewy old fellow, half-cut as often as not, always on a cocktail of rye, dry vermouth, and Campari—he called the concoction an "old pal." When he wasn't at the fights or the races, Sparrow could usually be found in Harry's Bar on the Rue Daunou. He styled himself as "a philosopher of sport." He could hardly string a sentence together—he'd conned his way into the job, his only previous experience being his work as a small-fry fight promoter and a one-time coach for the YMCA—but once the copy editors stopped trying to make sense of his copy, his twisted syntax earned him a cult following among the American ex-pats in the French capital. The poet and publisher James Laughlin, who lived in Paris in the 1930s, laughingly called Sparrow the "great living master of American prose" because he so loved the "literary pearls" he would slip into the "dignified account of the last boxing match at the Palais de Sport or a hailstorm of statistics about horse racing results in 1910." Reading Sparrow's Sporting Gossip columns in the *Trib* was part of the daily ritual. "Back at home we would never have read the sports pages at all as a matter of principle," Laughlin wrote in his autobiographical short story, "The River." "But there in Paris at the big cafés, sitting and sipping, watching and reading, we came to be liking that part best of all."

Sparrow, Jay had decided, was just the man he needed to help beat up a little publicity for the bobsledding teams. He invited him over for supper one evening. The only problem was, if you wanted anything from Sparrow, you had to give him something in return. He wasn't in the business of handing out favors for free. So Jay fed him a scrap of gossip for his column, a tall tale about a new sport he had encountered on the Riviera that summer. Sparrow didn't believe it, but it made for enjoyable copy. Not long after they met, the following snippet appeared in the pages of the Paris *Herald Tribune*:

> The writer spent a very pleasant evening at the Paris home of Mr. Jay O'Brien, who a few years ago was the best of the American gentleman steeplechase riders. Mr. O'Brien's bobsleigh and crew won the famous St. Moritz Derby last year, and also several other races at the Switzerland resort. It is the intention of Mr. O'Brien to organize two American crews for the Olympic championship bobsleigh event which will be given during the winter sport next year.

Mr. O'Brien spoke of the latest sport which is called balloon jumping. A balloon about six feet high is strapped to the shoulders and with that contrivance one can hop around like a ballad [sic] dancer. One of the most expert of the balloon jumpers, Mr. O'Brien informed me, is Arthur "Bunker" Vincent, who is also one of the best American amateur golfers in France. Mr. Vincent puts the balloon attachment to his shoulders when he goes out on the links to sock the little pill around, and Mr. O'Brien says "Bunker" has a regular la-la time hopping around the links, feeling light as air. "It is a great sport, balloon jumping," Mr. O'Brien says.

"It is a good story, even if it is not true," Sparrow wrote to a friend of his. And for him, that was all that mattered.

For Jay, well, now word was out. Sparrow soon gave him another plug, calling for young male volunteers to ride on the US bobsled team. You needed to be American, in Europe, and athletic. Anyone interested should contact the paper. There were three responses. One was from a man named Geoffrey Mason, a student who was traveling through France on his way to Germany, where he was going to university. The second was from a man named Nion Tucker, a businessman from Hillsborough, California, who had studied at Berkeley.

The last was from a man named Clifford "Tippy" Gray, and his isn't the kind of story you can sum up in a line or two. No, the life of Clifford Gray is one of the great mysteries of the Olympics.

From left to right: Jay, Eddie, Clifford, and Billy. Lake Placid, 1932.

CHAPTER 5

THE MUSICIAN?

She stared at the photograph, asked herself again whether the man in it really could be her father. When June Grey had first opened the envelope and read the note inside, it had seemed like such an unlikely story. He died when she was young, and she had pieced together his life from the little she and her sisters remembered, bits they had heard and read about him, tales he had left behind in his memoirs, which he'd never finished. There was so much she didn't know about him. But this was too much. Even he couldn't have kept this secret. Could he? But the more she looked at the grainy black-and-white image, the more she began to wonder.

She picked up the framed picture of him. Normally she kept it on her mantelpiece, but she had taken it down so that she could look from one photo to the other. The two men had the same full face, the same high forehead, the same hair swept back flat behind it, and those same deep folds in the flesh on either side of the nose, running down to the corners of a broad mouth. It must be him. But it just seemed so incredible. And besides, it was all so long ago. He had been dead for nearly forty years, and this picture was a decade older still.

Tim Clark had been waiting a long time to find a story as good as this. Scoops didn't come along too often in the monthly magazine trade. This one was fifty years old, but it was perfect material for a feature, a human-interest story.

It was 1978, and the Winter Olympics were coming back to Lake Placid in 1980. Tim was reading up on the last time the Games had been held there, back

in 1932. He had a connection to the widow of one of the athletes who had competed in the four-man bob. He planned to pull at the thread, see if he could
unravel an article or two. He began looking into the participants in that four-
man bobsled competition and the name Clifford Gray caught his eye. He had
been a member of the United States' team in 1928 and 1932. There wasn't too
much detail on Gray in the contemporary reports, but the few clues he could
find seemed pretty intriguing. Gray, known to everyone by the nickname
"Tippy," was described as a "song-writer," an "actor," and a "tune-smith." Tim
looked up the name in an old edition of *Who's Who of the Theater*. And there
was his man.

> **Clifford Grey,** born Birmingham, England, 1887. Died Ipswich, En-
> gland, 1941. Composed over 3,000 songs for stage and film in a 30-year
> career, notably If You Were The Only Girl (in the World), Spread a
> Little Happiness. Married Dorothy Gould, 1912.

Three things didn't fit. The first was the spelling: The bobsledder was
known as Clifford Gray, with an "a"; the composer was Clifford Grey, with an
"e." That could just have been an error, a slip of a pen somewhere, or a vowel
switched in translation between the UK and the United States. The second,
harder to explain, was that the composer, Grey, was English, yet he had been
competing for the United States. And the third, oddest of all, was that Tim
couldn't find any mentions of Grey's Olympic career in the reference books.
Curiouser and curiouser.

Tim pulled out a couple of photos of the two men, Grey and Gray. Side by
side, they looked so similar. But he needed proof. He had an idea. Someone must
be collecting royalties on Grey's songs, so he called the American Society of
Composers, Authors and Publishers. They refused to give out any contact details
but told him they would be happy to forward a letter. So he wrote, explained
what he had found, and sent it off.

The letter made its way to Riverview, Florida, and Mrs. Eugene Silver,
maiden name June Grey, Clifford's eldest daughter. June got in touch with her
younger sister, Jill. She had an older sibling, too, a half-sister from a relationship
her mother had before she met and married Clifford. But the half-sister, Dorothy, wasn't talking to June. They had fallen out over Clifford's estate. Dorothy,
whom they all called Babs, had been in England with him when he died and

had, June suspected, sold off a lot of his possessions and kept the proceeds. Then there was the issue of royalties and who got what from his songs. That always seemed to rumble on.

Jill contacted Babs about Clark's letter, and Babs remembered that Clifford had visited her in Lausanne, Switzerland, where she had been sent to finishing school between 1926 and 1928. Which meant he could well have been in the vicinity of St. Moritz for the 1928 Olympics. More tellingly, Babs recalled that their father "adored bobsledding." She even vaguely remembered meeting some of his teammates. That seemed to settle it. Of course there was the confusion over the spelling of his name, but that was a common enough mistake. It had been spelled "Gray" with an "a" in the latest edition of *Who's Who*. June finally felt ready to reply to Tim's letter with one of her own. "Dear Mr. Clark," she began. "More and more, it appears to be our father."

Clifford Grey never told his children that he had been an Olympian. It seemed so strange that he should keep such deeds secret from his own family. But, as June explained in her letter to Tim, it really wasn't so odd. Clifford was, she said, "a very modest man, gentle and quiet, he never boasted." June had only recently discovered that her father had once toured Russia and China with the great violinist Efrem Zimbalist. She and her sisters had never really known their parents. "They traveled a great deal," she explained. "I crossed the Atlantic 19 times before I was 12 years old—and never once sailed with my parents. So you see, English children do not always know as much as American children." She ended her letter to Tim, "Thank you for your interest. It is exciting—and, from the photograph, I find it hard to doubt." There was a final PS: "So many thanks."

Tim Clark had his proof, and his story. Clifford Grey, an English composer, had, unbeknown to his own family, ridden incognito on the United States' Olympic bobsledding team. The lack of evidence in the reference books and the discreet, fleeting references to his career as a composer in the contemporary newspapers began to make more sense: he was hiding a secret, one that, if exposed, would have disqualified him and his teammates. In those same Games in 1928, the US Olympic Committee refused to field an ice hockey team because the squad, drawn entirely from Augsburg College, included the five Hanson brothers, who were all born in Canada. Grey, born and raised in England, would surely have suffered the same fate if he had been caught.

Tim Clark's article was published in *Yankee* magazine in February 1980, the same month as the opening ceremony of the second Lake Placid Winter Olympics. It was a beautiful piece of writing. And its revelations about Clifford Grey's double life caused ripples that were still spreading years later. They were seized on by other historians from across sport, music, and theater. David Wallechinsky, president of the International Society of Olympic Historians, picked up on it. So did an academic, James Ross Moore, who was researching Grey's life for the *American Dictionary of National Biography*. Between them, working independently, they set about piecing together the jigsaw details of Clifford Grey's life. It was clear that he was a man who kept a lot of secrets—that, as Tim Clark said, "there were a lot of things his children did not know about him."

Clifford was born in Birmingham, England, in 1887, in "an unromantic spot," as he called it, on St. Luke's Road. His real name was actually Percival Davis. And this was the first real clue about the kind of man he was. He changed his name when he was twenty because he wanted to reinvent himself. He had grown up in a humdrum middle-class household.

His father, George Davis, was a whip manufacturer, and though he couldn't afford to send his son to university, he did at least allow him to stay in school till he was seventeen. "Quite a concession on his part," Clifford wrote. "He had been brought up in the sterner Victorian tradition and had been put to work at the ripe old age of nine."

Clifford found a job with the local water department for a while, but realized it wasn't for him when he confused two telephone calls, sending a gang of men with tools, horse, and cart to repair a leaky tap in a kitchen, and then dispatching a lone plumber, armed with nothing but a spanner, to cope with a burst water main in a public square. As funny as the ensuing flood was, he found the work pretty dry.

He had a young man's hunger for adventure. So he quit the office and threw in with a local musical troupe, the Refined Set. It was then he changed his name from Percival Davis.

His range was pretty limited. Clifford sang only a couple of numbers, "Violets" and "Love Me and the World Is Mine," but that didn't hinder him. Back then "no program was complete without some amiable young man in evening dress who dispensed drawing room ditties in a mildly amusing manner," so he got plenty of bookings to perform at parish halls and temperance parties—"I always had to resist the urge to run on stage and shout 'BEER!' at the top of my voice," he wrote. Finally, he began writing his own material, and "finding that I could get a laugh or two," he said, "began to think seriously of burning my amateur boots." He was being modest. Clifford had such a gift for writing comedy lyrics that he soon found work on the circuit.

While traveling, he met and fell in love with Dorothy Gould. He was twenty-five; she was a little younger, at twenty-two. She already had a child, the daughter who would grow up to be Babs. Clifford adopted her when he married Dorothy in London in 1912. Together, they popped up in shows all over the country, from Bath to Brighton to Bristol. Finally, in 1915, when he was twenty-eight, Clifford's first full revue, *Why Certainly*, opened in Morpeth.

The next year, Clifford got his big break from the West End producer George Grossmith Jr. He was commissioned to write lyrics to accompany songs by the American ragtime composer Nat Ayer for a new revue, *The Bing Boys Are Here*. It was a smash and then some. It ran for 378 days at the Alhambra on Leicester Square and played to full houses from the first night to the last. Even Queen Mary went to see it, at a special matinee performance in July. Grossmith and his partners eventually replaced it with a series of sequels, *The Other Bing Boys*, *The Bing Girls Are There*, and *The Bing Boys on Broadway*, wringing every last penny they could from the public's affection for their original show. The most popular song of the series was Clifford's collaboration with Ayer, "If You Were the Only Girl (in the World)," a sweet and sentimental tune popular with pining lovers pulled apart by the war. Clifford wrote the lyrics for it during a Zeppelin raid, finishing them off by candlelight after the electricity went off. He played down his contribution, said he "was lucky to have been handed a melody like this," but his lyrics became so peculiarly evocative of their era that it has been a staple of soundtracks for period pieces ever since, popping up most recently in *Gosford Park* and *Downton Abbey*.

Clifford Grey was now one of the hottest young writers in the West End. He teamed up with Ivor Novello, "very young and humming with energy." The two of them holed up in Novello's flat in Aldwych, huddled around his piano, and rattled out songs for the shows *Who's Hooper?* and *Arlette*. After that, Clifford worked with P. G. Wodehouse on *Kissing Time*. Wodehouse and Grey would come to be good friends, but at first, it has to be said, "Plum" had a low opinion of Clifford's writing, thinking him "a plodder who changed others' work slightly and claimed credit."

Truth was, Wodehouse's sniffiness owed a little to their professional rivalry. In 1920, the great impresario Florenz Ziegfeld, the man, and mind, behind the famous Follies of Broadway, was looking for a vehicle for his new star, Marilyn Miller. He bought the rights for a new musical by the great American composer Jerome Kern, for which Wodehouse had written the lyrics. But when Ziegfeld renamed the musical *Sally* and insisted on including a couple of songs that Wodehouse hadn't written, Wodehouse returned to England in high dudgeon. When he read in *Variety* that Ziegfeld and Kern had hired Clifford to rewrite his work, he wrote to "everybody in New York" demanding his original lyrics back. At which point . . . well, it's best to let the master storyteller take over. He described the "laughable imbroglio" in a personal letter: "I got a furious cable from Jerry. The sort of cable the Kaiser might send to an underling—saying my letter withdrawing the lyrics was 'extremely offensive' and ending 'You have offended me for the last time!' At which point the manly spirit of the Wodehouses (descended from the sister of Anne Boleyn) bubbled in my veins."

While Wodehouse squabbled with Kern, Clifford seized his opportunity. "My wife and I decided it was time we discovered America," he wrote. "I had been in rather indifferent health throughout the previous winter and the idea of a holiday seemed good." Which is one way of putting it. The move may also have had something to do with rumors that Grey had an affair with a London showgirl that same year. Either way, he and Dorothy moved to New York in a hurry, lured by the prospect of working on Broadway with Ziegfeld. Not that life there was any less stressful. "Ziegfeld has a great name among American showmen," Clifford wrote. "In any town in the United States the name of Ziegfeld on a playbill would pack a theater. Other management might have to advertise the names of the stars. Not Ziegfeld."

"Attempting to grasp Ziegfeld's genius," wrote Randolph Carter in his biography of the man, "is somewhat like probing a mist." Carter felt Ziegfeld had little feeling for music, and no real appreciation of comedy, but was "something of a Midas, who converted gross into gold to fashion a fitting crown for his own superb ego." It would be hard, Carter went on, "to say whether this alchemy was achieved at greater cost to himself, his associates, or his backers. In any event, Ziegfeld was not an easy man to work with." This was some understatement. Ziegfeld worked eighteen-hour days. He once sent two of his writers fifty pounds of loose paper covered with his indecipherable observations about their script. After they had finally reworked the draft to make it more in line with what they imagined he wanted, they arrived at the theater to find Ziegfeld had ordered the construction of a set that bore no relation to the scenes he had asked for. So they had to start all over again.

Ring Lardner was so exasperated by his own experiences of writing for Ziegfeld that he extracted revenge in an acid little short story, *A Day with Conrad Green*. In Lardner's version, Ziegfeld was too much of a tightwad to pay the paperboy, too lazy to attend a friend's funeral, and too self-absorbed to remember his wife's birthday. One of Ziegfeld's writers remembered that "we revolved like little moons around his sun, hoping to avoid the heat when we could." His leading ladies, on the other hand, could afford to give back as good as they got. Marilyn Miller, the twenty-one-year-old star of *Sally*, had a hot temper and a sharp tongue. In her memoirs, Ziegfeld's daughter, Patricia, remembered being taken backstage by her father to meet Miller after a performance.

"Hello," Miller said, "you lousy son-of-a-bitch."

"Now dear," Ziegfeld replied. "I brought my little daughter backstage especially to meet you. You've heard me talk about Patricia, haven't you?"

"Yes, to the point of nausea."

When Ziegfeld asked what was bothering her, Miller replied, "You know goddamn well what's bothering me. It's this piece of crap you call a costume. It weighs a ton, and as far as I'm concerned you can take it and shove it!" At that, Ziegfeld and his daughter hurried back out, closing the door behind them just in time to stop the jar of cold cream Miller had hurled from hitting them.

Clifford Grey, a modest and mild-mannered man making his first foray on Broadway, was beset on all sides. He was caught between Ziegfeld, Miller, and Jerry Kern, whom he loved and respected but who could, as Wodehouse said, be a right "blighter." It didn't help that Ziegfeld was wary about English writers. He'd refused to hire Noël Coward on the grounds that his songs were "too British" and therefore "too sophisticated." He expected Grey to produce something with plenty of pizzazz, like his work for *The Bing Boys*. "As the Americans say, I was in 'fast company,'" Clifford wrote. "However, I found they were more than willing to help a somewhat lame dog, so, in spite of the newness of my surroundings, things went along according to plan."

Another understatement. Clifford concocted one of the great song-and-dance sequences in the show. *Sally* tells the story of a scullery maid who smuggles herself into a party on Long Island by posing as a Russian ballerina. There she launches into the song "Wild Rose," in which she kicks, twirls, and swirls her way around the stage, flirting with members of the male chorus arrayed around her. Clifford penned the scene's back-and-forth patter:

Chorus: You're nothing tame / You're like a burning flame / We
know your name.
Sally: But all the same / I'm just a wild rose / Not a prim and
mild rose / Tame me if you can / I'm a rose to suit any man.

At which point Miller would run forward to the front of the stage and wink at
the audience. And of course all the men in the audience would think to themselves, "She's singing to me!"

Sally was a fantastic success and ran for 570 performances in New York
alone.

Clifford Grey was made. He and Dorothy bought a house on Long Island,
took up "tennis and motoring"—the two activities he listed as his "interests" in
Who's Who—and became regulars at the Lamb's Club in New York. Clifford
continued to work furiously and earned credits alongside all the great composers
of the age on a string of Broadway hits. There was a show in each of the years
1922 and 1923, a short trip back to Britain in that same year to help launch
George Gershwin's first West End revue, then two more Broadway productions
in 1924, and three in 1925.

The most intriguing of the lot was *Ups-a-Daisy*. It was only "a mild frivol,"
as the *New York Times* put it, with, in the words of the *Sun*, "trite lines, undis-
tinguished scenery, [and] costumes which fail to quite hit the mark." At first
glance, the most notable thing about it now is that it included a walk-on appearance by Bob Hope, one of the very first roles of his career. The plot, however, involves a married man who pretends to be climbing the Alps when he
is, in fact, living the high life in Paris. He dupes his wife by sending home
letters about his exploits in Switzerland, which he has copied, verbatim, out of
an obscure book by a real mountaineer. She is so impressed by her husband's
descriptions of his derring-do that she has the letters published. He returns
home to find himself a renowned climber and an acclaimed author. The original author, outraged, turns up at the impostor's house and promptly falls in
love with his sister-in-law. It all ends with the two men setting off to climb in
the Alps together, so one can save his reputation and the other can win the
woman.

Grey wrote the story in the summer of 1928, and it made its Broadway
debut on October 8 that year, just eight months after the Winter Olympics in
St. Moritz. This, then, is surely a story inspired by the author's own adventures,
a take on what Ross Moore calls "the secret life of this quiet, retiring, and

serious-looking man, so supposedly sedentary and shy behind his horn-rimmed glasses."

Clifford Grey must have known Jay O'Brien from around and about Long Island and Broadway. The two men certainly moved in the same circles. Both knew Flo Ziegfeld and his friends. In his short story about Ziegfeld, *A Day with Conrad Green*, Ring Lardner includes a character who is an "internationally famous polo player" who refuses to let his "pretty and stage-struck wife" pursue a career in Ziegfeld's Follies. It could well have been O'Brien and Mae Murray that Lardner was describing. In the early twenties, O'Brien ran with Herbert Swope, a member of the celebrated Algonquin Round Table. There's a record of his having gone for dinner at Swope's house along with Groucho and Harpo Marx and William Randolph Hearst. That was when Swope lived across the road from both Lardner and F. Scott Fitzgerald, in Great Neck, Long Island— which also happened to be where Clifford Grey was staying while he was working on *Sally*. He knew the Marx brothers, too, having once turned down their act on the grounds that it was too risqué for the stage.

In 1928, Clifford took a trip to Switzerland to visit his stepdaughter at her finishing school in Lausanne. From Lausanne it was but a short hop to St. Moritz, where he went in search of sport and society. His friend O'Brien must have introduced him to Fiske, who needed men to ride in his sled at the Olympics. So, as Ross Moore puts it, "with considerable skill, Grey invented an American persona, Tippi [*sic*] Gray," and it was under that name that he signed up to compete.

The secret stayed hidden for fifty years. Grey died of an asthma attack while he was staying in Ipswich in September 1941. His condition had been aggravated by smoke inhaled during a German bombing raid on the city a fortnight earlier. Obituaries appeared in newspapers across Britain and the United States. Many of them, taken from a template put out on the news wires, described him as "one of the best-known lyric writers of the last three decades." They all mentioned his beginnings in Birmingham, his hits with Nat Ayer, and his work with Grossmith in the West End and with Ziegfeld on Broadway. Not one made any reference to his Olympic career.

He was buried in the Old Cemetery in Ipswich, beneath a simple gravestone that read, "In happy memory of Clifford Grey." In 2005, Clifford's four grandchildren and about thirty others who knew the story as Tim Clark had told it gathered at the Old Cemetery in Ipswich to lay a new marble tablet at the foot of the original headstone:

HE "SPREAD A LITTLE HAPPINESS"

CLIFFORD GREY

LYRICIST

"IF YOU WERE THE ONLY GIRL IN THE WORLD"

"LET THE GREAT BIG WORLD KEEP TURNING"

"GOT A DATE WITH AN ANGEL"

OLYMPIC GOLD MEDALIST

4-MAN BOBSLED IN 1928 & 1932 (USA)

BORN BIRMINGHAM JAN 5TH 1887

DIED IPSWICH SEPT 25TH 1941

WHILST ON DUTY WITH "ENSA"

REDEDICATION BY FAMILY AND FRIENDS 2005

It felt like a fitting tribute. Seventy-seven years after he rode with Billy Fiske in the 1928 Olympics, sixty-four years after he died, and twenty-five years after Tim Clark uncovered his secret, Clifford Grey had finally earned the recognition he deserved.

There was just one problem. Clifford Grey never competed for the United States, and he never went to the Olympics.

The story of Clifford Grey, of how this rotund, asthmatic English composer came to be mistaken for an American Olympian, takes some untangling. The knots of the problem have been drawn tight over time, and now the idea that he led a double life as an Olympic athlete is fixed fast, because it has been repeated over and again in a range of reference books and newspaper articles.

There had always been those who were skeptical about the story. David Wallechinsky, the president of the International Society of Olympic Historians, was one. At first he accepted it to be true, but over time he began to have his doubts, largely because the records held by the US Olympic Committee listed Clifford Gray as having been born in Chicago in 1892. James Ross Moore was quite convinced that this was just part of Grey's deception, his ingenious invention of an "American persona." He appended his entry on Grey in the *Dictionary of National Biography* with a footnote insisting that the "the US Olympic Committee's records on Grey are inaccurate."

John Cross from Bowdoin College, in Maine, also had his doubts. He was researching the life of the third man in Fiske's sled from 1928, Geoff Mason, a Bowdoin alumnus. According to Mason's recollections, Gray was a "businessman" and an alumnus of Cornell. "The story of the British songwriter-turned-Olympic gold medalist appeals to the Walter Mitty in all of us," Cross wrote. "It persists, despite the absence of a scrap of evidence to support it."

Which isn't quite right. There was the physical resemblance in the photos, so strong that it swayed Grey's own daughter; the references in the reports from the 1932 Games to Gray's being a "song-writer" and a "tune-smith"; and the hazy recollections of Grey's adopted daughter, who recalled that he "adored bob-sledding." There are some circumstantial details too: the plot of *Ups-a-Daisy*, about a man with a double life and his adventures in the Alps, and the fact that he had already changed his name and created a new identity once before, when he dropped Percival Davis and became Clifford Grey.

But nothing definitive. What bound it all together into a story that stuck for so long was the fact that so many people wanted it to be true. June Grey wanted to believe it was her father in that photo because she regretted how little she knew about his life. June's niece, Vicki Barcus, wanted her grandfather to have led a secret life as an Olympian because it appealed to her romantic streak. Tim Clark wanted a good story for *Yankee* magazine, and was sure he had found one—the very same urge that led so many journalists to follow up on his work. James Ross Moore seems to have been driven by a biographer's desire to uncover every last detail about his subject; but he got so close to the story that he lost sight of whether those same details were true or not. So Clark's original, understandable, error spread. It is still being perpetuated today because no one has found a single piece of incontrovertible evidence that proves that it is wrong. Until now.

On page 11 of an old edition of the *Sarasota Herald-Tribune*, spread across six columns, sandwiched between an advert for a Bendix washing machine and a Hanes suede-knit shirt, is a profile of Clifford "Tippy" Gray, champion bobsled-der. The headline reads, "Bobsled Champ Writes Music for His Living." The date printed on the top of the paper is March 9, 1948. Seven years after the English composer Clifford Grey died in Ipswich, Clifford "Tippy" Gray, with an "a," was still alive and well. In fact, at the time he was on holiday in Venice, visiting his brother, having just come back from the 1948 Winter Olympics in St. Moritz. Gray told the interviewer he was forty-seven, which was a lie, by a good few years. He said, too, that he was in "peak condition"—a claim that we can chalk up to his sense of humor, since he wasn't ever what you might call a fit man, even in his younger days. He was still sledding though, and planned to "help coach" the United States teams at the world championship the following year.

It's curious enough that two men alive at the same time could have such similar names and also look so alike. They both had balding heads, thick jowls, and stocky bodies. But the twist that really threw Tim Clark, the first and foremost coincidence in the chain, was that there was so much overlap between their two careers. "The sportsman has another facet to his career which is hard to believe upon meeting him," reads the profile in the *Herald-Tribune*. "Tippy looks like a line coach or any number of things other than his real vocation—which is music." Gray, like Grey, was a composer, though considerably less successful at it. At the time of the interview, he was working for the Music Corporation of America, writing background music for the movies. This, too, caused some confusion, since Grey spent three years in Hollywood himself, working as a screenwriter. Both were songwriters, both moved in and around Broadway, and both worked in Hollywood. They knew the same people, frequented the same haunts and hangouts. Odd thing is, they seldom seem to have been in the same place at the same time. While the Englishman was working the concert party circuit in England, the American was making movies in Hollywood. When the Englishman came to work in New York, the American moved to England, and then went on to Paris. When the American moved back to the United States, the Englishman was already home in England. No surprise, then, that the two grew to be confused with each other.

It seems to have been a common enough mistake in their own lifetimes. Over time, Gray came to be forgotten altogether: much of his life and many of the things he did were attributed to his near namesake. Even Gray's friends thought he was a mysterious man. His good pal Odd McIntyre, the famous gossip journalist, once called him a "human question mark." (McIntyre worked, for a time, as Flo Ziegfeld's publicist—another curious link between the two Cliffords.) McIntyre took great pleasure in including little snippets about Gray's life in his famous column "New York Day by Day," which was syndicated in five hundred papers across the United States. In the 1920s, McIntyre was reckoned to be the most widely read and well-paid journalist at work anywhere in the world. He fed his readers tales of the city, "the drifters, chorus girls, gunmen," and, of course, the celebrities. He was who you read if you wanted to know how Amelia Earhart was wearing her hair, what Babe Ruth had been eating for dessert, who Ernest Hemingway had been squabbling with in a bar downtown. McIntyre's columns are the nearest thing we have to a record of Gray's comings and goings. But even he found his friend to be "as homeless as smoke and always adrift."

Let's start with what we know for sure. Clifford Gray was born in Chicago in 1892, the son of an English father and an American mother. He is supposed to have attended Cornell, where he was a member of the Psi Upsilon fraternity— at least that was how his teammate Geoff Mason remembered him; Cornell has no record of Gray ever having attended. By 1910 he was in New York, writing subtitles for silent movies made by Jesse Lasky's Feature Play Company. From there he made the leap into starring on-screen himself. He had a series of roles in short films and made his debut in a full feature in 1915. The film was called *Beulah*, "a slapdash drama," as one critic called it, which was unsurprising given the rate at which Hollywood rattled out its silent movies. Gray was in nine productions in 1916 alone. In 1917 he landed his first leading role, in *The Inspirations of Harry Larrabee*, "a breezy detective story" about a playwright caught up in a murder mystery. He followed that with *Alien Blood*, in which he shared the top of the bill. The best of the bunch of films Gray made was *Coney Island Princess*, in which he starred with Irene Fenwick (who, of course, went on to marry Jay O'Brien) and Owen Moore.

Moore remained a friend of Gray's for the rest of his life. Damon Runyon remembered hanging out with the two of them at a party in New York in 1933. Gray was passing through the city, having just returned from Paris. He had traveled back on the liner *Europa*, accompanying home the body of his fellow actor Jack Pickford. Gray, Pickford, and Moore all came up in Hollywood at the same time, a tight little circle of friends together through the 1910s. Moore had been married to Pickford's more celebrated sister, Mary, though they had long since separated. Gray didn't enjoy anything like the success of his two friends, though Moore tried to help him along, getting him work on a couple of bigger productions made by Myron Selznick's new studio. Moore and Pickford both earned their stars on the Hollywood walk of fame; Gray never came close to that. But in the long run he was luckier than either of his two friends, or perhaps just blessed with a stronger constitution. Moore was a lifelong alcoholic; Pickford was a notorious playboy who died at the age of thirty-six from neuritis brought on, rumors had it, by syphilis. They were the original Hollywood hell-raisers, as debauched and dissolute as any of the many who have followed in their footsteps.

In 1920 Gray and Moore were in Europe with Pickford and his wife, Olive Thomas. She had been one of Ziegfeld's girls from the Follies until she was signed by Selznick to star in his film *The Flapper*. "Two innocent-looking children, they were the gayest, wildest brats who ever stirred stardust on Broadway," wrote their friend Frances Marion, who worked with Gray when he starred in the film *The Heart of a Hero*. "Both were talented, but they were much more interested in playing the roulette of life than in concentrating on their careers." Gray was with the two of them in Paris when Thomas, after a night out at Le Rat Mort in Montmartre, drank a bottle of mercury bichloride. Pickford, rumor had it, had been prescribed it as a cure for his syphilis. A hotel valet found her the next morning, naked on a sable opera gown spread out on the floor of the Royal Suite.

Moore, Gray, and Pickford stayed by her side at the American Hospital in Neuilly-sur-Seine. She died five days later. The American papers were full of wild innuendo. Even the *New York Times* reported "rumors of cocaine orgies intermingled with champagne dinners which lasted into the early hours of the morning." The story spread that she had been out trying to score heroin for her husband and that they had fallen out after she had failed to find any. Pickford never escaped the idea that Thomas had committed suicide after having a row with him, though the coroner ruled it was an accidental death. The very same day that the verdict was announced, Gray, Moore, and Pickford traveled together to a memorial service at the Church of the Immaculate Conception in London.

Gray stayed in the UK. Pickford traveled back to the United States. He would soon marry Marilyn Miller, the star of *Sally* who had been working with Clifford Grey only a year earlier. It may have been a small world they were moving in, but it is still striking how the lives of the two Cliffords intertwined. Another odd link: the reason the American Clifford stayed on in the UK was so that he could make a film, *Carnival*, with Ivor Novello, who had been working with the English Clifford only a few months beforehand. It was Novello's first feature film, a remake of *Othello*, shot in Venice and, a touch more prosaically, Twickenham, in south London. Gray had signed on to make three films with the Famous Players–Lasky British Producers. *Carnival* was the first of them, and then he had small parts in *Dangerous Lies*, whose production crew included a young Alfred Hitchcock, and, in 1922, *The Man from Home*. It was the last film he ever made, and the last time he ever acted. He was staying at the Hotel Cecil on the Strand when he was arrested after being caught, bizarrely, in possession of an opium pipe and a Colt automatic pistol. He told the police that the pistol had been given to him by a friend who had just left for America, and explained, a little unconvincingly, that he used the pipe as a cigarette holder.

After that little scandal, Gray drifted, away from London and away from films. He became, in Odd McIntyre's words, "the most consistent of the international gadabouts." A professional playboy, to put it another way. "Wherever there is excitement," McIntyre wrote, "Tippy is more than likely to bob up suddenly, look about pleasantly, and as suddenly vanish." McIntyre took great delight in regaling his readers with installments of the adventures of this "most ubiquitous New Yorker." "Tippy fits the vague classification of a man-about-town. Everybody knows Tippy and he seems to know everybody. Wherever you go—Palm Beach, Paris, London, Hollywood, or New York—you will find him. He is natty, boyish, and a wizard thumping piano keys. He appears every inch the irresistible movie hero, and while I have known him a number of years his profession, save that of having a good time, is as nebulous as fog. A sort of human question mark is a fitting description. Tippy is always just arriving or just going somewhere. Not so long ago I talked to him in Los Angeles. He was hopping on a train in 10 minutes for New York. A week later at a New York pier he was going up the gangplank of a liner for Europe. He never seems to light. One night he might be found dining at a lunch counter with a vaudeville acrobat, and the next in immaculate evening dress at the Ritz with a group listed in the social register."

Of course Gray was a friend of Jay O'Brien's. They knew each other through Irene Fenwick, O'Brien's second wife and an old pal of Clifford's from his Hollywood days. He and Jay were both regulars at Harry's Bar in Paris. Both men claimed to have concocted the Sidecar cocktail, a mix of cognac, Cointreau, and lemon juice, while drinking there. The records are patchy—as McIntyre wrote, Gray was "not the publicity seeker often seen among his ilk. He is just a play-boy, and seemingly having heaps of fun at the job"—but if anywhere was home, it was Paris. A month after he wrote the column in which he described Gray's profession as "nebulous as fog," McIntyre was surprised to receive an envelope stamped with a Paris postmark that contained only a single business card. It read, simply:

Clifford Gray
Compositeur de Musique
Moulin Rouge Music Hall
Paris

"Tippy" McIntyre wrote, "has put me right."

In the mid-1920s Gray was working at the Moulin Rouge, writing revue songs for the famous French singer and showgirl Mistinguett. She had just returned from her first US tour and wanted to incorporate a few jazz numbers into her show. Clifford wrote a couple for her, including a foxtrot that he called "California Rose." He had always been, as McIntyre noted, a wizard at the piano: "For appreciative listeners he will often occupy the piano chair all night to improvise." Mistinguett was almost fifty then, "an old lady with young ankles," though as famous as ever. And as flirtatious too. Not that there was ever a suggestion she and Gray were involved. McIntyre stated his friend was "not a roaming Don Juan. In fact Tippy seems to appeal to the maternal in all women. He is the sort they trust."

Certainly one did. In 1929 he married Clara Louise Cassidy in Paris. She was the heiress of Charles Whelan, who owned United Cigars, a man then reckoned to be worth around fifteen million dollars. The Whelan family moved to Paris and began living high on the hog. They had started poor but had done so well in the tobacco business that they were able to spend one hundred thousand dollars on the wedding of their second daughter, making it, in the words of the *Schenectady Gazette*, "one of the most elaborate society affairs seen in years." Clara had been married before, to her father's business partner, John C. Cassidy, and had five children with him. They'd divorced after seventeen years together. It seems she latched onto Clifford, or he onto her, in the immediate aftermath of the separation. The brief marriage notices described Clifford as a "musical comedy producer from Chicago," which seemed as good a formal description of what he did as any other. With Clifford Gray, the details are always vague.

The marriage didn't stick. Neither did the Whelan family fortune: they lost everything in the fallout from the Great Crash of 1929, almost at the time when Clara and Clifford were getting married. Clara's grandnephew, Frank Whelan, remembered how his grandfather used to tell stories about "yachts, big houses, and servants," but he always ended them with the phrase "but that was before 1929." Frank remembered how he'd once seen "my father look at the paper one day and throw it down in disgust and stare into space. In the space of one day he had lost several million dollars." The family had to cut their cloth to suit after that. "We're all going to have to live a little more simply now," Charles told his children. It was, Frank wrote, "Bye-bye Paris, hello Jersey Shore."

Clara had a nervous breakdown not long after and ended up in hospital. Clifford Gray drifted away. Soon he was back, McIntyre wrote, living as "a plump bachelor," "a lone wolf among globe trotters. He knows almost everybody but nobody seems an intimate. He is a side-line looker-on at life, gazing with the detachment of a modern Punch and murmuring the same immortal line, 'What fools these mortals be!' " It's not clear if he and Clara actually divorced. She was still going by the name "Whelan Gray" as late as 1938.

Gray returned to what McIntyre described as "the blow-torch life," only now it was more extravagant than ever. McIntyre claimed to have heard reports of people bumping into Tippy "moseying out of a movie theater in the Bronx," "on the veranda at Shepherd's in Cairo," "casually strolling the Shanghai bund," in "the South Seas, Singapore, and the Arctic circle," and a "Gibraltar bazaar." Gray was, McIntyre added, "the man-about-the-globe," a "zooming devastator of space." And of course he met him in St. Moritz, too, where Gray "won trophies for his skiing." Which was news to at least one of his pals, the journalist Arthur "Bugs" Baer. "I never knew Tippy to go in for the outdoor life unless it was an estaminet table or a garden party. Even at the Coconut Grove, he benched out every dance." But then we shouldn't be surprised by the contradictions and confusions. Gray was the "anthology of human paradox," noted McIntyre. "Loving life, he seems constantly fleeing from it."

There were few faster ways to flee than by riding a bobsled—which could well be why Tippy responded to Sparrow Robertson's column when he saw it, in one of those idle estaminet moments, in the *Tribune*. In January 1928 he set off for St. Moritz, to meet up with Jay O'Brien, his drinking buddy from Harry's Bar. Jay duly roped him into the US bobsled squad. Gray was a big man after all, his waist well upholstered after all his hard living, and the sleds needed ballast.

As for his English namesake, who knows? He may have been in Switzerland that winter—it wouldn't be the most surprising of the many coincidences in this curious tale. One thing is for sure though: Clifford Grey never got into a US bobsled, and he never raced with Billy Fiske.

Sunny Corner, St. Moritz, 1927.

CHAPTER 6

THE RACE

T he envelope was slim and stamped with a Paris postmark. Geoff Mason guessed it was from the offices of the *Herald Tribune*. He had written to the paper a few weeks earlier, putting himself forward as a volunteer for the US Olympic bobsled team. Mason had never been near a bobsled, but he had been a fine athlete and football player in his college days. And besides, he had time to kill. He had come over to Europe from the United States the previous summer to take up a place at the University of Freiburg, in Germany. He'd brought his family with him, his wife and their two young daughters. They had done a little traveling. Now they had settled down in their new hometown, only a short distance from the Swiss border. The new term wouldn't start till later that winter. So when Geoff saw Sparrow's column, his first thought had been "Why not?" His second had been . . . well, he hadn't had a second thought. He'd sent off his letter and forgotten all about it.

He opened the envelope and took out the short note inside; it was signed "Jay O'Brien" and sent via Sparrow Robertson at the *Trib*. Geoff skimmed his eyes over it once, and again, slower, a second time. He was on the team. It didn't mention anything about a physical exam or a trial run in a sled. It just said, "Come down to St. Moritz, soon as you can." It was late January 1928, a little over two weeks before the opening ceremony of the Winter Olympics.

Mason took a morning train to Zurich, and a second on to St. Moritz that same afternoon. By the time he got in, it was ten at night. He trudged through the snow to the Palace Hotel, where, so the letter told him, his new teammates were staying. It looked a little grand for his budget, but rates had been fixed for the Games: $1.50 a day for the cheap rooms, $4.50 for a suite. It was already full, so Mason made his way down the road to a cheaper place. He found he was sharing it with the Canadian ice hockey team. He was over six feet tall and weighed two hundred pounds, but for once, he wasn't one of the bigger men in the room.

The next morning, Mason walked back through the town to the Palace. He passed the ice rink, where an army of carpenters was working on the new grandstand, and went on through the busy streets, where painters and decorators were prettying things up, hanging up bunting and flags. He met with the rest of the US team at the Palace. First, Jay O'Brien. He was whippet thin, with a fine pencil mustache that hung over the long ebony cigarette holder that was always tucked between his teeth, cigarette smoldering at the far end. It was such an effort to keep it there that his face, already leathery from the sun, often seemed to be bunched up in a scowl. But he was a friendly man, and he made the introductions. There were a couple of other men who had replied to Sparrow's column: Nion Tucker, an unlikely-looking athlete, a portly chap with pebble-lens spectacles; and Clifford Gray, whom everyone called "Tippy," short and stout but with a warm grin and a wickedly quick sense of humor. And then there was Billy Fiske, youngest of the bunch by far. O'Brien and Tucker were both in their forties, Gray was a little younger, Mason was twenty-five, but Fiske was just a kid. Nonetheless, he struck Mason as "an extremely mature young man," "very sophisticated," "very smart but not a smart alec." And he was, they said, "a crackerjack bobsled driver." The others seemed to have "utter confidence" in him.

Mason would soon come to think of Billy as "unquestionably the best anywhere." O'Brien, who had to pick three teams for the Olympics—USA 1 (the top sled), USA 2, and a reserve crew—didn't quite agree with that. Jay was a good friend of Billy's father, and he felt that the boy, talented as he was, was still a touch too young to be No. 1. Billy had, they said, actually approached Jay and asked to be his sled driver in the Olympics. When Jay knocked him back, Billy had replied, "Well, sir, what shall I do with the bobsled my father gave me?" He was certainly sure of himself. But Jay had an idea that either Jennison or Jack Heaton would be the best pilot. The three of them were all good friends; Jennison was still dating Billy's sister, Peggy.

The two big questions were who would get to drive which sled, and who would have to sit it out, and Jay decided that the best way to settle the issue was to wait until the Derby was run on the St. Moritz track, just a week before the

Olympic race was due to take place. Billy had won it the previous year, on his very first attempt. And he had made an astonishing start to the Olympic season. He had already won the Netherland Cup on January 9 and the Argentine Cup on January 17. That very week, with Mason watching, Billy triumphed in the prestigious Gold Cup, the ornate trophy presented to the club by Jay's good friend Princess Vlora. So Fiske was the man in form. But O'Brien insisted on basing his decision on the results of the Derby. As the UK *Times* reported, "The Derby is the biggest race of a normal year, and will provide an excellent pointer for the Olympic race, since most of the crews competing in it are to engage for Olympic laurels." The top two Americans to finish would be Jay's first and second drivers for the Olympics, and the third would be the reserve.

There was always a little gambling action around the bob run. Couldn't but be, what with all the money around the town, the idle rich spectators with nothing else to do for kicks till the bars opened and the balls started in the evenings. The St. Moritz Bobsleigh Club made most of its money that way, running auctions and sweepstakes on the results of the races. The 1928 season, though, was something else. St. Moritz was overflowing. The Olympics tourists were spilling out into the nearby towns of Celerina, Samaden, and Pontresin. The crowds weren't too popular with the regular guests. One British journalist complained about the new breed of swells, the "fur-collared males" and the "painted lady with her dog, her fat ankles, discontented face and bejeweled sports clothes." But the townspeople loved it. Especially the bookmakers. The big money on the Derby was behind Jack Heaton. Second in the running was the crazy Belgian Ernest "Henri" Lambert. Fiske, despite his good form so far that year, was fourth. He was only sixteen, after all, and no one knew how he would handle the pressure of the competition.

The race was scheduled for a Thursday. On Wednesday night, someone— and no one ever discovered who it was—broke into the shed where the sleds were kept and fiddled with Henri Lambert's bob. Or so Lambert said once he had finished the race. He came in second, in the end, behind Jack Heaton. Billy finished third, though he did win the Olavegoya Cup, because he recorded the single quickest run during the competition. Each sled had taken four runs, and the winner was the one with the lowest combined time. None of which mattered much once Lambert's story got out. The journalists swilling around town, who had never seen a bobsled race before, smelled a more interesting story than the straight results of the race. "Here's fun," wrote John Kieran in the *New York Times*. "It appears that some miscreant, under cover of night, strolled into the stall in which the Belgian bobsled expert keeps his iron steed and gave the runners a severe twist. It is most important, of course, that the runners of the sled should be parallel, otherwise the speed is much diminished, and there is a tendency on the part of the sled to separate into several segments. Should the sled divide itself into several segments, the rider has a choice of evils. He can slide the next forty yards either on his nose or on his ear. Neither method is particularly comfortable, especially if the icy coating is inclined to be rough and bumpy. There are straw mats to catch those who fall off their sleds at various points, and the telegraph poles along the route are wrapped in many thicknesses of burlap placed for the reception of distinguished guests. Even so, many rich Americans and titled Englishmen miss the mats and the upholstered telegraph poles and have to be dug out of the common or garden variety of snowdrift." It was no joke, this, as funny as Kieran made it sound.

Lambert had spent the morning of the race readjusting the runners on his sled, but still felt that the delicate calibration was out of kilter when he started. One punter won twenty thousand dollars on Heaton's victory. The rumor ran around town that someone was trying to fix the results of the races. Afterward, Jack Heaton declared, "This bob is going under lock and key. Anyone tampering with it must pick a lock and know the combination of my safe deposit box." The *Times* reported that the sleds were "guarded like thoroughbreds . . . locked up in sheds as a result of heavy betting on the international event." Billy certainly took the threat seriously: Peggy remembered that he spent the next few nights sleeping in the stall with his sled, buried beneath a mound of fur blankets, to make sure no one could get their hands on his equipment before the Olympics.

Jay O'Brien knew a thing or two about fixing from the days when he ran with Arnold Rothstein in New York, betting on racing and baseball. He wasn't surprised by anything. And all that aside, he now knew what his teams would be for the Olympics. John "Jack" Heaton would drive USA 1, Billy Fiske USA 2. He began to assemble their crews accordingly. He would ride as brakeman in the No. 1 sled himself, alongside Heaton and three men he seemed to pick on the strength of their social credentials as much as their sporting ones. Two of them were financiers: Lyman Hine, president of the American Cotton Oil Company, and David Grainger, a trader who had just bought a seat on the New York Stock Exchange for $143,000. (They had contrasting fates ahead of them. Hine died in a car wreck in Paris in 1930, at the age of forty-one. Grainger ended up holding on to that NYSE seat for seventy-six years—a record. He was still going to work in his Wall Street office in his nineties.) The final member was Tom Doe Jr., only fifteen but an athletic lad, and, just as pertinently, the son of the president of Eastern Air Transport Inc. The second team would take the three rookies, Nion Tucker, Geoff Mason, and Clifford Gray, with old hand Dick Parke as brake.

Billy had the disadvantage of racing with a largely green crew, most of whom had never even been on a bobsled until they arrived in St. Moritz, and in Mason's case had only had a fortnight to prepare for the Games. They were an unlikely lot—a sixteen-year-old pilot and three men who had only just taken up the sport. They were racing ventre à terre, though, which meant that their inexperience wasn't quite the handicap it might have been otherwise. When you're lying down, overlapping like slates on a roof, there's a limit to how much you can roll from side to side, so sudden movements or miscalculations don't have the same dramatic effect on the momentum of the sled as they do when you're sitting up. But while such things wouldn't actively hinder the sled, they wouldn't do much to urge it on either. A well-drilled crew, one that knows how to bob in rhythm before the corners and lean in concert as they go around them, can add vital speed and help trim those crucial tenths of seconds from the time. The man in the middle seat of the five has to be able to absorb the bobbing of the two riders behind him and, by clenching onto the rails of the sled, convert their rocking into extra speed for the vehicle. This was the role Mason had taken on. He had been practicing it with the Polish crew, who had lost a member to illness, as well as with the Americans, because he wanted to put in as many hours as he could before the big race.

Billy encouraged him to do exactly that. He knew Jack Heaton well. In fact, the two of them were pretty much best friends. So Billy had a keen awareness of Heaton's flaws. Once, writing in his journal, he described "a damn good dinner" the two of them had eaten together, during which "Jack made the statement that 'Independence is the only thing worth striving for.'" Billy thought there "was something in it" but found it "a bit far fetched" since Jack "hasn't strived very hard so far, but he certainly seems to have reached his end." He felt Jack was talented, but a little lazy. Billy knew that if he had an edge, it would be in the effort he and his crew put in. So he set the five of them to work, making them take run after run after run down the course at St. Moritz, drilling them until they knew each of the turns intimately and could anticipate whether they needed to lean left or right without waiting for Billy to shout it out. They had only a week to get ready for the Olympic bobsled race. Billy wanted to be sure they used the time wisely. He insisted that Gray and Parke bob together on the straights, and Parke bob alone going into the corners. He taught Mason how to absorb the shock of the two riders behind him throwing themselves onto his back, and how to transmit that energy into the sled. Tucker's job, in the No. 2 seat, was simply to hold Billy fast and act as a buffer between the driver and the bobbers behind.

Billy came to be quietly confident in his crew, but he wasn't the only rider who fancied his chances. A lot of money was being bet on Lambert, spoiling for a second shot after being foiled by sabotage prior to the Derby. The British papers were talking up the chances of their riders, the current world champion Henry Martineau and Cecil Pim, the captain in the Scots Guards. Pim had crashed in practice, shooting his sled over the top of Sunny Corner into a group of spectators, but he had recovered. And he had won eight races on the track the previous year. The outspoken Argentine Arturo Gramajo gleefully told the press that he could "certainly beat" Heaton's winning time in the Derby, and that he expected the winning order to follow on from the alphabetical one, with Argentina in first place. From out of town there was the German crew of Hans Kilian, a crack driver, but one who had precious little experience on the St. Moritz track. And of course there was Heaton with his crew, composed of Jay's pick of the US riders.

On Saturday, February 11, the Olympics opened, and the weather broke. A strong wind came rushing down the Majola pass. It carried a heavy snowfall with it. And so the athletes were forced to march. Five thousand turned out to watch what should have been an impressive parade, but not many stayed till the end. It was seven degrees below zero. "The prevailing cold effectually prevented the presence of that dignity so essential to its success," noted the *Times*. Most of the athletes were kitted out appropriately, in long fur coats, thick jerseys, and woolen stockings, but the International Olympic Committee's officials were "clad immaculately in lounge suits and bowler hats," a state of dress so ill suited to the conditions that it "moved the small crowd present to mirth rather than the desired solemn exaltation."

An official named Godfrey Dewey led the American team and carried the flag. Billy Fiske hardly knew him then and could have had no idea how much he would come to hate him in the years ahead. Gustavus Kirby followed him, with the ski jumpers, speed skaters, and figure skaters in short order behind, and the bobsled crews bringing up the rear. There were only twenty-six of them altogether, twenty-four athletes and two officials.

The weather didn't get any better for the next two days. It was so bad, in fact, that the uncovered stands were mostly empty at the figure skating and hockey rinks because the fans stayed packed into the hotels. Some of the athletes wished they could do likewise. There were, as was typical in the early days of the Olympics, some strange events on the program. Oddest of all was the military patrol, which was junked from the Olympics after 1948. Teams of athletes had to ski a twenty-mile course while carrying a rifle, rations, and other field equipment. It was open only to soldiers on active service and had been included largely as a sop to the Norwegians: they were aggrieved that the Olympics was competing with their own Nordic Games, but appeased by the fact that the program had been tailored to include plenty of events they could win. Like the military patrol. No one else had much of a chance. The event took place on a course that was so grueling that the papers reported that most of the athletes collapsed face-first into the snow once they'd crossed the finish line. One young Frenchman fell down, delirious, three miles from the finish, and was carried on the shoulders of his teammates for the rest of the way. Two of the four members of the Finnish team passed out after the race. All three were sent to hospital, where, according to one report, "hot grog and other stimulants were administered." The Norwegians, on the other hand, felt in such fine fettle at the end of the four-hour-long race that they burst into a spontaneous rendition of their national anthem "at the top of their lungs."

On Tuesday, the sun emerged, and a thaw started. When everyone woke, they found it was raining. The snow on the streets turned to thick brown slush, and the ice at the skating rink was water. The 10,000-meter speed skating had started at midday. The competition was being run in heats, with the athletes split into pairs for the individual races. Whoever set the fastest time of the day would win the gold. The hot favorites were two Norwegians: Bernt Evanson, who had already won a gold in the 500-meter sprint, a silver in the 1,500-meter, and a bronze in the 5,000-meter; and Armand Carlsen, who had broken the world record for the event a fortnight earlier, with a time of 17:17.4.

Evanson was drawn in the first heat. He would be racing against an American, Irving Jaffee. Jaffee came from a Russian Jewish family who had immigrated to the United States at the turn of the century. He had been brought up in the Bronx and had dropped out of high school when he failed to make the varsity baseball team. He took a job as a cleaner at the Gay Blades ice rink on West 52nd Street in Manhattan, not least because it saved him the seventy-five-cent cost of admission when he wanted to go skating. He was good at it. In 1927 he won the national five-mile race, which earned him selection for the Olympic team. Jaffee was only nineteen, and it was the first time he had ever traveled outside New York.

Good as Jaffee was, he was still the underdog for this 10,000-meter heat. Evanson duly took a decent lead over the first half of the race. Jaffee slipped three seconds back, but he managed to hold the gap there; then, as the two of them continued to circle around, over the slushy ice of the stadium, he began, ever so slowly, to pull his way back toward Evanson. And then, as they entered the home straight, Jaffee snapped into a lightning sprint. He caught Evanson almost exactly as they crossed the line. The tip of the skate on Jaffee's front foot was an inch ahead, and he was awarded the victory by a tenth of a second, the smallest margin the timing mechanism would allow.

It wasn't just the best race of the day; it also turned out to be the only good race of the day. By the time the next heat was under way the temperature was up around 75 degrees Fahrenheit, and there were large puddles across parts of the track. Carlsen, the world record holder, finished with a time of 20:56.1—nearly four minutes off his personal best—which put him 2:20 behind Jaffee. Another Norwegian, Roald Larsen, gave up when he saw that his split times were two minutes behind Jaffee's. No one could get within ninety seconds of Jaffee's time. The pace grew so slow, and the ice so wet, that during the fifth race the referee decided to cancel the event.

The Americans protested. They argued that the race should simply be postponed until the track was in a better condition. But the referee stood by his decision to scrap all the results so far. Jaffee's race had been in vain. Most people agreed that it was the wrong call. The UK *Times* opined, "This surprising decision virtually robbed the United States of winning the event." It led to a day of "bickering and dispute," reported the *New York Times*. Gustavus Kirby led an appeal, and that evening the executive committee of the IOC ruled that Jaffee was the Olympic champion. Their decision was then overturned by the International Skating Federation on the grounds that Kirby's appeal had been made more than three hours after the race and was therefore technically invalid. The results were wiped from the books, and outrage ensued.

The officials from the ISF suggested that the race be rerun on the weekend. The only problem with this plan was that the Norwegian athletes left town the very next morning. They stopped off at Jaffee's hotel before they went and congratulated him on a victory they felt he had earned, if not been awarded. Kirby, who had come down with a bad cold, addressed the press from his bed. He had just fired off a furious letter of complaint. "You may call this a real protest," he thundered. "Yesterday's complaint was merely a friendly suggestion." As for Jaffee, he simply said, "This is a tough break, but I will race them again on skates, skis, or at foot-running." Plucky in public, privately, of course, he was pretty despondent about what had happened. And who was there to throw an arm around him? Billy Fiske. The two kids had never met each other before, but they struck up an unlikely friendship that week.

Billy and Irv came from opposite poles. Irv was a Jewish kid from the Bronx too poor to afford a skate at his local ice rink. Billy, he said, "was a blue-blood, and he was absolutely fearless. He'd try anything. He always had a lot of money, and he was always gambling. I still don't know why we hit it off." That night, Billy took Irv to the little casino in St. Moritz. "I'd never bet a nickel before," Irv remembered. "So he handed me a $100 bill, which was big money in those days. Billy saw by my expression that I thought it was a put-down. Then he said, 'Come on Irv, just because I've got money and you don't is no reason not to have some fun. I'm going to lose anyway, so what's the difference?' He jammed the money in my hand, and I saw in his face that he was very sincere. From then on we became very close."

Billy, Irv, and the other athletes could afford to stay out late, living it up. The warm weather continued through the week, and the Games ground to a halt. "The temperature has gone up and the ice has gone down so rapidly that the rest of the program may be abandoned," noted the *New York Times*. The rinks were under an inch of water. Canada refused to play its ice hockey game against Sweden on the grounds that, as one of the players said, "we came here to play hockey and not water polo." The figure skaters, the paper noted, were "roaming about disconsolate." And there were real doubts about whether the two showpiece events of the Games, the bobsledding and the skeleton sledding on the Cresta Run, would take place at all. The tracks just weren't fit: The Cresta needed a good night's frost to harden it up. The state of the bob run was sorrier still.

With the rise in temperatures, the *Times* noted, there had been a rise in tempers too. "The extraordinary decision of those responsible for the control of the 10,000m speed skating event to abandon the race when it was already half over has caused a great deal of comment and not unjustified criticism. Whether the frost comes back or not, the United States and Jaffee, their representative, can claim, justly, a moral victory."

Jaffee and the rest of the American speed skating team left St. Moritz on Friday. Dozens of their fellow Olympic athletes turned out to cheer them off, including a little group of Swiss competitors who carried a banner that read,

"Jaffee, winner of the 10,000m race. Long live America." The Finnish skaters sent him a farewell telegram that said, "Congratulations. The American victory in the 10,000m was well earned." But he didn't have a medal to show for it, and the records of the race had been scratched from the books. Jaffee's abiding memory of it all, other than his night out with Billy, was a meeting he had with Count Clary, president of the French Olympic Committee. Clary, a venerable old soul, sported a fine flowing mustache several inches long. He grasped Jaffee by the shoulders, pulled him close, told him that "as far as France is concerned you are the Olympic champion," then kissed him on both cheeks. "That," Jaffee remarked afterward, "was even worse than racing Evanson."

That same night, a frost fell. "It undoubtedly saved the Games from being a complete fiasco," noted one report. "But the IOC must consider itself extremely lucky. Even now the events are being carried out in circumstances which mitigate against the enjoyment of the spectators." The organizers seized the opportunity to run the skeleton race on the Cresta Run. Two of the Heaton brothers, Jack and Jennison, were competing in it for the United States. In the years to come, Billy Fiske would become one of the great Cresta riders himself, but at that point the only experience of it he'd had was in a novice race, starting from midway down the run. Of course he'd won it. But for now he was concentrating on the bobsledding—if it ever got under way. The firm favorite for the Olympic skeleton title was the Englishman Lord Northesk. It was, his supporters said, going to be "a walk-over." But he blew it. "He was palpably off form," noted the *Times*, "and on the day was perhaps lucky to have taken third place." The Heatons finished ahead of him, Jennison in first place and Jack in second. The result, the *Times* reckoned, was "humiliating both to Lord Northesk himself and Great Britain."

Finally, on the penultimate day of the Games, the organizing committee decided to try to run the bobsledding contest. It had been a long week for the athletes, though one enlivened, it's true, by the nightlife at the Kulm and the Palace. After two nights of frost, the track was just about usable again, and the bobsledders snapped back into action. Jack Heaton had been injured during his final run on the Cresta, so Jay switched him with his brother Jennison; Jack dropped back to the reserves. Jennison would take the No. 1 sled and Billy stuck with the No. 2 team. There was so little time left before the closing ceremony that everything happened in a hurry. The organizing committee decided to cut the number of runs per team from four to two. The competitors felt that the decision made a mockery of the contest, much as golfers might feel if they were told the Open was going to be settled over two rounds. Major races, like the Derby, always included four runs. "With the reduction came the feeling that the race was reduced to the level of very minor races," reported the *Times*. "This, it was rightly argued, was scarcely fitting to the dignity of an international event, supposedly the amateur championship of the world." It would have been better, they said, to cancel the event altogether.

With the number of runs cut from four to two, the advantage would be with the quickest crew rather than the most consistent. One great run coupled with another ordinary one could be enough, whereas over four it would take more than a single freakishly fast run to win. The flip side was that there would be a reduced margin for error, since the riders would have only one extra run to compensate for any mistakes first time round. So whoever wanted to win would need to switch on quick, to push all distractions to one side and rush out two fast runs in succession. There would be no time to ease into the contest. The long wait for the race, the St. Moritz nightlife, the brouhaha over referees' decisions— all of this would need to be put out of mind, sharpish.

Luck would play a part too. Since the running order counts for a lot in a bobsled race, the riders drew lots to decide it. Anyone with an early position typically gets to ride on a pristine track. But at St. Moritz, where it is carved out of the snow, the course still has a little too much loose powder on it to be run as fast as possible. Draw a late starting position, and that same snow is long gone, but then the ice underneath is creased and rutted from the passage of the sleds ahead in the order. In a typical contest, that same order is then reversed for the second run, so that everyone's luck evens out. The IOC's organizing committee, however, insisted on holding separate draws before both runs. It was another unpopular decision. And after the thaw and the hasty rebuilding work, the track was in a terrible condition, so bad that two sleds crashed on the first run. The driver of the Luxembourg crew lost control, and the two riders bobbing in the backseats slammed into the third man and broke his ribs. The second British sled, driven by Cecil Pim, whistled into a skid going into Sunny Corner, and though Pim was able to keep his sled upright, the collision cost him crucial seconds.

The times were slow—slower than Jack Heaton's when he'd won the Derby a week earlier, and almost ten seconds down on the track record. Jack's brother Jennison, in the sled with Jay O'Brien riding brake, could clock only 1:42.3. Martineau managed 1:41.7. Kilian matched that. Gramajo was a little quicker at 1:40.3. Henri Lambert was the first to break the 1:40 barrier, the outer limit of what the bobbers considered to be quick. And then came Billy and his rookie crew, Nion, Geoff, Clifford, and Dick. Billy, one reporter wrote, "took chances streaking down the bobsleigh chute that would make a man smoking a cigarette sitting over a powder magazine appear a first rate insurance company risk." When they cut the thread at the finish line, the clock stopped at 1:38.9. He had a lead of nine-tenths of a second over his nearest rival, Lambert.

The going may have been slow, but the sport still made a hell of an impression on John Kieran. "The safest way in which to watch one of these bobsleighs is to run down behind it," he wrote in the *New York Times*. "Dress is optional, but the best costume for bob sleighing is a suit of thirteenth century armor. Incidentally no one had yet covered the course in a one-piece bathing suit. The ordinary costume is of heavily upholstered leather with large metal cups for the elbows, and smaller metal cups for the hands and wrists. The helmets worn by the riders are like football helmets, only more so." The easiest and most common way to get injured on the bob run was to lose your foothold on the sled. The rider's leg would slip out and get caught, bruised, and snapped between the bob and the ice wall. Kieran concluded, "These courses at St. Moritz, by the way, were built by the theorists for their own enjoyment. The Swiss natives do not use them. The Swiss are a sensible people."

That night, Billy was sensible too. He got to bed early. He had been told that the odds on him had been cut to 3 to 1. He would start the second, and final, run as the favorite for the gold medal. That brought a different kind of pressure. The race started at 8 a.m. on Sunday. Over an early breakfast, the sledders discovered that the organizing committee had made yet another bad decision: they had canceled the ballot for the second half of the race and decided instead to follow the normal procedure and reverse the starting order from the previous day. Jay O'Brien had talked them into it, out of fairness, he said, to the other teams. Not least his own. The decision seemed sound. It is what they should have done from the start. But the late switch threw everyone out of kilter again. The riders complained. Some insisted that they had taken it easy on the first run because they knew they had a good draw for the second, and so would take their risks that time round.

Billy had had a late draw on the first day; now he had an early one. He finished it in 1:41.6. That gave him a combined final time of 3:20.5. With nothing to lose, the other riders cut loose. Martineau crashed, like his compatriot Pim had the day before, and though he managed to keep his sled upright and running, he lost so much speed that he finished in 1:44.5, six seconds back overall. Pim was even slower. Both British riders were out of the running.

Lambert, second overnight and therefore Billy Fiske's biggest rival, was a wild driver. His attitude was that his team would either crash or win, which is why Hubert Martineau once described him as "a source of tremendous danger." He was right too: Lambert died three years later from injuries sustained when he crashed on the Cresta Run. He also pushed his sled too hard on this February day in 1928, and it slipped into a skid that slowed it to a neat halt, skewing it sideways across the track. He finished in 1:44.7. Gramajo drove well, but was still too slow to best Fiske's second run, let alone his first. Among the contenders, only Hans Kilian managed to pip Fiske's time: he was 1.4 seconds quicker. That wasn't enough to make up the deficit from the day before.

Billy had counted off his rivals, one by one. He was still leading as the day's racing moved toward the bottom of the running order, and by then there was only one man left who could beat him, his great friend Jennison Heaton. They say that the spectators cried, "What nerve!" as they watched Heaton race his sled down around Sunny and on into Horseshoe. It was the fastest run of the day—of the competition—at 1:38.7. But it wasn't fast enough. Billy Fiske was Olympic champion, by half a second. Jennison Heaton was second. It was a one-two for the United States.

There was no ceremony and no formal celebration. There wasn't even an official medal presentation. The bobbers broke up for the day and met again at the closing ceremony later that afternoon. Truth was, by then the Olympics had become a bit of farce. The organizers had a Swiss brass band play all the anthems at the closing ceremony. The French delegation was especially offended by their ear-rending rendition of "La Marseillaise," which provoked great gales of laughter from the spectators.

"Can't you play the Marseillaise?" bellowed the secretary of the French Olympic Committee.

"It's been so long since you won an Olympic event that we've forgotten it," the bandleader shot back.

While all that was going on, Billy and his team were given their medals. Geoff Mason remembered that an official approached him in the crowd and handed him a box, with the words "Here, Mason, here's your medal." Billy liked it that way. He wrote in his journal, "In Europe someone wins an important sports event and no one cares a damn and very few hear about it; in America somebody wins a pole-sitting competition and they immediately become honored citizens of their community—by way of the newspapers." He didn't even let slip the fact that he was only sixteen, which is why not one of the newspapers mentioned it in the reports the next day, though they all made great play of the fact that Sonja Henie, who had won the women's figure skating for Norway, was only fifteen. Billy's record as the youngest male gold medalist in the Winter Olympics stood for sixty-four years, until 1992, when in Albertville the Finnish ski jumper Toni Nieminen beat it by a single day.

It had not been a successful Games. The *New York Times* observed that its chief feature seemed to be all the protests made by the athletes against the officials' decisions. The *Times* agreed that "the Olympic spirit of good will is not so apparent here at St. Moritz as it was four years ago at Chamonix." In fact, the paper was one of several that doubted whether the event even had a future: "To the casual and unbiased observer a grave doubt must come whether these Olympiads are not a colossal mistake and a gross waste of money. It would seem that the thaw, had it remained, might not have been so great a catastrophe."

As for Geoff Mason, well, the wife of one of the Canadian hockey players told him later that he should take the American flag from the closing ceremony home with him as a souvenir. So he slipped it into his bag, then went back to his hotel, settled his bill, and caught the next train out of town. He never went near a bobsled again. He ended up becoming a Latin teacher in Pennsylvania. "In most pursuits," he said later on in his life, "success is achieved by starting at the bottom and working one's way as swiftly as possible to the top. In bobsleighing, particularly in my case, one starts at the top and works his way as swiftly as possible to the bottom."

PART TWO

The world was divided into those who had it and those who did not. This quality, this it, was never named, however, nor was it talked about in any way. As to just what this ineffable quality was ... well, it obviously involved bravery. But it was not bravery in the simple sense of being willing to risk your life. The idea seemed to be that any fool could do that, if that was all that was required, just as any fool could throw away his life in the process. No, the idea here (in the all-enclosing fraternity) seemed to be that a man should have the ability to go up in a hurtling piece of machinery and put his hide on the line and then have the moxie, the reflexes, the experience, the coolness, to pull it back in the last yawning moment—and then to go up again the next day, and the next day, and every next day, even if the series should prove infinite.

—from *The Right Stuff*, by Tom Wolfe, 1979

Godfrey Dewey, Lake Placid, 1931.
In the photo above, he is shaking hands with IOC
President Count Baillet-Latour.

CHAPTER 7

A MAN WITH A MISSION

W ork started on August 4, 1930. The first thing they did was lay a
track, running up from the brand-new Cascade Road right up to
the top of the mountain. Once that was open, the workers could get access. They
had a couple of hundred laborers up there, working with picks, shovels, saws,
and more. First they cut a path through the pine forest, chopped the trees down
flush with the ground, and trimmed the overhanging branches. They set dynamite into the ground, blasted apart the rock and earth. Then the shovel parties
got to work shifting the debris, all thirty-six thousand tons of it. It wasn't just
these workers who needed to get up there; the public wanted to come too. There
was such curiosity about the colossal earthworks on the edge of town that, according to the local newspaper, "all during the fall many motored out daily to
watch progress of the construction." And what they saw unfold was a mile and
a half of winding dirt track, six feet wide at its narrowest points, almost thirty
feet at its widest. Then the joiners came. They erected intricate spiderwebs of
wooden beams around the corners. These were filled in with rocks and rubble,
forming solid banks that stood, the tallest of them, thirty feet high, each capped
with a two-foot-tall stone wall. The joiners then set to work on the huge wooden
grandstands in the crooks of the two biggest turns, Shady and Whiteface, and
the new lodge up at the summit. The plumbers laid the drains, and then the
pipes to carry the water that would provide the ice, eight thousand feet of them,
from the new reservoir through the pumping station and all the way up the

slope. Then engineers strung up phone lines connecting the way stations along the route. By the end of December, the work was done. Lake Placid, a little town in the Adirondacks, had just become home to America's first purpose-built bobsled run, the only one of its kind in the world outside central Europe.

The locals had always known that piece of land as South Meadow. It was just another of the many picturesque peaks around their town. Now that it had a new purpose, they decided it needed a new name. They settled on Mount Van Hoevenberg, a fine tribute to an early pioneer of the Adirondacks, and suitably grand too: the run would, after all, be the central attraction of the 1932 Winter Olympics. And, though they didn't know it yet, within a year that mile-and-a-half patch of ground on the side of the mountain would become the single most publicized, criticized, and dramatized stretch of terrain in the entire United States.

Lake Placid, three hundred miles north of Manhattan, way up beyond Albany in the Adirondack forest preserve, was, and still is, a one-street town. The main road runs around the west side of Mirror Lake, where, in the winter, children gather, as they always have, to skate, sled, and play pickup games of hockey. In 1930 there were around three thousand residents, which meant that the entire population could have been seated in those new grandstands on Mount Van Hoevenberg with room to spare. The bob run had cost $227,000 to build, the single largest chunk of the $2 million that had been spent to bring the Winter Olympics to this little quarter of New York State. It had seemed a vast sum even when the plans were first drawn up, and that was before the Great Depression hit. A large part of it was public money, supplied, after much wrangling with Governor Franklin D. Roosevelt, by the state legislature in Albany. Another sizable portion had been raised by issuing community bonds. The per-capita cost was almost sixty dollars per resident—about three weeks' wages for the men working on the construction of the run. The Los Angeles Summer Games that same year, by way of contrast, cost the citizens of that city less than a dollar each.

Not that the cost had been evenly shared around the citizens of Lake Placid. Even a small town has its divisions. And in the 1930s the split was drawn on either side of the Central School on Main Street. Anything south of that was considered downtown; anything north of it, uptown. An uptown address gave a family a certain standing. At the heart of the ritzy half, on the far side of Mirror Lake, lay the grand old Lake Placid Club, the fiefdom of the Dewey family. And if you want to understand the extraordinary accomplishments of this little town, how it came to be the home of America's first bob run and the host of both the 1932 and the 1980 Winter Olympics, the Lake Placid Club is where you have to start looking. The residents liked to think of Lake Placid as "the little town that could," echoing the can-do attitude of the little engine in a story familiar to all American children. And while it's true that many had a hand in their organization, the 1932 Winter Olympics were, ultimately, one man's work. His name was Godfrey Dewey, a fellow of singular vision and steel-strong will.

When the United States Olympic Committee first asked Dewey, in January 1928, whether he thought Lake Placid would be willing and able to host the 1932 Games, his answer was "absolutely not," though he put it in slightly more polite terms than that. It was, Dewey felt, an "impossible" job, because it would require cooperation "not merely by the civic bodies and community of Lake Placid itself," but also by "many others thruhout the region and state." Nevertheless, the USOC persuaded him to think the idea over. They arranged for Dewey and his wife to take a six-week trip to Europe to visit St. Moritz that February. They even gave him a job, as manager of the United States' three-man skiing squad. Dewey inveigled his way into carrying the American flag, and he took the Olympic oath on behalf of the team in the opening ceremony, that long and comical march through a freezing blizzard. These were honors typically reserved for distinguished athletes. Dewey, at forty, was, in his own words, "an ardent and capable winter sportsman," but not so capable that he was picked to compete. He did persuade Jay O'Brien to include him on the reserve team for the bobsledding competition, even though, like Geoff Mason and a couple of the others, he had never ridden a sled before. There was a sense, even then, that he wanted to impose his will on the American team.

Dewey spent those weeks taking fastidious notes on "the housing, the budget, the facilities, organization, committees, health and safety, and policing" of the Olympics. And of course the St. Moritz Olympics were a mess, beset by bad weather and spoiled by slapdash organization and amateurish administration. By the time Dewey returned to America in March, he had changed his mind. He had decided that Lake Placid could "match the highest standards set abroad." Fired by enthusiasm, he addressed the local worthies at a meeting of the Kiwanis Club. He told them, "What St. Moritz could do, Lake Placid can do." He felt the town should bid for the Games, and would win the Games. There was only one major obstacle that he could see: they would need to build a bobsled run.

Dewey thought the town could have a winter tourism season, just like those enjoyed by the leading French and Swiss resorts. The Games would be the great catalyst. "They are not an end in themselves, but a means of accelerating development of winter business so that the economic life of the town was transformed." The central attraction wouldn't be the downhill ski slopes—the sport had not yet become that popular—but a new bobsled run, the first of its kind on the continent. He had been so taken with his first taste of this new sport in St. Moritz that he now considered a run to be "indispensable," a "matter of necessity for Lake Placid regardless of the Olympics." The cost, he guessed, would be around fifty thousand dollars; but once it was up and running, drawing curious tourists from far and wide, the town could expect to make between one million to two million dollars of extra income each and every winter. Dewey firmly believed that Lake Placid could become the first great winter sports resort in the United States. At first, noted the official report of the '32 Games, "many residents were aghast that there was even a remote possibility of this little mountain resort of less than 4,000 people entering the winter sports world in 1932. The responsibility seemed too heavy, the task too great. But to hear Dewey tell about what St. Moritz had done and what Lake Placid could do was to be anxious to start doing it."

To make sense of Godfrey Dewey's vision, to understand how he came to harbor such grand designs, and was able to wield such influence on the community he lived in, we have to go back further still, to his roots. Godfrey's grandparents were, one biographer wrote, from "typical pioneer stock." There was nothing typical about Godfrey's father. His name was Melville Dewey. In time he would cut off the last two letters of his first name, because the first and most enduring of his many obsessions was simplified spelling. He insisted that the English language was too complicated, and adopted a phonetic system he used in all his correspondence right through his life. He did his utmost to encourage everyone else to follow suit. He actually changed the spelling of his own surname to "Dui." But he could never make it stick: by that point, the original spelling of his name was already too well known, too widely used.

The Dewey family was "religious to the point of austerity." Melvil was raised to believe that, in his mother's words, "praise to the face is an open disgrace." Pride was a sin. So was smoking. And so was drinking. Melvil had a "fanatical hatred" of both. As a young man, he actually made his father stop selling tobacco in the family's little corner store, even though it was one of the most lucrative bits of the business. "I told him," Dewey wrote in his own inimitable way, "Yu hav no ryt to sel tobako & cigars in yur store as yu hav for so many years." He flogged the stock at cost to the rival shop across the way.

The simplified spelling makes him look illiterate. In fact he was a very bookish man. When he was twelve, he worked odd jobs until he had saved ten dollars, then he walked eleven miles to the nearest town and spent it all on an unabridged copy of *Webster's Dictionary*. It was only after reading it through from first page to last that he decided that the English language needed to be reformed.

Melvil Dewey went to Amherst. He wasn't one of the brightest pupils there, but he was blessed with a work ethic and, as his biographer wrote, "an unquenchable belief that life deserved to be approached with high seriousness." He didn't drink, smoke, or socialize. "I shall mingle in society very little during the next four years; in term time almost none," he wrote. "I have no time for party-going." After graduation, he took a job in the Amherst library. They needed someone to sort through two collections of four thousand books each, which had just been donated to the college. And it was there, among the full boxes of books and the heaving shelves, that Melvil had the idea that would make him, in his own peculiar way, famous around the world. At Amherst, and most other major libraries, books were given permanent shelf locations based on the order in which they were acquired rather than on the subject they concerned. Dewey spent months trying to find a better system. Then, while he was in church one Sunday, enduring an especially long sermon, "the solution," he wrote, "flasht over me so that I jumpt in my seat and came very near shouting 'Eureka!'" What he'd seen in his mind were the little strings of punctuated numbers you find tacked to the ends of library shelves around the world. He divided all knowledge into nine classes, those classes into nine subclasses, and those nine subclasses into further subdivisions. So class 7 would be the arts, subclass 8 would be music, subdivision 2 would be songbooks. Anyone who wanted to find a hymnbook would now know exactly where to look.

The decimal system was Dewey's enduring achievement. Today, it has been translated into thirty languages and is used in more than two hundred thousand libraries spread across 135 countries. Melvil duly became the secretary, treasurer, and "chief moving spirit" of the American Library Association. In 1884, he was hired as librarian in chief at Columbia College. He persuaded the college to let him start a training school for librarians, America's first, and took the title "Professor of Library Economy." At Columbia he introduced a number of innovations that would, over the years, become the hallmarks of how to run a library.

He fixed ladders to the shelves; he had rubber stops fitted to all chairs and tables; he put a coat check at the front door; he banned all talking "but in low tones"; and, of course, he outlawed smoking.

Columbia was the prototypical modern library, but Dewey was not a prototypical librarian. He had a zeal for reform. He wore cuff links stamped with a letter "R" as a reminder that "I was to give my life to reforming certain mistakes and abuses." His colleagues at Columbia found him insufferable, "boastful," one put it, "to a degree not in accordance with academic propriety." They thought him "abrupt, haughty, self-righteous, and self-serving." His mother's lessons about pride were long forgotten. But vanity was the least of his sins. Dewey actively encouraged women to enroll in his new library school, even though the college wasn't co-educational. This so infuriated the governing board that they refused him the use of a classroom. So he arranged impromptu lessons in a storeroom above the chapel.

Dewey was, all through his life, a passionate and sincere supporter of women's rights. The trouble was, his enthusiasm for female company in the workplace often crossed a line and led him to act in an inappropriate manner. He was, in his way, a womanizer, even at Amherst: he would often describe in his diary how he would "call on" two or three women, some of them married, in the space of a single evening. Eventually, in 1906, scandal forced him out of the American Library Association. He was seen hugging, squeezing, and kissing several female association members at a conference. Some of the women accepted his "unconventional and familiar" manner; others didn't. Four in particular were so outraged by his unwanted approaches that they threatened to expose him unless he was fired from the ALA. The association had received, one member said, a string of "tearful confidings" from female students who had been disturbed by Dewey's behavior.

Oddly, or perhaps not so very odd at all, depending on your worldview, Dewey's marriage was a model of probity. He and Annie, another librarian, had became husband and wife in 1878. Their relationship, Annie wrote, was based on "intellectual companionship and friendship stronger than the usual tie." They devoted themselves to self-improvement. At the beginning of each month they would write lists of goals, and when the month was over, they would grade each other on how close they had come to achieving them. A typical list of his included "be more patient," "think twice before speaking," "dress with more care," and "rise early and eat slowly." She drew up "time budgets" that broke days down into chunks: "Exercise 1 hr; Self-Culture 1 hr;

Sing 15min." This was the household Godfrey Dewey was born into, in September 1887.

The Deweys were so enamored with their way of life that they decided, ultimately, that they should make it the basis of a new model community. Each summer they would scout likely locations. In 1893, they settled on Lake Placid. Annie's sister already lived in the village, and Melvil fell in love with the place while he was visiting her there. He bought seventy acres on the eastern shore of Mirror Lake and an old ramshackle mansion on a neighboring plot. They planned to pay for the upkeep by letting cottages to their friends. Melvil imagined that this new property would become a kind of cooperative vacation resort, a "university in the woods." He invited a select group of friends and acquaintances to join him there, explaining in a letter that "we are intensely interested in getting for neighbors people whom of all others we would prefer." The group began to buy up land all around, to protect against "undesirable neighbors."

By then Melvil had moved on from Columbia. He and Annie had moved to Albany, where he became the secretary for the Board of Regents at the New York State Education Department. He continued to act, his nephew Freemont Rider wrote, like "a fifty-ton tank, riding roughshod over all sorts of obstacles toward its chosen objective." In 1888, he was appointed the New York state librarian. It was a remarkable achievement for a man from such a humble background. Melvil Dewey was now a man with a measure of wealth and influence.

In 1895, the Lake Placid Club was formally launched. That April, Dewey wrote a letter to James Laughlin, a professor of political science at the University of Chicago, listing the names of some of the professors who were already members—H.A.P. Torrey from the University of Vermont, Herman Neil from Amherst, Jeremiah Jenks from Cornell. Laughlin's eye stopped at Jenks's name. "Socially he would not be agreeable to me," Laughlin wrote in his reply. "And if more of his kind come I think I should be more comfortable elsewhere." Laughlin thought, mistakenly, that Jenks was a Jew. Once Melvil had corrected him, Laughlin joined the club.

Melvil realized that "the club shall get a bad name by taking them in"—and by "them," he meant Jews. He later told Jenks, "I have some Hebrew friends who are very charming. But I should dare not break the rule barring them from Club membership." Those rules, of course, had been drawn up by Dewey himself. The club operated, in the words of Dewey's nephew, as a "kind of proprietary enterprise," with the man himself "absolute dictator." Every last detail of it bore his mark, from the timing of the evening "lights out" (at 10 p.m.) to the choice of Protestant hymns at the Sunday sing-alongs to the simplified spelling used on all the signs and official documents. The breakfast menu in the restaurant at the "loj," as Dewey insisted it was called, offered "kiperd herin," "bredcrum gridl cakes," "stud apricot" and "egs to order." Alcohol, tobacco, and gambling were prohibited. Tipping was banned, as were all guests "against whom there is physical, moral, social, or race objections." And just in case that wasn't clear enough, the club's literature added, "It is found impracticable to make exceptions for Jews to others excluded, even when of unusual personal qualifications."

There was a history of anti-Semitism in the Adirondacks. Hotels and boardinghouses tended to be divided into those that accepted Jews and those that didn't. The latter would carry signs in the window: "Hebrews will knock vainly for admission." But the Lake Placid Club was, as the academic Peter Hopsicker wrote, "the mountains' flagship resort for bigotry." It became a target. Dewey had repeatedly refused admission to an acquaintance of his, Henry Leipziger, though he had never once given him a good explanation as to why. When Leipziger finally realized why he was being blackballed, he recruited a prominent Jewish lawyer from Manhattan, Louis Marshall, and the two of them set out on the warpath together. Marshall filed a petition with the Board of Regents calling for Dewey's dismissal from his position as state librarian. They argued that a public official had no business propagating such anti-Semitic material, especially when there were three-quarters of a million Jewish taxpayers in New York, all of them contributing to his salary, all of them offended by his prejudices. At first Dewey and his friends thought Marshall was "an evil genius." Dewey said, "It seems a crime to wreck my life work." He fought back. He wrote to the local papers protesting his innocence; he put together a forty-page pamphlet of evidence for his defense; he sent letters to two hundred prominent Jewish figures around the state arguing his case. He even started writing to all the individuals who had signed the petition, asking that they withdraw their names. The one thing he never did was apologize. He was too proud. Marshall dismissed Melvil Dewey's pleas as "nauseating slobber."

The Board of Regents decided to allow him to continue his work on the condition that he realized his private business was incompatible with his public position. In short, he had to give up his presidency of the club. He couldn't do it. In fact, he sent out another pamphlet to the club's members explaining that while the club retained the right to "reject membership to any person not desired at the club," they would be excising all specific mentions of Jews from the rules on the extraordinary grounds that "the Jews are too important an element nowadays to be discriminated against by anybody who holds a public position. Jews may be despised, but their votes are respected." It was all the ammunition Marshall needed. In September 1905, the Board of Regents asked for Dewey's resignation.

Dewey tried, for a time, to pursue another old interest: language reform. He met with the millionaire Andrew Carnegie and tried to persuade him to fund a body that would work to promote simplified spelling. Carnegie was keen on the project, but he had no desire to work with Dewey. Especially when, nine months after Dewey lost his job as state librarian, he was accused of "violating the standards of Victorian social conduct" by the four women he had molested at the ALA conference the previous year. In the space of a year, Dewey had lost his job, his ambitions, and his reputation. His life's work had been wrecked, just as he'd feared it would be.

Godfrey was seventeen when his father resigned from office, eighteen when he was dismissed from the ALA. He had convinced himself that his father was simply "indifferent to appearances" and had a "well-known disregard for conventions." The father was such a strong personality that his only son was always going to bear his impress. The public humiliation fueled Godfrey's desire to reclaim his father's legacy by carrying on his work.

The family retreated to Lake Placid. If Melvil Dewey could not shape the wider world around him, he would work, instead, to make a new society on the shore of Mirror Lake. One molded in his own image, matching his exacting specifications. One of his employees actually believed that Dewey had grown so bitter that he was determined to "build a community wealthy Jews would covet but could not join." By 1909, a decade and a half after it had been founded on a seventy-acre plot, the Lake Placid Club owned six thousand acres and 225 buildings, including three sawmills, a creamery, a milk plant, a chicken factory, and twenty-one farms, all of it in a thirty-five-mile radius of the club lodge. It had an annual income of five hundred thousand dollars, but Dewey had stretched the finances so far that the club was heavily in debt. He decided the solution was to keep the club open all through the year. His associates thought it a lunatic idea. But it worked. At first only "a few adventurous souls remained thru the season to see what an Adirondack winter was like," but the group grew in number with each passing year, and got to be so large that the club laid out cross-country ski trails and erected two toboggan slides on the banks of Mirror Lake that sped riders over the ice and across to the village. Bolstered by the winter income, the Lake Placid Club went from strength to strength.

Vindicated by these successes, Dewey became more entrenched in his prejudices. He issued diktats reminding members that "new-rich groups" like "many Cubans" would also be denied entry because of their "lack of refinement" and stipulating that "negroes can be admitted only to servant's quarters"—all this despite the club lying in the very same valley as the farm of the famed abolitionist John Brown, whose body still "lies a-moldering in the grave" on that very site. In the early 1850s Brown brought families of freed slaves north to form a farming community in the Adirondacks, just a half mile from what would become the Lake Placid Club lodge. Dewey even bought up a stretch of land on the road leading to John Brown's farm because he was worried the owner "wd sell to Jews."

Melvil seemed to view people much as he did books. He broke them down into five official classes, ranging from type "A," who were "admirably suited to the ideals of the club," through to "C," "common clients," and "E," "unsuitables who must be excluded for the protection of the rest." This last group included women who smoked and families who allowed their children to dance cheek-to-cheek. "Whatever fashion allows drinking, smoking, and gambling by women yung or old wil no more be tolerated at this family club than wud contajus diseases." This attitude, oddly, didn't stop him from hiring a "dainty litl flapper" to work as his private stenographer. After spending a single summer working for him, she quit, and then filed a lawsuit against him demanding damages for what would today be called sexual harassment. He had repeatedly tried to kiss and caress her. This was when Dewey was seventy-eight. He settled out of court, for $2,147. "I have been very unconventional," he admitted. "As men ar always who frankly show and speak of their liking for women."

By that time Godfrey had grown into an adult, if not into his own man. He and his father had the same hard, square jaw, but Godfrey's build was lean and slight where his father had been big and bearish. Godfrey went clean-shaven, wore his hair in a tightly cropped side part, and sported small wire-framed spectacles. His skin seemed somehow to be stretched too tight across his bones. After graduation from Harvard he had studied for a master's degree in education. He wrote his thesis on the "Relative Frequency of English Speech Sounds," devoted himself to furthering his father's campaign for simplified spelling, and devised his own "fonetic alphabet," which he insisted would be of "constant and general usefulness." He wrote endless books, many of them self-published, and articles encouraging people to use it.

He was, in his own way, obsessed with speed, just like Billy Fiske. Of course he thought himself something of a sportsman—a bobsledder, a skier, even a racing driver. He was inordinately proud of the fact that in 1904, when he was still a teenager, he had driven from Albany to Lake Placid in twelve hours in a new Thomas Flyer automobile that his father had bought for the club. He was traveling at an average speed, the papers reported, of over 10 mph. But for Godfrey Dewey, speed was a means of achieving greater efficiency, not finding new thrills. He loved shorthand because it "saved 2/3s of your time and effort." Like his father, he felt efficiency was a moral issue. "Time wasn't merely money," wrote Freemont Rider. "It was, to him, a portion of an all-too-short life in which so much more for the betterment of mankind had to be accomplished than one could possibly achieve at best."

After completing his master's, Godfrey returned to the family roost at the Lake Placid Club. He was married himself now, and he brought his family with him. He accepted his father's invitation to take on the management of the club. He and Melvil set up the Lake Placid Club Education Foundation together, to advance the cause of simplified spelling and other eccentric schemes including promoting cremation, prohibition, women's suffrage, and eugenics. They transferred many of the club's assets to the foundation. Godfrey became the vice president of what was now the largest residential club in the world. It owned 10,600 acres and had its own three-thousand-seat theater, twenty-one tennis courts, five golf courses, a resident orchestra, a chapel, stables, garages, shops, stores, tearooms, restaurants, cafés, a cinema, and a post office, as well as all those dairy farms, poultry farms, cattle farms, laundries, sawmills, and lumberyards.

Godfrey's mother, Annie Dewey, died in 1923. His father did not remain a widower for long: two years later he was married again. He was seventy-four now, and it was starting to show. He fell severely ill soon after the wedding. Godfrey began to take on more and more responsibility in the running of his father's empire, but Melvil did not make the succession easy. Bad blood began to flow between them, ill feeling sparked in part by Melvil's inappropriate behavior toward Godfrey's wife, Marjorie.

Enmity exploded between them in 1926, when Melvil and his new wife went south for the winter and decided to found a new Lake Placid Club in Florida. He bought a three-thousand-acre plot in the Florida highlands, near a town named Lake Stearns. He even persuaded the Florida legislature to rename the town Lake Placid. The new club was to be run on the very same lines as the old one. He sought to reassure prospective members by telling them that "Florida has fewer negroes" than most Southern states, and that "we have no colord help" in the club. The Florida venture was a bust. Most winters, Melvil could count the number of paying guests on his fingers. So he turned to his son for help turning it around. Godfrey had assumed control of the original Lake Placid Club. He thought the Florida project a monumental folly and was convinced that his stepmother, Emily, was exploiting his father, driving the Florida club on so that she could take control of its finances. So Godfrey refused to release funds from Lake Placid North.

Melvil wrote letters to prominent members of the club, briefing them against Godfrey. He told them his son was "a spendyr & not a provyder" and criticized his "peculiarity" and "lack of altruistic spirit." Melvil was old, and many of the members knew that his Florida venture was a foolish one, but he still had a lot of clout. Many of the club's directors were persuaded that Godfrey was not his father's equal and would be unfit to take on the presidency of the club.

Godfrey had been serving as the de facto head of the club in Melvil's absence, but he would have to fight for the right to succeed him when he died. Godfrey was forty-one now and had committed the best years of his career to the club. And now his fellow directors had been turned against him by his own father, who was hell-bent on stopping him from ascending to the presidency. Godfrey decided that he needed a grand plan, a project that would eclipse anything his father and stepmother were doing in Florida and secure his position as heir apparent. And then the United States Olympic Committee got in touch.

The USOC wasn't asking the town to bid for the Games; it was asking the club. The club was the single largest employer in Lake Placid, and the single source of revenue too. And while plenty of the locals objected to the Dewey family's bigotry and their pomposity, no one would question their importance. The Deweys weren't just pillars of the community; they were poles that kept the roof propped up. So they trusted Godfrey Dewey when he promised them the Olympics, believed him when he told them that, as great as the cost seemed, they would earn it back over and over again because the Games would establish Lake Placid as America's first winter sports resort.

But of course it wasn't just the locals Dewey needed to win over. The club and the community couldn't carry the cost alone, and he spent a lot of time in Albany lobbying Governor Roosevelt and the New York State Legislature. In January 1929, a couple of months before the IOC was due to make its decision on which city would host the Olympics, Dewey won what he wanted: both the state senate and the state assembly passed, unanimously, a bill pledging to support the bid. At the end of March, Dewey went back to Switzerland to present his bid to the IOC in Lausanne. He traveled with the backing of the members of the club, the citizens of Lake Placid, and the politicians in Albany, if not of his own father.

Los Angeles was the only city bidding for the Summer Games in 1932, so that decision was done and dusted before the conference had even started. The competition to host the Winter Games, on the other hand, was fierce. There were nine bids. Two of them, from Lake Tahoe and Yosemite Valley, had the advantage of being in the same state as Los Angeles: the Californians were keen to hold both the Summer and Winter Games. There were bids, too, from both Duluth and Minneapolis, Denver, and Bear Mountain, a hundred or so miles away from Lake Placid, down in the Hudson Valley. Oslo in Norway, a city that could cite its experience of hosting the Nordic Games, had also declared its candidacy. The smart money, however, was on Montreal. The US press had already reported that the Games were going to be held there, forcing the USOC to issue a denial. It had one clear advantage over the American contenders: there was no prohibition in Canada. The pundits seemed to think that the promise of legal liquor would help oil the wheels at the IOC. But then, Dewey had an ace of his own: his was the only bid that included the specific promise to build a bobsled run for the Olympics. This, he said himself, was the "keystone" of the Lake Placid bid.

Dewey had prepared with a diligence that did him credit. The IOC was impressed that he had traveled to Switzerland to present the bid himself, and the four-page sales pitch he brought with him seemed strikingly professional when set against, say, the efforts of Lake Tahoe, whose representative said, simply, "We have the requisite terrain and climate and we are prepared to spend anything up to $3m to provide whatever facilities may be necessary."

When word came, it wasn't from the president of the IOC, or any of the other officials on the bid committee, but the stenographer. Dewey was tight with anxiety, waiting outside the boardroom. The stenographer passed him. And couldn't resist stopping to whisper in his ear, *"Vous avez gagné, Monsieur."* You have won.

Godfrey Dewey returned to Lake Placid a hero. When he arrived back, in early May, a testimonial dinner was thrown in his honor, the largest in the history of Lake Placid. "From Lake Placid, from Saranac Lake, from Bloomingdale, Albany, St. Regis Falls, Wilmington, Plattsburg, and the Valley towns," reported the local paper, "men and women gathered to show by their presence their appreciation of the efforts of Dr. Dewey." Later that same week the people of nearby North Elba voted, by a count of five to one, in favor of issuing a two-hundred-thousand-dollar bond to raise funds for the Games. "Such united support," the local paper noted, "was the most encouraging sign to officials." Dewey did not dwell long on his successes. He had too much to do. He needed to start work on the "impossible" job.

To build his bobsled run, Dewey needed more than just an empty stretch of mountain. He had to find a slope with a vertical drop of around two hundred meters over a distance of two miles, with a downhill gradient of between 4 and 12 percent, a northerly exposure so that the sun wouldn't melt the ice, and space for the big banks at the turns and an access road running alongside the track. Dewey hired the best designer he could find, a German named Stanislaus Zentzytzki, who had laid out several bob runs in Europe. Lake Placid is surrounded by the highest mountains in New York: Marcy, McIntyre, Haystack, Colden, and Whiteface. In and around the peaks and their foothills, Zentzytzki found three possible sites for the new run. The best of them, at Mount Scarface and Mount Jo, were on public land. Lake Placid is in the heart of the Adirondack forest preserve. The land around the town is fixed, by state law, to be "forever kept as wild forest land," which "shall not be leased, sold, or exchanged, or be taken by any corporation, public or private, nor shall timber thereon be sold, removed or destroyed." Dewey argued that a "liberal interpretation" of the law would allow him to construct "sport and recreation facilities," but what seemed "liberal" to Dewey was unacceptable to the environmental lobby. The Association for the Protection of the Adirondacks launched a campaign to stop the construction of the run. For the next two years, Dewey had to fight the AFPA in the back rooms of the legislature and, ultimately, the courts of New York State. He didn't make it easy for himself. He had an opportunity to meet with the head of the AFPA to negotiate before the argument escalated, but he was too proud to ask for an audience. Instead he waited for a formal invitation, which never came.

At the same time, Dewey was in Albany, lobbying politicians to try to obtain state funding for the Olympics. He had secured their backing before traveling to Lausanne, but the bill they had passed contained precious few details about financial support and made no mention whatsoever of the bob run, despite Dewey's plea that they promise to pay for it. In the end, he persuaded Assemblyman Fred Porter to introduce a bill authorizing the construction of a run on public land and appropriating seventy-five thousand dollars of funds to that end. The AFPA blocked it by appealing directly to Governor Roosevelt. A second, simpler, bill was passed. This made no mention of state money, or public land, but simply authorized construction of a run. Even then Roosevelt felt he had to consult with Attorney General Hamilton Ward before he could bless it.

Dewey needed more. He had Porter introduce a third bill, one that reintroduced the idea that the run should be built on state land, with state money. He had found what he thought was a loophole in the law: he felt he could sell the run on the idea that it would encourage people "to visit and enjoy the wild forest lands," thus fulfilling one of the purposes of the forest preserve regulations, which was to "stimulate public interest in preserving them for scenic and recreational purposes." The legislature bought it. But the AFPA didn't. It declared the bill to be unconstitutional and took its challenge to the Appellate Division of the Supreme Court of New York.

Dewey grew ever more anxious. He needed the run to be ready a year before the Games started so that he would have time to test it properly. It was already nearing the end of 1929 and construction hadn't even begun. Instead, he had spent his time trying to negotiate his way around the "serious obstacles" and "unwarranted complications" the environmentalists had put in his path. If he couldn't deliver the bob run, the IOC would have to reconsider its decision. Every extra day of delay, he knew, made it more likely that Lake Placid would have to forfeit the Olympics.

And then, Black Tuesday. On October 29, 1929, the stock market crashed, and the Great Depression started. It hit Lake Placid hard. Barbara Tyrell Kelly, who grew up in the town, a "child of the Depression," remembers in her memoirs how "the [Lake Placid] Club was the engine that provided employment. It kept many citizens afloat in those hard times prior to the 1932 Olympics, but there were not enough jobs to go around. Many families moved in together and shared what money there was. Most families had gardens, and many raised chickens. Those that had extra space often took in paying boarders. Barter for goods and services was common." Kelly slept in a bed with four of her cousins, all of them spread widthways across the mattress. The citizens were hungry for the work the Olympics would provide. But they knew, too, that unless Dewey was right and the Olympics did establish the town as America's leading winter sports resort, it would be only a short-term fix, and one that would leave them with a lot of long-term debt.

Public enthusiasm for the project began to wane as the costs started to mount. The estimated budget had escalated to well over a million dollars. It grew further when the IOC president, Count de Baillet-Latour, visited Lake Placid in 1930 and announced that, in his opinion, "when the Games are over, something tangible and physical must remain in Lake Placid as a memorial to the Games." He decided that an indoor ice rink would be just the thing, and made it clear, in private, that this wasn't a suggestion but an order. The rink added another $200,000 to the bill. Desperate for cash, Dewey and the organizing committee hired a firm to conduct a fund-raising drive around the northeastern United States, in New York, Philadelphia, and Boston. They hoped to get $250,000 in donations. While they met with "good will and good wishes" wherever they went, they raised only $37,000—just enough to cover their expenses.

While Dewey's team was conducting its fruitless fund-raising drive, the courts were still weighing the matter of whether or not the bob run could be built on public land. The lower court had ruled that the AFPA was right, that building the bob run on either of the two public sites Dewey and his architect Zentzytzki had in mind would undoubtedly be a violation of the "forever wild" law. Dewey, with the support of the attorney general, appealed the decision. Just as he had done with Roosevelt, Dewey tried to bend the appeal court to his will by arguing that the wrong decision "would compel the abandonment of the Olympic Winter Games in New York State, and undoubtedly for the United States in consequence." The threat didn't work. The judge told Dewey that if the decision cost Lake Placid the Olympics, so be it, since "constitutional provisions cannot always adjust themselves to the nice relationships of life." On March 18, 1930, the Court of Appeals upheld the original decision: the land must remain "forever wild." Less than two years out from the Games, Dewey didn't have the money to pay for his bob run, or a stretch of land to build it on. The AFPA was triumphant. The association had staged what the academic Peter Hopsicker describes as "the first major environmental protest of any Games in modern Olympic history," and it had won.

Dewey wasn't ready to quit yet. He found a spot on the north slope of South Meadow Mountain, a mile and a half outside the town. The land there was owned by the Lake Placid Club, which meant that he was free to build on it. The problem was that it would cost a lot more to build there than it would on either of the two public sites. Dewey had already fought to persuade the state legislature to set aside $125,000 to cover the cost of the run—double the original estimated cost. If construction went ahead on South Meadow, he would need to double that sum all over again. And the organizing committee was so broke that Dewey had to borrow the money to fly Zentzytzki back out from Europe to draw up a fresh set of plans for the new site.

So Dewey was forced to return to Albany, cap in hand, to plead for another $375,000 of the state's money. Governor Roosevelt had one eye on the presidential run he was planning for 1932 and was loath to commit so much money to facilities that would be used for only "about a week or two." He decided to veto the bill for additional funding. Dewey was furious. He had been foiled again. He questioned Roosevelt's "good faith" and said publicly that the governor was "the one man who can seriously jeopardize the very holding of the Games." Roosevelt wasn't going to be bullied. He put Dewey back in his place, told him there had been, to this point, "no suggestion that the State would be called upon to appropriate any large sum," and that the idea he was under any "obligation" to grant another $375,000 was entirely wrong. Dewey was wise enough to realize he had picked the wrong fight. He apologized to Roosevelt and sought instead to convince him that saving the Games would be the shrewd political move, "much more popular than otherwise" with the electorate. Roosevelt relented. At last, Dewey had a private site for the run, and the promise of public money to pay for it.

Just weeks after the first shovel of earth was turned, a scandal erupted. On September 25, Roosevelt received a letter from David Mosessohn, the editor of the *Jewish Tribune* and an executive on the Jewish National Council. Why, Mosessohn asked, was the state using taxpayers' money to pay for a bob run on land owned by the Lake Placid Club, an organization that was "un-American" in its promotion of "race and religious hatred?" He warned that the Jewish community of New York, two million strong, would "not sit idly and see State funds spent on property from which they are now barred." He hired a lawyer, Mark Eisner, to represent the Jewish community of New York, and instructed him "to prevent improper use of State funds and to seek recovery of such funds as have been expended without legal warrant." When Godfrey learned of the complaint, his mind flashed back to 1905, when, as a young man, he had seen his father drummed out of his job as state librarian.

But Mosessohn was right. Life at the club continued much as it always had. No drinking, gambling, or "dancing declared offensiv of good taste or morals," no "conduct, dres, or manners which might justly offend the refined family life"—and no Jews. Godfrey refused entry to one woman, the wife of a member, because she had a single Jewish grandparent. He shared his father's prejudices, but he was, as he told his father, always mindful of "the importance of regarding not merely facts but also appearances." He was a hypocrite who cloaked his bigotry in kind words. He told Otis Peabody Swift, who had been hired to run the publicity campaign for the Olympics, that "personali, it hurts me veri much to seem to hav a relijus or racial prejudice." But in private he revealed a different side of himself. He told his confidants that this "nu Jew attak will giv us much valuabl publiciti" because it would show "why our members have always de-clyned to admit them." He couldn't have been more mistaken.

The *New York Times* and the *Herald Tribune* picked up on the *Jewish Tribune*'s story. Public opinion turned against Godfrey Dewey, just as it had turned against his father. And there were indeed plenty of people in the town who ob-jected to the Dewey family and the way they ran the club. But very few were willing to speak out against them publicly. The *Tribune* found one, local post-master Sol Feinberg, but even he would only go so far. Nonetheless, he thanked Mosessohn for "having raised the standard of the Jewish people of that section in the eyes of their neighbors."

Dewey argued that the Lake Placid Club had actually signed up to an ease-ment on land in South Meadow. It would be transferred to the state, which would be allowed to operate the run without interference from the club. This, Mosessohn countered, was a "transparent subterfuge," since the deal also stipu-lated that if the state failed to maintain the run, ownership would revert to the club. Eisner, meanwhile, prepared a solution. He suggested that the club should forfeit all claims on the land in South Meadow, and that if the state did fail to maintain the run after the Games, ownership should be transferred to the Parks Commission, and by extension the citizens of the town, not the members of the club. If that happened, the Jewish National Council would withdraw their pro-test. Dewey had been utterly outmaneuvered. He had no choice but to accept Eisner's terms.

On December 4, shortly before construction was finished on Mount Van Hoevenberg, a meeting was held in New York between members of the Olympic Organizing Committee, the Jewish National Council, representatives from Roo-sevelt's office, and the Lake Placid Chamber of Commerce. "Harmony was es-tablished." The new land agreement was signed, and the council officially withdrew its protest. Godfrey Dewey did not attend. He was too angry and too busy, and, to be blunt, his views were too toxic for his presence there to be any-thing but a hindrance. He had been pushed to one side.

————

Just as his father had done before him, Godfrey Dewey responded to defeat by turning inward, toward things he felt he could control. He began to focus more of his attention on the bob run. He had always thought that the Olympics, and the future of the resort, depended on its popularity, and, after he had fought so hard to secure it, he became obsessed with ensuring its success. He began to micromanage its every detail. Around him, Lake Placid was alive with work-men. Construction crews were working twenty-four-hour shifts to get the ice arena done. The foreman remembered "men so thick they looked like ants crawling over each other." At their worst, the shifts stretched for seventy hours straight without sleep, with breaks only for meals. All the while, Dewey worried away at the run, fussing over the sleds, the course, and even the teams that would be riding them. He spent hours working on blueprints for a new type of sled, one with flatter runners and finer steering. He had, of course, a little experience as a bobsledder himself: he had been a reserve on the US team in 1928. He also had some firm ideas about who should be representing the country this time round at what was, he felt, his bob track, in his Olympics. For two years now he had been liaising with officials on the United States Olympic Committee and the Amateur Athletic Union (AAU), whose representative was proving to be partic-ularly recalcitrant. His name was Jay O'Brien.

Godfrey Dewey knew Jay a little from St. Moritz. He had written to him in 1928, asking for his help in persuading the IOC to award the Games to Lake Placid. "Any influence you can bring to bear will be most welcome." Jay wasn't especially inclined to do Dewey's bidding. Since 1928 he had been running the AAU's bobsleigh program as a private concern. He paid all their expenses for the 1931 World Championship out of his own pocket. And he didn't much ap-preciate Dewey's interference.

You could scarcely find two men of such similar station yet more different in manner and mind-set than Dewey and O'Brien. This was the beginning of a delicious rivalry. In February 1930, the International Bobsledding and Tobog-ganing Federation held a congress in Paris. They met to discuss, among other things, the new style of sledding, in which riders sat upright, and the technical specifications of the sleds and the run to be used in the Lake Placid Olympics. Minor details, these, but important ones—things like the width of the sleds and the rules governing the running order for competition. Of course Dewey had fixed ideas about all of them, and was anxious that he should get his way. The trouble was that the Lake Placid Organizing Committee had no jurisdiction over the federation. "Neither a vote, nor a voice, nor even an assured right to attend," Dewey complained. "This is a manifest injustice." So he had the Amateur Athletic Union pass on meticulous orders to O'Brien. He was particularly keen for O'Brien to hammer home the point that there would not be a separate skeleton sled competition in 1932. It had been hard enough to secure money for the bob run; the idea of building another course for a different competition was anathema to him. As, to Jay, was the idea of being Godfrey Dewey's errand boy. He didn't just disagree with the instructions; he ignored them. In fact, he didn't even turn up for the first part of the congress, figuring, presumably, that there were better things for a man to do with his time in Paris than debate bobsled gages.

When Dewey discovered this, he fired off a series of furious letters, one to his architect, Zentzytzki; another to the head of the United States Olympic Committee, Brigadier General Charles Sherrill; and another to Daniel Ferris, secretary-treasurer of the AAU. They all read the same, more or less. He complained that his instructions "were too explicit to be overridden." O'Brien, he decided, had been "determined to defeat their purpose, regardless of his official obligations." It was, Dewey said, "discourteous, dishonorable, and a deliberate betrayal of trust." Dewey was certain the AAU would be horrified enough to discharge O'Brien. For neither the first nor the last time, he was horribly wrong. The AAU didn't discharge O'Brien. Instead, it made him chairman of the Olympic Bobsled Committee.

He and Dewey now stood square in opposition to each other. Dewey was sure of one thing: whoever was going to win the gold and the glory on Mount Van Hoevenberg in 1932, in the United States' very first Olympic bobsledding competition, it wasn't going to be Jay O'Brien. He would do everything he could to make sure of that. Jay, of course, had his own ideas. He wasn't planning on just managing the US bobsled team; he also wanted to be a member of it. He was forty-seven now, and he knew this would likely be his last chance to win a gold medal. In his mind, he was already putting together a crack team to drive the United States' No. 1 sled. He wanted Billy Fiske to be his driver and Tippy Gray to be the No. 2. He would be the brake himself. Now that bob teams had four men rather than five, he had one spot left to fill. He needed someone strong, to provide power for a running start. And heavy, to provide the weight to haul the team down the mountain. And cool, able to keep his head even as the sled's speed shot up to 70 mph. In short, he needed someone who knew how to live fast.

Jay knew just the man.

Eddie Eagan.

CHAPTER 8

THE BOXER

E ddie saw the punch coming, but that didn't make him feel any better when
it hit. The six-ounce glove, soppy with water and stained with blood, caught
him high on his cheek, and a flaming sunset flashed in front of his left eye. Eddie
had just enough sense left to make sure he fell forward into his opponent's chest.
He held on in a clinch and waited for the sweet relief of the bell, which he knew
was about to sound. When it came, it cut through both the buzzing in his head,
and the screams and shouts of the thousand or so fight fans inside the Opera
House.

Eddie staggered off toward his corner and slumped down onto his stool. He
could feel his cheek starting to swell. "Hell," he thought, "what a shot that was."
He sniffed at the smelling salts his brother was waving under his nose, opened
his mouth, and sucked in what little good air there was in the smoke-filled room.
And he asked himself, again, just what the hell he was doing here in Cripple
Creek, a sixteen-year-old kid in the ring against a bigger, older, stronger man.

The answer, Eddie knew, was foolish pride. He had already beaten Lum
Myberg once before, in the welterweight final of the Denver Athletic Club
Championship just a few months back. The victory had won Eddie his first
amateur title. It had been close—he got it on points, not by a knockout—but
Eddie had long since forgotten that. In his mind it had become "a clean-cut and
decisive victory." Ever since that day the local press back in Myberg's hometown
of Victor, just outside Cripple Creek, had been goading Eddie. Longmont,

where Eddie lived, was about a hundred miles away but Eddie's acquaintances made sure he saw those papers. "Did you see what they're saying about you, Eddie?" It seemed, Eddie remembered, that "almost every issue contained a challenge for me to defend my new-won title. It was a real wrench to ignore those items." Eventually, he snapped. "Eagan apparently is satisfied to rest on his questionable victory over our champion," one paper stated. "Eagan is afraid to fight."

Eddie never could abide an insult. He was born poor and raised proud. He liked to say that the first blow he ever had was the slap on the bottom from the doctor right after he was born, and that the doctor always joked that the baby Eddie had taken a deep breath and hit him right back. That was in Denver, on April 26, 1898, the day after the United States declared war on Spain. Eddie's mother, Clara, always believed that her boy was bellicose because he had been born at a time when the public was being whipped up into such a patriotic fervor by the yellow press.

John Eagan, Eddie's father, was Irish American, a big, burly man. He died in a railroad accident when his boy was still a baby. His train ran off the track while crossing a trestle and fell thirty feet into a ravine. Clara, a hot-blooded little slip of a lady, raised Eddie and his four brothers by herself. She had emigrated from the Alsace and spoke both French and German. She started working as a language teacher and washed laundry when she couldn't find any paying pupils. As soon as he was old enough, Eddie was sent out to start pitching in, running errands, sweeping floors, selling papers, collecting scrap. "Life," he said, "was a fight for bread."

Clara moved her family from Denver to the new town of Longmont, looking for a better life. Longmont had only been founded a couple of decades before she arrived, on the spot where the Cherokee Trail from Denver crossed the St. Vrain Valley. It began to grow when the Colorado Central rail line arrived in 1873, but by the time the Eagans got there, it was still, in the words of its local paper, the *Longmont Call*, "an overgrown country village" of around three thousand people, "with nothing to support it but agriculture." As soon as he was old enough, Eddie started working chores on a ranch, under a bruiser of an Irish foreman named "Big" Tim Healey. "He supported his authority," Eddie said, "with kicks, cuffs, and blistering profanity." As Eddie remembered it, Healey once made the mistake of picking on a ranch hand named Abe Tobin, a little bowlegged cowpoke who knew how to work a lasso and who, it was said, had done a little prizefighting in the past. "All I recall," Eddie said, "is Abe's brown bare arm suddenly lashing out with the speed of a rattlesnake striking. Crack!" Healey got back to his feet, and Tobin skipped around him, hitting him at will. When Healey charged, arms flailing, Tobin took an easy sidestep and shot his right into his gut. Healey lay in the dust, gasping. "Quits! I'm licked." Healey was a different man after that, and didn't offer Abe Tobin or the other hands any more trouble.

Eddie watched, wide-eyed. "To say that I was thrilled by that fight was putting it mildly. In Abe I had seen grace, rhythm, science, music, in action." He fetched Tobin a bucket of hot saltwater so he could soak his bruised knuckles. Eddie knew then that he wanted to learn to box. He nagged at Tobin to teach him, but the older man insisted that "it was a mug's game." Eddie didn't quit— he never would—and eventually Tobin gave in. So the two of them started training together, boxing barehanded. Tobin would never punch Eddie, just hit him with an open palm, hammering his lessons into his pupil's head. "After one of his slaps, my cheeks would burn for hours." As often as not, Eddie would walk away thinking that the pain "wasn't worth the candle," that he wouldn't come back for more the next day. But he always did. Tobin taught him how to duck, weave, and feint, and how to lead with his left hand, sending it in ahead of his right like artillery in front of cavalry. That stuck. It became his signature punch. Years later the great Damon Runyon would call it "Eddie's steamshovel."

Abe Tobin quit Longmont to head south to Mexico in September 1912. His last lesson for Eddie, delivered as he leaned down from the saddle of his horse, was "Eddie, you're a good scrapper. Don't be a mug and go pro. You'll be in high school next year. Stick to your books and get brains. Fighting is fun so long as you take it for just that. With pros money comes easy and goes easy. Eddie, my boy, always just fight for fun." Then he rode off into the sunset. At least, that's how Eddie told it.

It would turn out to be the single most important piece of advice Tobin ever gave him. Eddie did stick to his books. He loved to read and spent the few spare cents he did have on dime novels. His favorites were Gilbert Patten's Frank Merriwell stories. Patten was one of the best-selling authors of his day. He churned out one twenty-thousand-word story a week. The Merriwell tales, all about the adventures of a clean-living all-star athlete who studied at Yale, sold by the millions. Patten, who drank plenty, smoked more, and got through three marriages, once said that his clean-living hero "had little in common with his creator or his readers." But then, he never met Eddie. "Frank Merriwell's superhuman virtues were to me precedents far more impressive than the ten commandments," Eddie wrote. "To this day I have never used tobacco, because Frank didn't. My first glass of wine, which I do not care for, was taken under social compulsion in Europe. Frank never drank."

With Tobin gone, Eddie took to sparring with a local boy who had just moved to the town, Earl Rice. His family, unlike Eddie's, was just rich enough to be able to afford a couple of pairs of boxing gloves. The two of them set up a little makeshift gymnasium in an abandoned saloon uptown, across the railroad tracks. They shoved the old bar to one side to make room for a ring, and strung up a punctured tin bucket to use as a shower. Eddie's first real fight was against Earl. The two of them boxed a three-round bout at a local fund-raising event. The friends knocked each other silly, forgetting the little they'd learned about the art of boxing in the excitement of fighting in front of an audience for the first time. "At the end of the second round," Eddie remembered, "I was gasping for air. My arms and legs ached in weariness. It didn't seem possible I could get up for the third round." Then he heard Abe Tobin's voice in his head: "If you feel tired in a fight, always remember that the other fellow is just as tired as you are. Smile at him and he'll think you are fresh and strong." So Eddie shot Earl a smile, "a lying, hypocritical" grin.

By the time the bell rang, Eddie had mustered enough energy for one last round. He flailed wildly, planting punches all over Earl, none of them with much force. It was enough. He won the fight. "Gosh, Eddie," Earl told him later. "I was so darn weak when you smiled at me before the third round! That's what took the fight out of me." As Eddie wrote in the *Denver Post* years later, "Many a battle has been won by a straight back, a grin, and a barrel of American nerve." That night Eddie accepted the compliments and congratulations offered by the audience, and was more grateful still for the sandwiches, doughnuts, and coffee he was given as a reward for winning.

He was still living a hardscrabble life. He was fired from a job at the Kuner-Empson pea cannery when he got into a fight with his foreman, a hulking bully of a man by the name of Bolt, who had, Eddie said, "punched his way into his profession." John Howard Empson liked to claim his factory was the biggest cannery in the world. Certainly he was clearing twenty-five thousand dollars a year, and paying his workers as little as ten cents an hour. The workers were unhappy and, according to the *Longmont Call*, "agitating the matter of organizing a labor union." Tensions were high. Eddie said that he had seen Bolt shove a man who was suffering with a hernia. Bolt reckoned that Eddie spent too much time shadowboxing when he should have been working the hulling machine. The two of them got to squabbling. Bolt snapped and slapped Eddie. And Eddie shot that steamshovel left straight back at him, knocking him flat to the floor. "A thrill went through me!" Eddie remembered. "What a punch I had!" Eddie walked away. But word spread. As he said himself, "When a boss has been licked by a worker, the news travels fast."

Eddie was now the cannery's unofficial champion. He was soon challenged to a fight by Kid West, self-proclaimed champ of Longmont's other major employer, the Great Western sugar beet factory. "Of course I accepted," he wrote. So a few hundred employees of the two firms packed into the Longmont Armory. "There was little interest in the personalities of the contenders," Eddie admitted. "The fans were pro-sugar or pro-canned peas." Until the two of them got into the ring, that is. Eddie was a head shorter and a load lighter than West, and when the fans saw them side by side, there weren't too many willing to root for him, whether they worked at the cannery or not. "Why does mere size count for so much with fight fans?" Eddie once asked. "It never should." He knocked West down with an uppercut to the gut in the third round. The punch stupefied West, left him sitting there "with a stupid, pained expression on his face."

The victory earned Eddie his first write-up in the *Denver Post*. "Eagan had his opponent completely outclassed," the paper said. "Although he was handicapped by twenty pounds in weight." It was the first of many stories about Eddie's successes. Six weeks later he won the welterweight championship at the Denver Athletic Club. He fought five times just to get to the final, where he met that man Myberg for the first time. It was, in the words of the *Rocky Mountain News*, "a hot four round session," and Eddie's victory, on points, marked him out as one of the brightest prospects on the local circuit. It wasn't long, though, before Myberg started hollering for a rematch. Eddie had to bite his tongue for a time and swallow all the insults that came his way, because he was studying for his exams, with his heart set on winning a scholarship to Denver University. Besides, he had already beaten Myberg once; there was no real need to fight him again. Until the papers said Eddie was afraid to fight.

Eddie took the train to Cripple Creek, having sent word ahead that he was ready to fight Myberg on his turf, in front of his people. The trouble was that Cripple Creek is almost ten thousand feet above sea level, and almost as soon as Eddie stepped off the train, he grew short of breath and his head began to swim in the thin air. He wasn't helped by his reception committee, who insisted on taking him to the bar for a drink—he made sure to order a root beer—and then showed him to his quarters in the local fire station, where he was sharing a bunkroom with a bunch of firefighters. The night before the fight, Eddie was woken in the early hours when the crew were called out to deal with a fire. He lay awake, hoping that it was the Opera House that was burning, just so he'd have a little more time to acclimatize before the fight. No such luck.

Everywhere Eddie went in the town he heard whispers. "He's just a kid! Myberg will kill him." "It won't be a fight, it'll be plain murder." Myberg was a miner, one of many who had moved to Cripple Creek in the wake of the last Colorado gold rush, in 1890. He was eight years older than Eddie, and eight pounds heavier too. They called him "Blue," because that was the color of the ribbon he wore around his waist when he fought. He had won that Denver Athletic Club Championship four years straight until Eddie had stopped him in the spring of 1914. He was a slow, powerful fighter whose favorite ploy was to wait for his opponent to walk into his vicious right hook, which Eddie reckoned "had the effect of a hand grenade."

It was that same right hook that hit Eddie at the end of the fifth, drawing forth roars from the horde of hostile faces, "weather beaten, hard bitten, there wasn't a smile in a car-load." They were all convinced that their man had been robbed when Eddie beat him the first time round and had come to see justice done. Eddie had never felt so lonely in his life as he did in the middle of that ring. Until he heard one friendly voice call out, "Kid, snap into it in this last round!" It belonged, Eddie later learned, to a man named Lenihan, a gambler who had backed him at odds of 2 to 1. His only interest in the fight was a mercenary one, but it made all the difference to Eddie to know there was someone out there rooting for him.

Eddie did snap into it. Typically he liked to fight light on his feet, to flit around his opponent flicking out his jab. Now, though, he was too spent to move like that. So he and Myberg stood toe-to-toe. When Eddie saw Lum readying that big right of his, he slipped in two quick shots of his own and followed them with a hook left. It was the best punch Eddie had. And it hit Myberg flush on the chin. He dropped, struggled to stand, and sagged back down. When the bell rang for the final time, he was holding himself up on the ropes. After that, there could only be one winner. The ref lifted Eddie's hand high as he announced the result. "It was well he did," Eddie said. "I didn't feel I had the strength to do it myself."

In the dressing room after the fight, once the well-wishers had cleared out, Lenihan cornered Eddie. "You're good," he told him. "But you need a manager.

Why don't you turn pro? I've handled fighters before. Come with me and we'll clean up."

Eddie was tempted. "If I proved a success," he thought, "it would mean the end of worries for my work-worn little mother, no more manual toil, and good educations for my brothers." But again he heard Abe Tobin's voice in his head: "Don't be a mug and go pro." Eddie said no. "You see," he explained to Lenihan, "I'm going to college in September and I have to stay amateur to play in the teams." Lenihan gave him a pitying look.

Truth is, Eddie probably protested a touch too much here. He probably came closer to going pro than he ever let on. He fought for serious money on a couple of occasions for the Colorado Athletic Club, under the management of a man named Delaney. And certainly he needed the money, even though his scholarship covered his tuition. He took a job as a physical instructor, just because it offered board and lodging, and another as an athletics teacher at an elementary school. He was, he said, "busier than a flea on a houn' dog's ear," and loving every minute of it. Eddie finally had his Frank Merriwell life. He was studying, running on the university's track team, dabbling with football, doing teaching and social work in his spare time, and trying to raise money to build a boxing gym for underprivileged kids on the west side. And, of course, he continued to box.

He entered himself in both the middleweight and heavyweight divisions of the Denver Athletic Club Championship in 1918. He won both titles, beating, as he put it, a bunch of "muscle-bound laborers, boiler makers, plumbers, brick layers, and piano movers." Eddie reckoned himself to be a class above these part-timers and amused himself by trying to knock out his opponents as quickly as he could. His gung ho fighting style won him a lot of fans. "He's a hard hitter, game all the way through, and is always after his man from start to finish," reported the Rocky Mountain News. Ike O'Hara, a copy boy at the Denver Post, said, "This Eddie Eagan is the best fighter I ever saw in a tournament, because he could use his left." According to the Post, Eddie's middleweight final, against Tommy Tierson, "was a real thriller and brought out the very best boxing of the tourney."

The heavyweight final against George Blossom was harder still, because Eddie was duped into thinking that his opponent's father had gotten out of his sickbed to come and watch his boy box. "You can lick George with one punch," Blossom's manager told Eddie before the fight. "But I am going to ask you not to do it." He said he was worried that "the shock of seeing his son knocked out might be too much for his weak heart. I'm just appealing to you to spare the old man's life by not kayoing George." The truth was that George Blossom's father had been dead for five years already, but Eddie was so green that he swallowed the story. The plan backfired when Blossom called Eddie "a sentimental sap" during a clinch in the first round. Eddie realized that he had been fooled and, infuriated, "tore into George full throttle." The *Post* reckoned that Eddie "fought like a wildcat," and the *News* noted that "angered, he boxed with a determination that could not be stopped, his usual smile gone." Blossom weighed over two hundred pounds, but Eddie knocked him clean through the ropes and out of the ring.

Well, after that, Eddie was a regular hero. The *Post* hailed him as "one of the cleanest-cut and best sportsmen Denver has ever boasted," and it signed him up to write a series of twelve articles all about the art of boxing. They were pretty pompous, mixing as they did advice for aspiring boxers and opinions about the state of modern America. Later in his life Eddie had the good grace to admit that he blushed when he thought about the things he had had written. "The idea that a Christian shall be a pusillanimous backboneless jellyfish is becoming antiquated," Eddie advised. "Boxing is the perfect sport to take all of the girl-like ways out of boys and make men of them." This from a kid who hadn't yet turned twenty. Eddie advocated a life of "constant unending strife" and a regimen of rising at 6 a.m. to run twice around the block while wearing "your father's biggest boots" followed by a cold bath and a brisk rub with a towel.

If Eddie had a big head, well, perhaps that was unsurprising. He was the heavyweight champion of the city and hadn't yet lost a fight, or even come across someone who seriously threatened to be able to beat him. That was about to change. Early in the summer of 1918 Eddie was asked to take part in a three-round exhibition fight as a fund-raising evening for the Red Cross, at the Empress Theater. The organizers were so sure that he would agree that they put a notice in the paper announcing the fight before they had even asked him whether he was free and willing. The opponent, they explained, was an out-of-towner by the name of Jack Dempsey.

Now, in 1918, Dempsey was still an up-and-comer. Of course Eddie had heard of him, as had most fight fans, but he was just another heavyweight contender, one of many queuing up for a shot at the world champion, Jess Willard. He was still some way away from winning Willard's title, which he would do the following year, let alone being seen as one of the greatest heavyweights in history, which is what he would become. In 1950 the Associated Press would vote Dempsey the "greatest fighter of the last 50 years," and even today both the *Ring* magazine and *Sports Illustrated* rate him as one of the ten best heavyweights of all time. Back then Dempsey was billed on the vaudeville circuit as the "Coming World's Champion," but Eddie reckoned that was just so much baloney. He knew that in 1917 Dempsey had been knocked down in the very first round by "Fireman" Jim Flynn, in a fight many now suspect was fixed by the mob. Eddie himself had watched Flynn box in Denver and been underwhelmed by what he had seen. Besides, he had seen pictures of Dempsey in the papers, and Dempsey wasn't nearly as big as George Blossom, whom Eddie had licked in that Denver Athletic Club final.

The fight had been arranged by Otto Floto, a man Eddie generously described as a "famous sportswriter." Floto did work as the editor of the *Denver Post*—and had taken on Eddie as a columnist—but even the paper's co-owner, Harry Tammen, admitted that he had hired him only because he thought Floto was "a beautiful name" and he wanted to use it for a dog-and-pony show that he owned. Which he duly did. Floto, who weighed the best part of three hundred pounds, was, in the words of *Post* columnist Woody Paige, a "drunk, barely literate loudmouth." He also dabbled in the fight game, and knew Dempsey from way back when he was growing up in Manassa, down near the border with New Mexico. Floto volunteered to act as referee for the evening.

Eddie started serious training. As he told his readers, "The law of the boxing life is the law of work. Not the law of idleness, of self-indulgence, or pleasure, merely the law of work." He ran five miles each morning and spent his afternoons sparring in the gym. This work wasn't for Dempsey's benefit—Eddie was convinced he had his measure—but because, for the first time in his life, he was going to be fighting in front of women as well as men. "Several beautiful co-eds from the University were to sell programs," Eddie remembered. "And one of them was The Girl." He was tingling with anticipation picturing "her awe at my display of skill, speed, and punching power."

The Empress, down on Denver's old theater row, seated around 1,400, and it was full that night. The fight was at the top of the bill, which meant that Eddie and Jack had to wait until the other acts were over. Eddie stood backstage, quivering with excitement. Finally Jack Kearns, Dempsey's manager, strolled out into the ring that had been erected on the stage and called the fighters out to join him. Eddie came first, blinking in the bright lights. "And now," Kearns announced over a drum roll and a flourish of trumpets, "ladies and gentlemen, let me introduce the Mauler from Manassa, Colorado, future heavyweight champion of the world, Jack Dempsey!" A ripple of applause ran around the theater, though the ovation was not so generous, Eddie reckoned, as the one that had been given to him, the hometown champ.

Floto called the two men to the center of the ring. Jack ran his eyes over Eddie, apparently unconcerned by what he saw. "Now boys," Floto said, "a nice fast exhibition. And Jack, remember there are women out there, so don't hit hard." Eddie wondered why Floto hadn't given him a similar warning. Irritated at being underestimated, he resolved to hit Dempsey with a straight right at the first opportunity.

"Knock him stiff as a railroad tie, Eddie!" someone shouted.

And then the bell went. Eddie rushed out of his corner and, just as he had planned, threw his right fist at Dempsey's chin. Eddie knew it was a good shot, the kind that had put bigger men flat on the canvas. It caught Dempsey on the jaw. A look of surprise flickered across his face.

"Keep it up, Eddie!"

Next, Eddie feinted to throw his left, then shot out another vicious right. That one caught Jack's jaw too. His head bobbed backward. Trying to knock Dempsey down, Eddie now realized, was as futile "as trying to swim up the Niagara Falls." He stepped around, looking for another opening. And then he heard something underneath the sound of the crowd. Eddie did a double take, asked himself whether his ears were deceiving him. They weren't. Dempsey had started to sing to himself, underneath his breath. It was "Everybody Two-step." He began to shuffle his feet, keeping time with the beat. "Oh my dear, don't you hear the latest music hit? Oh gee! The orchestra is playing it!"

Then the roof fell in. A rafter fell on the back of Eddie's head. At least that's what he assumed had happened, until he came to. He felt the taut ropes behind him, cutting into his back, and two padded gloves underneath his armpits, holding him up off the canvas. As the ringing in his ears faded and his hearing returned, he heard the cries of the crowd and, below those, the voice of the referee. "Hold him up a little longer, Jack. And for heaven's sake go easy on your punches." When Eddie opened his eyes, he saw Dempsey standing there, left eyebrow cocked upward, lips twisted into a wry little grin. Eddie was shoved back into the center of the ring.

"Let's two step and dance in old Havana style."

Whop—Jack threw out a jab at Eddie's head.

"Just act like you were made of rubber, child."

Bop—another jab.

"Glide along the floor and slide your feet a little bit, that's it!"

Bang.

When Eddie came to, he was still on his feet, but only because Dempsey was holding him there and doing his best to make it look like the two of them were locked in a clinch. It was, after all, an exhibition, and he had to make sure the crowd got their money's worth. Eddie suddenly realized he was in far over his head.

"If you hit me again, Jack," he said, "you won't be able to hold me up."

Dempsey smiled. "All right kid, but don't try any more of your funny rights."

A friendship was forged during that fight. Dempsey nursed Eddie through the three remaining rounds, even allowing him to land a few jabs for appearances' sake. The following year Jess Willard, then the reigning champ, asked Eddie to work as his sparring partner ahead of his title fight with Dempsey, telling him he could "name his price." Eddie turned him down because he wanted his friend Jack to win the fight, which he did.

After the exhibition, he and Jack had a chat in Dempsey's dressing room. He taught Eddie a few of his tricks, showing him how he tucked his chin down into his shoulder, a style Eddie adopted himself. "You're a good puncher," Dempsey told him. "You know how to box and you'd be a good professional. But Otto Floto tells me you're in college. Stick to it, kid. I wish I had your chance. The professional gets darn little money and lots of punches."

Eddie didn't stick to it. He decided to drop out of university and join the army, enlisting as a private in the infantry. He won a commission, funnily enough, after he was challenged to a fight by his drill sergeant, who, just like the foreman at the cannery a few years earlier, made the mistake of picking on the wrong man. The two of them got to arguing after he refused to grant Eddie weekend leave. Of course Eddie knew better than to hit a sergeant. But the man told Eddie to "disregard the stripes on his shoulder" because he was going to "give him the licking of his life." Eddie promptly knocked the sergeant flat on his back. He assumed he was in for it when he was called in to see the regimental commander a few days later, and was a little surprised when his colonel told him, "Eagan, I'm ordered to send ten privates to officers' training school. Your captain says that if you can't command 'em, you can lick 'em. Report there this morning."

By the time Eddie finished at artillery school, the war was already over. He was discharged and took up a place in the Officers' Reserve Corps as a second lieutenant. His brief time in the army broadened his horizons. He met and be-friended a couple of men who had studied at Yale. Their descriptions of life in New Haven reawakened his childhood dream of studying there, just like his hero Frank Merriwell had. He resolved to apply, and though he was turned down at first, on the grounds that his "Latin was too weak," he persuaded Dean Corwin of Sheffield Scientific School to take a chance on "an athlete and a scholar." It helped that Corwin had played a little football as a young man, some-thing Eddie knew from a photo he spotted on the wall of the dean's study.

Eddie was utterly out of his element at Yale. His gauche, garrulous manner was at odds with the "stiffness and restraint" of his fellow students. He couldn't afford a suit and spent the first semester of his freshman year wearing his old army uniform. People assumed he wanted to show off the badge on his shoulder, but he was just too proud to admit how poor he was. He took a job as a physical instructor at the local YMCA, where he lived in a skinny little room. Struggling to adjust, Eddie got on with what he knew how to do—studying and boxing.

In April 1919 he decided to compete at the National Amateur Champion-ship. He was too self-effacing to say he was representing Yale, so he entered himself as a member of the Denver Athletic Club. He scraped together his rail fare and traveled alone, without seconds or support, to Boston. Eddie had put himself in for two categories, light heavyweight and heavyweight. That meant he had seven four-round fights in the space of two days. He had grown into quite a fighter now, with a style all his own. He was clever and cunning, using his quick feet to maneuver around the ring. He loved to attack, and was always pressing forward. He looked to fight inside the reach of his opponents, who were invariably bigger than he was. And when he was on the back foot, though he would never admit it, he knew a few dirty tricks that he had picked up back when he was roughhousing around Colorado. There were at least a couple of occasions when, in a clinch, he wrestled his opponent out of the ring. He did that in his light heavyweight semifinal, against a man named Al Roche, and the crowd booed him because of it. "No more of that rough stuff," the referee warned him, "or I'll disqualify you." He didn't need to do that: Eddie lost the fight, on points. Even the *Denver Post* said that he was "decisively beaten," though Eddie, bullishly confident in his own abilities, said he knew in his heart that he had won.

Eddie needed to tell himself that, whether it was true or not, because the heavyweight final was scheduled to take place that same night. Only a few hours later he was back in the ring, squaring up against Jim Tully, a policeman from

New York who knew a couple of tricks of his own. Tully's seconds had tried to bring the final forward so that Eddie wouldn't have any time to recover from his first fight. He saw through that. Then at the start of the fight Tully told the referee, "If you see I'm killing him, stop it, I don't want to hurt the lad." Eddie didn't fret. He could smell whiskey on Tully's breath, taken for Dutch courage. He knew then that he had the measure of the man. He stepped in close, inside the range of Tully's long arms, and pummeled his stomach. In the clinch, Eddie whispered, "I must win, I must win, you hear, you big Harp? I will win." And he did, on points. When Eddie returned to Yale, his eyes were swollen almost shut, both his brow and lips were cut, and his nose was broken. But he had a gold medal in his pocket. He was the amateur champion of the United States. Word soon spread. Eddie, still a freshman, became a hero around the campus.

The victory won Eddie an invitation to try out for the US team at the 1919 Inter-Allied Games in Paris. He traveled to Europe that spring, after taking a temporary job in the sports and recreation department of the American Expeditionary Force. His first fight came as a surprise. He was attending a Franco-American boxing night at the Palais de Glace and had only just finished his meal—he'd had a bellyful of sole, shrimp, and oysters—when he was asked if he would step in to an empty slot on the card and fight a French middleweight. He won, just, but decided that he'd best start taking his training a little more seriously. After that he spent most of his time running the roads in the Latin Quarter, where "every window framed a girl's head." They would call out to him as he passed: *"Chéri! Où allez-vous? Restez ici."*

"A sock on the nose or soft caresses?" Eddie wrote. "It was, at times, hard to elect the socks."

One of his teammates was a sly "will-o'-the-wisp" named Gene Tunney, who would go on to make his name by defeating Jack Dempsey to become the champion of the world in 1926. Tunney was certain to be picked to represent the United States in the heavyweight division, which left Eddie competing with Al Norton for a slot in the next category down, the light heavyweights. Norton was a pro. He had fought Dempsey three times himself, and he'd had little more luck at it than Eddie in his exhibition. US coach Spike Webb arranged for the two of them to face off for the spot.

Norton got the edge over Eddie right from the get-go. Eddie, amateur that he was, began the fight by stretching out his arm so the two men could touch gloves. Which they did, briefly, before Norton, the gnarled old pro, clobbered him with a left hook that knocked him down for a seven count. The blow had caught Eddie unawares and left him so concussed that he suffered from amnesia for three days after the fight. When he fully came to, he was told that he had fought on, furiously, for ten rounds, and that the fight had been called a draw. But seeing as Eddie finished it unable to remember his own name, let alone what day of the week it was, the team had entered Norton for the Games. Eddie was offered the middleweight slot instead, as long as he could sweat off nine pounds. He did it, just. He had more of a struggle making the weight than he did winning his first fight, against an Italian named Negri: it took Eddie thirty-two seconds to knock him out. The Belgian Eddie fought in the second round fared only a little better. The two knockouts made such an impression that Eddie's two remaining opponents withdrew, "cowed into submission," as the *New York Times* put it, "merely by his demonstration in the preliminary bouts." Eddie became the Inter-Allied champion by a walkover.

Sweet as the win was, Eddie was even more pleased with two other rewards that came his way. The King of Montenegro, Nicholas I, was so taken with Eddie's pugilistic prowess that he gave him a medal and made him a member of the Order of Prince Danilo I. "The Montenegro coach says that you fellows that got medals are Counts of Montenegro," Spike Webb told Eddie afterward. "See to it that you ain't ever Count Ten." Better yet, Eddie managed to wangle a press ticket to see the signing of the Treaty of Versailles. He took his place at the back of the Hall of Mirrors, but got so fed up with looking over the backs of so many heads that he pushed his way toward the front. He watched history unfold from thirty feet away. Not that he was all that impressed with what he saw. He expected the great statesmen David Lloyd George, Woodrow Wilson, and Georges Clemenceau to seem "splendid and godlike" and was disappointed to find them, as he wrote later, "acting like a lot of Oxford boys at a coming of age party," each seeking the autograph of the other.

Eddie wasn't long back at Yale. He lost his national title in the spring of 1920, beaten on points by a heavyweight named Karl Wicks. There was a similar result in the light heavyweight final, when he took on Jack Burke. The *New York Times* reckoned that Eddie fought "with the bulldog spirit for which Yale is noted," that he had "backed his man into all four corners of the ring" and had Burke "virtually defeated" when he was caught by a lucky punch. He weathered out what was left of the fight, but lost on points. Burke, Eddie said, had a right uppercut that hit like "a rock catapulted up from the floor." He once used it to knock down Jack Dempsey in a sparring session. He lost in the final of the heavyweight category, too, on points again.

Eddie had changed in the space of the past twelve months. This time around he was a proud Yalie. He'd traveled to the tournament with his fast friend Sam Pryor, a wealthy young man who would go on to become the vice president of Pan Am. They spent the morning before the Burke fight studying John Singer Sargent's murals at the Boston Public Library. Eddie actually thought the defeats did him good: "They brought me back to my main purpose at Yale." He knuckled down and passed his Easter exams with honors. The only fighting he did was during Yale's mock political convention ahead of the 1920 election, when he was chosen to serve as the sergeant at arms. "He is expected," the *Times* reported, "to insure peace and quiet." That, Eddie gleefully recounted, is exactly what he did. The convention was crashed by a group of socialist delegates calling for "free love, free beer, and no work," and Eddie, together with the varsity football team, enjoyed a "good rough-house." By the time it was over, "the intruders were repressed and order was restored." He did such a good job that he was hired to serve in a similar role at the real Republican convention in Chicago that May.

By July 1920 Eddie was back in the ring. He traveled down to New York to take part in the qualifying bouts for the 1920 Olympics, to be held in Antwerp, Belgium, that August. He hoped to avenge the two defeats he had suffered in Boston, but Burke had since turned pro, which meant he wasn't eligible for Olympic competition. Eddie remained resolutely amateur, though there were plenty of times when he was tempted. He was offered a guarantee of $1,500 to fight Mike O'Dowd for the middleweight championship of the world, a "sum that loomed as large as the Allied Indemnity bill." But accepting it would have compromised his education and committed him to a career as a prizefighter. He turned it down, mindful of what both Tobin and Dempsey had told him in the past, but he spent the rest of his life wondering whether it had been the right thing to do. If Eddie couldn't fight for money, he would fight for glory. And the most prestigious prize available to him was the Olympic title, so that was what he set his heart on. He won all four of his qualifying fights and took his place on the US team in the light heavyweight category.

The team traveled out on the *Princess Matoika*, a rusty old tub that had served as a troop carrier. The trip was a farce, and the ship became infamous when a group of athletes mutinied in protest at the poor conditions on board. The men were packed into the sweltering hold, where plenty were struck down with seasickness. As for training, the runners had to practice on a sixty-yard-long cork track on deck, the javelin throwers were forced to tether their spears to the side of the ship and toss them out into the sea, and the swimmers made do with a leaky canvas tank full of saltwater. Eddie didn't much mind. As a boxer, all he needed was a little patch of deck to exercise on and a space to spar in. Besides, he had endured worse in his time. "Star athletes can put prima donnas to shame when it comes to demonstrating displeasure."

To win the Olympic title, Eddie needed to beat three men. The first of them was a South African, Tom Holdstock. The fight was nip-and-tuck until the last round, when Eddie knocked Holdstock down with a left hook. Next came an Englishman, Harry Franks. He was clever and quick, but, as Eddie's coach Spike Webb put it, "he couldn't punch his way through a spider's web." Eddie had planned to rush him, but found himself like a bull charging at a matador's red rag. Every time he closed in, Franks would sidestep and shoot out his jab. At the end of the first round, Eddie was well behind on points.

"Show him you can dance the tango too," Webb told him.

And Eddie did. He switched his stance, putting his right foot and fist out in front instead of his left. It was a neat trick, and it foxed Franks. While he was blinking in confusion, Eddie caught him with an uppercut. By the third and final round, Eddie had the Englishman's measure. He won on points. "If you'd only made up your mind which way you were going to stand," Franks told him after the fight was over, "I'd have done much better."

They say there is a difference between a brawler and a boxer. One relies on aggression and instinct, the other on art and technique. Eddie was both. His childhood in Colorado had left him with rough edges, but he had learned his craft. He had beaten Holdstock with brute force, and then he had outwitted Franks.

Eddie spent the day before the final in the Royal Museum of Fine Arts, looking at the paintings by Rubens. That night he slept in a feather bed for the first time, in a room he had rented so he could be away from the noise and bustle of the team camp. His opponent was a Norwegian, Sverre Sørsdal, a giant redhead, "tireless and game," with a body that looked like it had been cut from marble. Eddie was cagey. He held himself back in the first two rounds, standing off and allowing Sørsdal to come at him. Each time Sørsdal closed in, Eddie would block and parry the blows he delivered and then pick him off. In the third, Eddie switched up a gear. "I cut loose with every remaining ounce of energy in my body. I tore into him." If Sørsdal was still landing blows, Eddie couldn't feel them. When the bell sounded, the two men embraced each other. It had been a great fight. And Eddie had won it. He was the Olympic champion.

Modern Olympians often talk of the slump they experience after the Games are over. They expend so much time, energy, and effort in the four years running up to that one event that afterward they are left feeling spent, wondering what to do next. Eddie's life was too full, too rich, for him to waste time worrying about that, but he did decide to step away from the ring for a while and see what else life had to offer during his senior year at Yale. He decided to try out for the varsity football team and played a few games as a tight end. He won good reviews, too, from both his teammates, who reckoned him one of the "most popular members of the squad," and the *New York Times*, which reported that he "played a wonderful game" against a scrub team and that "with the rapid strides he is making, in another season he should be a star." That didn't happen. Frank Merriwell may have been able to excel at everything he turned his hand to, but Eddie found football a stretch. He did, however, win a coveted "Y," as captain of the boxing team, and he was elected class secretary and class orator. He had come a long way in the three years since he'd arrived in New Haven, penniless, intimidated, and unsure of whether he was worthy of a place there.

Eddie graduated with honors in the summer of 1921 and enrolled at Harvard Law School. He celebrated by taking a tour around Europe with his friends Sam Pryor, Mike O'Brien, and Mace Thompson. The other three could pay their way, but Eddie had to work his passage. He wangled a job as entertainments officer on board the ship. They cruised the fjords of Norway, climbed the Alps in Switzerland, and went to the bullfights in Spain. The place that made the biggest impression on him was Oxford, England. He decided to apply for a Rhodes scholarship so he could study there.

He had an extraordinary interview back in Denver, where he was grilled by a group of old Oxford men.

"What club would you use if you were in golf and 100 yards from the green?"

"Suppose at Oxford some of the students decided to debag you in the college quad, what would you do?"

"Will you drink tea should you go to Oxford?"

Eddie's answers were the right ones.

"That depends on the lie of the ball, but if it's good then take a mashie [wedge]."

"If a group of students tries to pull your trousers down, the obvious thing to do is try and debag as many of them as possible before they succeed in stripping yours off."

And, yes, of course he would drink tea.

A few days later the *Denver Post* announced of the city's favorite son, Eddie Eagan: "Denver's athletic and scholastic ace and king of the amateur light heavyweight boxers of the world has been awarded Colorado's Rhodes scholarship."

If Yale had seemed outlandish to Eddie, Oxford was altogether another world. He enrolled at New College, where he was welcomed by the warden William Spooner, an elderly albino who read Eddie's letters of recommendation with the aid of an oversize magnifying glass. Spooner, of course, was famous for his habit of muddling up his consonants when he spoke.

Eddie's rooms had no heating or plumbing. Everything about the place felt antiquated. He was woken each morning by his elderly, gap-toothed scout, who would bring him a cup of tea and sing him a music hall song. His law tutor had served in the war and was riddled with shrapnel. "At frequent intervals he would be laid up while bits of metal worked their way out of his body." Eddie was never more a fish out of water than when he was invited to a party held by a group who studied at Christ Church and called themselves the "Oxford Wits." Their ringleaders were Brian Howard and Harold Acton, who provided the inspiration for the character of Anthony Blanche in Evelyn Waugh's *Brideshead Revisited*. Waugh had been part of the esthetes' set himself, and lampooned them in his 1945 work. Acton, just like Blanche in the book, liked to stand on his balcony and recite T. S. Eliot's *The Waste Land* through a megaphone to people passing below.

Eddie wanted to get to know all "types and classes" of the British, so he had accepted the invitation to visit. As he entered, Acton rushed up to greet him with a flower in his hand.

"Oh, we're so glad you came!" Acton said. "Have a lily."

Eddie, somewhat embarrassed, was struck dumb for a moment. "What shall I do with it?"

"Oh, nothing," Acton replied. "Just look at it. Isn't it beautiful?"

Eddie, a little lost among the "artistic" crowd, as he euphemistically referred to them, fell into conversation with a poet, most likely Brian Howard. "He was dressed as I had seen pictures of Byron; a velvet jacket, an open-throated shirt, and he wore his hair long and brushed back." Howard complimented him on his prowess as a boxer, and Eddie politely replied that his feats were "no more glorious than being the champion poet of Oxford," and jokingly suggested that the two of them should consider switching hobbies. "You come out for boxing, and I'll write poetry." Eddie explained, "There's poetry in any good fight. And if I could write how I've felt about some victories they would be epics." Howard, an earnest fellow, took him at his word. Eddie was mortified when he saw an article in a London newspaper the next day under the headline "Boxer Becomes Poet," explaining how Eddie was going to "sing about the thrills of prizefighting in metric cadence and rhyme." His main worry was that word would spread back to Denver, "where they would blame Oxford for ruining a good boxer."

In the end, Eddie decided that he was more comfortable in the company of the three fellows from the Oxford boxing club who had come to see him shortly after he arrived. One was Douglas Douglas-Hamilton, the Marquis of Douglas and Clydesdale. Just as it had done at Yale, boxing opened up a new world to Eddie, one that would perhaps have remained unavailable to him if he hadn't been so skilled in the ring. He and the Marquis of Clydesdale—"Douglo," as Eddie knew him—became sparring partners, and, eventually, firm friends. Eddie taught Douglo to box, and with some success: he won the Scottish amateur middleweight title. Douglo, in turn, took Eddie under his wing, bringing him to his estate in Scotland. Eddie learned that "beneath the veneer of social customs they were the same fine men I've met everywhere in the world." A little later in his Oxford life, Eddie dined with the Prince of Wales and found him to be "a pleasant, smiling young man" and an enthusiastic fight fan.

The marquis and his two friends had come to ask Eddie to join the varsity team for the match against Cambridge. Eddie's reputation preceded him. He had given little thought to the sport since winning his Olympic title, fighting only twice, but he found himself unable to turn them down. "Boxing is in my blood," he wrote. "And like an old cavalry horse smelling burned powder, the call of battle was proving irresistible." He was soon back in the ring, though he struggled to find worthy opposition. Eddie once explained that the kindest thing to do to an inferior fighter was to put him quickly out of his misery. "A knockout," he wrote, "is the most generous treatment" because "a man with fighting spirit will take punishment so long as he remains conscious." The alternative, he pointed out, was to "bludgeon an opponent until he is goofy." He was in an especially charitable mood during Oxford's match against Sandhurst military college, when he fought the team's coach and knocked him out in the first few seconds of the opening round. In the varsity match, Eddie made such short work of his opponents on the Cambridge team that the *Daily Mail* published a series of cartoons showing his adversaries pleading for mercy. "Unlike most heavyweights Mr. Eagan likes it," read the caption on one. "He is willing to box the whole of Cambridge or anyone who goes there."

Eddie's ambitions didn't stop there. The *Mail*'s boxing writer, Trevor Wignall, persuaded him to enter the British Amateur Championship in London. Wignall pointed out that while the competition was open to all comers, the title had "never been won by an American." That was all the incentive Eddie needed. He fought his way through the preliminaries easily enough, in front of a "strange mob" of sailors and navvies who cried out, "Kill the Yank!" when he came into the ring. He was only really tested during a bout against a policeman named Arthur Clifton. Eddie won the crowd over by beating him, the police being even less popular with the crowd than visiting Americans. Clifton would get his revenge a couple of years later.

The finals were held at Alexandra Palace, where the crowd was of a different cut. "Around the ringside were monocled toffs, with high silk hats, broad white shirt fronts, leaning on canes. Flashily clothed gentlemen, bowlers atilt, were sandwiched between the men about town." Eddie, ever the glutton for punishment, had again entered himself in both the light heavyweight and the heavyweight divisions. He fought twice in the morning, winning both times, and then popped into town to eat a steak at Simpson's on the Strand. Fortified, he returned to the Palace and fought twice more. His battle with Harry Mitchell for the light heavyweight title was, the *Times* said, "the fight of the day." Eddie came out swinging. "He sailed into his man with a fury that left Mitchell with a cut eye by the end of the first round" and carried on in similar fashion in the second. But he made the mistake of easing up in the third, as he believed himself to be well ahead on points. His opponent "landed some stinging counters and followed them up with a right to the head." Mitchell won on points, though both Eddie and the *Times* agreed that the decision was something of an injustice. In the heavyweight final he was matched against Henry Hulks, a good boxer "with a long, poking left." Eddie pulled that old trick of his, the one that foxed Harry Franks in the Olympics, and switched his stance midway through the fight. He sold a feint with his right, and as Hulks moved his hands up to cover his face, socked him in the belly with a left hook that put him flat on the canvas.

Eddie was now the Olympic champion and the British champion, and had been, not so long ago, the US champion too. He could fairly claim to be the greatest amateur heavyweight in the world. Inevitably, he received more offers to turn professional, including an especially tempting one from the promoter Tex Rickard, the Don King of his day. Rickard had arranged the first million-dollar fight, between Eddie's old pal Jack Dempsey and the handsome French-man Georges Carpentier. Rickard licked his lips at the prospect of selling a "Rhodes scholar pug" to the punters at Madison Square Garden. There had been a similar ballyhoo when Eddie had made a couple of casual remarks to a reporter from the *Tribune* about how he would be willing to fight Louis Mbarick Fall, known to all as "Battling Siki," the Senegalese heavyweight who became champion of the world after he defeated Carpentier in 1922. "Will Rhodes Scholar Go after the Big Money?" asked the *Daily Mail*. Eddie actually helped train Mike McTigue, the Irish heavyweight who took Siki's title, but he never did go for the "Big Money." Instead he went back to Oxford, and his books.

Douglo did talk Eddie into defending his Olympic title at the 1924 Games in Paris, and Eddie was duly drafted onto the team at late notice. It was a poor decision, and one he regretted. He was out of shape and soon struck down with food poisoning. He lost, on points, in the first round to Arthur Clifton, the very same man he had beaten so easily when he fought him at Hoxton Baths a couple of years earlier. Oddly, Eddie never once successfully defended any of the titles he'd won. He seemed to be too busy looking ahead, for new challenges to con-quer, and to find little motivation in the idea of repeating feats he had already accomplished. The defeat in Paris helped Eddie make up his mind. He knew then, at the age of twenty-six, that he never would turn pro. He still dreamed of greater glories, though, of becoming a world champion. He was just going to take a different route to the title.

In the summer of 1925 Eddie was made an offer he felt was too good to refuse: the Chicago businessman John Pirie asked him to chaperone his two sons, John Jr. and Robert, on a world tour. Eddie decided that his bar exams could wait. He had one more fight before the party left England, an exhibition in Brighton against his old friend Jack Dempsey. When they were done punching, the two of them chewed the fat. Eddie told Jack about his plans. "Ah ha," Dempsey said, "so you're going to box the compass? I envy you. Here I am, world champion, and I've never been around the world. Keep your eyes open for good scrappers. But don't send 'em to me. You lick 'em, Eddie."

Of course Eddie planned to pack a few pairs of gloves. Boxing would be just one of the things he would teach the two young men on their travels, and be-sides, he had an idea he might do a little fighting himself along the way. After all, he wrote, "a man can't live without meat, and a fighter can't live without scraps."

Which is how Eddie ended up in a jail in Naples. His hot head had gotten the better of him again: he had clobbered an Italian policeman who wanted to question him about a jewelry theft in Rome. Once Eddie was out of that fix, with a little help from the US consul, he and his wards quit Italy and hotfooted it to Africa. Not that his luck got much better. He suffered severe food poisoning in Egypt and lost fifteen pounds while he was laid up in hospital. When he was better, he made his way to Nairobi, where he caught malaria. After that, Eddie headed into Tanganyika, then northern Rhodesia, to do some big-game hunting. He bagged a lion or two and a black sable antelope, whose head was hung up in the grillroom of the Yale Club in New York. But he made a mess of his elephant hunt and ended up being chased across the plains by a stampeding herd, angered by the poorly aimed potshots he had taken at their bull. He escaped only when, in the rush, he tumbled head over heels into a river and the elephants lost his scent.

From Africa it was on to India, where Eddie met up with the Marquis of Clydesdale. The two of them put on a series of boxing exhibitions across the continent, the first as part of a fund-raising evening organized by the governor of Bombay. Eddie fought, and thrashed, the light heavyweight champion from the Indian army. The audience made more of an impression on him than his opponent did. "I had seen many strange fight fan audiences," Eddie remembered, "but I doubt that ever again I will look out upon such a range of humanity in caste, fortune and races assembled under one roof. The ringside glittered with uniforms of red and gold, the rank of the British Army. Ladies in décolleté were sandwiched between the men. Here and there an opulent, turbaned maharaja sat, bejeweled and immaculate in evening dress. In the background were the olive drab uniforms of Tommies and their native brothers-in-arms. Packed against the walls were Parsees, Hindus, and Muslims in native dress, ranging from loin cloths to tattered rags." Eddie sent word ahead that he was ready to take on all comers in each city he traveled to. He won fights against the local army champions in Colombo and Bangalore. In Calcutta he beat Milton Kubes, heavyweight champion of India, over four rounds. After that, Eddie struggled to find anyone bold enough to take up his challenge, so he fought a series of exhibitions with Douglo, in Delhi, Kabul, and Jaipur. The Maharaja of Udaipur was so impressed with their display that he offered Eddie a job as a bodyguard.

In Australia, on the other hand, a suitable opponent was waiting in Sydney. News had made its way from England about Eddie's deeds against Jack Dempsey. The story had grown in the telling, and by the time he arrived, he was known as the man who had knocked Dempsey down "15 times in the first two rounds" during their fight in Brighton. Eddie, it has to be said, didn't do anything to disabuse anyone of the idea that he had battered the greatest boxer in the world. His opponent was J. D. Brancourt, who had won the amateur heavyweight championship of Australia in both 1922 and 1923. Brancourt was six foot eleven and weighed 250 pounds, which made him a foot taller and seventy pounds heavier than Eddie, who prepared for the fight by nailing a padded board to the wall of his gym seven feet off the floor. He threw "two or three hundred" left hooks at it each day, until he had a "little knot of muscle in the back of [his] left shoulder blade as hard as steel."

In the ring, wrote the correspondent of the *Sydney Sporting Sun*, "it looked like an encounter between an alarm clock and the Post Office tower." An attendant had to come out with a stepladder and tie up the strings hanging from the overhead clock because they were brushing against Brancourt's head. Brancourt stood, almost immobile, in the center of the ring. Eddie threw a feint with his left, and suckered Brancourt into slipping out a straight left of his own. That was as much of an opening as Eddie needed. He slipped in and socked him on the jaw with that hook of his. Brancourt collapsed to the canvas. He got back to his feet, utterly stunned, and Eddie sold him the same trick all over again. *Thump.* "Mr. Brancourt," as the *Sun* put it, "reclined gently on one ear with a look of ineffable peace." They had to shove him out for the second round. One more blow, and he was done, "down to sleep with an air of determination." Jack Munro, the man who had organized the fight, later remembered, "They say in boxing that a good big man will always beat a good little man, but boxing axioms are very like the rules of grammar—there are always exceptions." Brancourt's father collared Eddie after the fight and told him that he felt the victory was "unfair." No one had ever had the temerity to hit his boy in the face before. Eddie reckoned the big lump had been entirely overawed by the stories he had heard about all those knockdowns Eddie had scored against Jack Dempsey.

His next stop was Saigon, then Hong Kong. Eddie beat the local champions he fought in both cities. He took particular satisfaction from the win in Saigon, since his opponent was Amadou Diop, a gangster who had been extorting protection money from the local shopkeepers. And as Eddie said, "If a good fight also presented the prospects of teaching a bully a lesson, that was an added incentive." He beat Diop so badly that he announced his retirement from boxing in the next day's papers.

From there it was on to Manila, Shanghai, Peking, and Tokyo, then across the ocean to Buenos Aires and up through South and Central America. By the time Eddie and the boys docked in Los Angeles in the summer of 1927, they had been traveling for nearly two years. "I had done what most young men would like to do—explored the world, sailed the seas, and had adventures in all lands."

Eddie's mother didn't care about any of that. She hadn't seen him in five years, and she was just happy to see him back safe and sound, even if his cheeks were puffier, his ears thicker, his nose a little more bulbous and broken in the middle. He had changed, and so had the world he came back to. Denver itself seemed to him so small now. The boys he had once taught on the west side were now all working the railroads, like their fathers before them. His Yale classmates had started their careers. And his friend Gene Tunney was the heavyweight champion of the world, having taken the title from Dempsey. Eddie found that especially hard to swallow. He still thought of Tunney as the little kid he had known back in 1919. Now he was readying himself to defend his title in a fight that would earn him a million dollars.

The money was too much. Eddie found himself wrestling with that old dilemma again, wondering whether he should become a professional boxer. This time it was Tunney who talked him out of it. "It's not worth it, Eddie," he said. He told him how long and hard the road to the top would be. "If you were broke with no other talent I'd not only advise you to turn pro, I'd help you get matches. But you're ready to tackle law." Instead, Tunney made him an offer: he asked him to be his sparring partner for the upcoming fight and suggested that when it was all over, the two of them should take another trip around the world together.

The pair headed up to New York together, but Tunney found that he had no privacy there, no rest. So they moved again, up to the small town of Speculator, across the Adirondacks from Lake Placid. There the two of them settled into a routine. They would run in the morning, eight to ten miles, and spar in the afternoons. At lunch and after supper, Eddie would study his law books and revise for his bar exams. At least that's what Eddie says he was doing.

On September 22, Eddie had a ringside seat at Tunney's victory in the rematch with Dempsey, one of the most hyped fights in history. Behind him at Chicago's Soldier Field stretched row after row of spectators, 145,000 in all, so many, said Hearst papers journalist Westbrook Pegler, "that you couldn't see them on the last rows, you could only sense that they were there from the combers of sound that came booming down the slope of the stadium out of the darkness." The *New York Times* reported that the city's bookmakers had taken three million in bets. The wise ones had backed Tunney, who won it on points. But the fight was remembered for the long count he was given in the seventh, after Dempsey had knocked him down. The referee, Dave Barry, didn't start the count to ten until Dempsey had retreated to a neutral corner, as was specified in the rules of the fight. The referee's count was on eight when Tunney got to his feet, but he had been down for fourteen seconds in all. By standing over Tunney as he lay on the canvas, Dempsey had allowed his opponent a few extra seconds to recover. Eddie felt Jack had penalized himself. He swore that he saw Tunney smile to himself as he lay on the floor. Asked to split his two pals afterward, Eddie diplomatically suggested, "Jack is the greatest fighter and Gene the greatest boxer in ring history."

If Eddie stayed out of the ensuing controversy, it was because he had other things on his mind. On his way back from Chicago, he called in at Cleveland, where he met up with Peggy Colgate, whom he had been courting that summer. The two of them drove up to the Adirondacks together and were married in Saranac Lake on October 1. Peggy's family had a house there, Camp Beachwood. Her brothers Gilbert and Robert had been on the Yale boxing team with Eddie, and her father, Sydney, was the grandson of Samuel Colgate. He and his brothers still ran the family cosmetics company. The papers said that the couple had eloped, but that wasn't quite right. They had simply kept it quiet. News only broke a fortnight later, when they were holed up in a Fifth Avenue apartment in New York.

After that, life did begin to settle down. Eddie and Gene never did take that world tour they had planned. Instead, Eddie passed the bar exams and began his career as a lawyer. He still did a little sparring, when work allowed. His first daughter, Caroline, was born in March 1931. By then, Eddie was beginning to feel a little like he was gathering cobwebs. At the age of thirty-three he was starting to itch for another adventure and was considering the idea of making a return to the ring to try to win another title in the following summer's Olympics when the phone rang.

Eddie told Peggy he would be out for dinner that night, catching up with an old friend from around and about, Jay O'Brien.

"That night," Peggy remembered, "Eddie came rushing home and said, 'Guess what? I'm on the US bobsled team!' I thought that was pretty strange, because he had never been on a bobsled before."

Hank Homburger and his Red Devils, Lake Placid, 1931.

CHAPTER 9

THE NEW US TEAM

The snows came late to Lake Placid that winter. There was a single heavy fall at the beginning of the season, which was reckoned by many to be a good omen. It wasn't. November turned to December, Christmas and the New Year came and went, and all the while the few citizens of the small town grew ever more anxious. The land was colored in bleached-out browns and greens—wet mud, dank grass, and bony trees, their brittle branches shorn of leaves. Above, blue skies and bright sun. The few clouds that did come carried rain. No one could remember a winter quite like it. The New York State weather bureau said that it was the warmest they'd recorded in the 147 years they had been taking measurements.

The athletes began to arrive. They traveled from New York by train up the Hudson Valley. The river was open water all the way up to Albany. The Norwegian team was the first to get to Lake Placid, followed closely by the Japanese. The locals were happy to see them. The Depression had grown so severe that a lot of countries had been having second thoughts about coming. Great Britain was sending only four athletes, all figure skaters; Argentina wasn't sending anyone at all. Godfrey Dewey had dispatched a special envoy from his organizing committee on a six-month tour of Europe to whip up enthusiasm overseas. Even so, some of the national Olympic committees had even suggested postponing the Olympics until the economy had begun to recover. In the autumn of 1931, using the contacts he'd made through the club, Dewey persuaded the North Atlantic

Steamship Line to grant a 20 percent reduction on round-trip tickets and the New York Central Railroad to cut the cost of a return trip from Manhattan to Lake Placid to fifteen dollars. Even Congress got involved: a resolution was passed exempting foreign athletes and officials from the usual visa requirements, waiving an eight-dollar tax, and granting free entry to baggage and equipment. They were extraordinary measures. But then, there was an extraordinary amount at stake. The townspeople were in for around $1.5 million, all told. "The tiny village has gambled in an effort to establish itself as the winter sports capital of America," wrote Edward J. Neil of the Associated Press. "Every merchant, every citizen, has in one way or another contributed to the total."

That January of 1932, the town itself was ready. The streets, Dewey wrote, "were a riot of color," decorated with flags, colored lights, and sprigs of evergreen. "It was in gala attire. The flags of nations flew everywhere. Great hotels and clubs, cottages and private homes, and business hotels were brave with bunting. There was a tenseness in the air as of something impending." The one thing they didn't have was cold weather. The organizing committee actually started to bring in wagonloads of snow from across the Adirondacks so they could spread it around the ski trails.

Billy Fiske arrived in New York on January 6. He paid for his own ticket across from England on the SS *Europa*. For Dewey and the residents of Lake Placid, so busy getting ready, the four years since St. Moritz had flown by. But that's a long time in the life of a young man. Billy had been a boy when he won the gold in St. Moritz. He was only twenty now, but he had changed. He had graduated from Cambridge University the previous summer, with a degree in history and economics from Trinity College. And he was full of himself, thought he knew best, as only a young man can. His time abroad had given him a different perspective on America. He admired the "bulldog" spirit of the British, and thought the French were "children" because "when they get on top they like to gloat over it." It was, Billy had decided, "part of their character, just as self-sufficiency is part of an English character." He hated New York, thought it was "without doubt the most expensive place in the world" and "full of the damnedest snobs, not for anything but money . . . the sort of people one ought to see I can't stand." The curious thing is that everyone who knew Billy, however slightly, agreed that he "never had a bad word to say about anybody." It's a phrase that occurs over and again in descriptions of him. And it's wrong. He had plenty of bad words for plenty of people—he was just too polite to share them. He confined his thoughts to his diary. He was, in some ways, a diffident man. "Bashfulness," he wrote, "gives rise to self-sufficiency in an intelligent person and boredom in a stupid one."

When it came to politics, Billy was convinced that America needed to have more influence in Europe, and that Europeans "treated her like a weak child with lots of toys to be taken away from her." He had a peculiar notion that the United States should "develop Spain as a buffer state in Europe," something he felt "could be done in 12 years or so by clever capitalisation." He would often talk stocks and shares with his father, who hoped that his son would come to work with him at Dillon, Read & Co. But Billy had other ideas. Three years of study left him hungry for adventure.

Not that it had all been early mornings, exams, and lectures. He'd spent a lot of time whizzing about the country lanes in that Bentley of his. Students were meant to be in bed by midnight. Anyone out later than that, as Billy often was, had to sneak around the college constables, the "bulldogs," as the students still call them. The trouble was, one luxury that Billy's Bentley didn't exactly allow him was inconspicuousness. There was one bulldog in particular who used to wait in the little village of Melbourn, at a tiny bottleneck on the road to London, to ambush anyone returning to the city after hours. And he knew there was only one man in town driving a supercharged Bentley. After he had been caught once too often, Billy hatched a plan. He popped along to the pub, where, he had been told, the bulldog could usually be found on his free afternoons. He bought him a couple of "dog's noses"—a cocktail of gin and beer so potent it made Billy's nose wrinkle—and after some polite small talk mentioned, in passing, the subject both men knew to be the only one that had prompted this casual meeting in the bar. They soon came to a happy arrangement. Whenever Billy was out late in his car from then on, the next day he would stop by that same bar for a round of "dog's noses," bringing with him a couple of gramophone records as a gift for his new friend. After that, he wasn't busted again.

Allowed to come and go as he pleased, Billy spent what free days he had at Royal Worlington golf course in Mildenhall. He was a good golfer, with a handicap down around four, but golfing didn't come as naturally to him as racing did. The tempo was wrong. The thing with Billy, his friend Henry Longhurst reckoned, was that "having driven us there in his monster at an average speed of something like 65 mph for 20 minutes, he could never understand why he found it so difficult to hole out from five feet." He had too much adrenaline in his veins. He toyed with the idea of entering the British Amateur Championship but never felt his game was quite good enough. At other times, he was out on the horse-racing circuit. He loved to gamble and reckoned himself "an excellent judge of horse rump." In the evenings, as often as not, he was in London. "Bill was a superb dancer," said his sister, Peggy. During his holidays he would travel over to France to stay with his family, and the two siblings "would spend hours whirling around the dance floors of Paris nightclubs, doing the Charleston and all the other dances to the sounds of big bands and small combos."

Peggy was now married, to Jennison Heaton, but Billy was still single. And while he still didn't much care for drink or tobacco—"everything in moderation," Billy wrote in his diary; "balance is the essence of good living"—he was, as his friend Harry Hays Morgan put it, "quite the ladies' man." Which was, in itself, quite the understatement. The only rule he had was that he didn't care to date anyone who was too much taller than him. He became an expert, he said, "at measuring a girl's height before asking her to dance."

By the time Billy got to New York, his two old friends Jay and Clifford were already up in Lake Placid, along with their new recruit, Eddie Eagan. When it came to people, Billy was a great believer in gut feelings. "I find one's first opinions of a person based entirely on appearances are usually correct," he wrote, "and a clever person should have the vision to keep these in mind and not let them be warped by a stronger relationship." He took to Eddie from the first moment they met. The two of them couldn't have had more different childhoods, but there was a keen kinship between them—both were educated in England, both were Olympic champions.

Eddie was a bull of a man, as brave as any. He had fought Jack Dempsey and stalked big game. But that first run down Mount Van Hoevenberg with Billy scared him more than anything he had ever known. "That run," Eddie said later, "will always be vivid in my memory. It took only about two minutes to make, but to me it seemed like an eon. I remember the snow-covered ground flashing by like a motion-picture out of focus, speeding a few inches away while I hung on to the straps without any sense of security. My hands seemed to be slipping. But still I clung. We hit a turn. My head snapped first to the right, then to the left. FINALLY we neared the bottom."

He had so much nervous energy in him that he couldn't stand still after the run was over. He and the other three were supposed to sit in the sled while it was tied to the back of a tractor and hauled up the mountain to the start of the run. The driver was a local farmer by the name of B. J. Cook. "I was pulling back their sled to the starting line," Cook remembered, "and I noticed one of their fellows standing up in the sled, shadow-boxing. I stopped the tractor, went back, and told him to sit down. He said he wasn't going to. So I told him a second time, and I said I was going to knock him down if I had to. A little smile came over his face, and he sat down. The rest of the fellows on the sled looked pretty amused." A little later, Cook learned he'd just threatened a former Olympic boxing champion. He was pretty embarrassed about it, so he made a point of apologizing. Eddie just smiled and called him "one tough little hombre." It cracked Billy up. He didn't quit kidding Eddie about it for a fortnight.

Godfrey Dewey, on the other hand, was a man Billy never warmed to. He had met him before, of course, back in St. Moritz, though their paths had barely crossed because they kept very different hours. But in 1932 Billy and the other bobbers were staying at the Lake Placid Club, Godfrey's fiefdom. And while they were there, they had to abide by his rules: no drinking, smoking, or gambling, and no noise after 10:30 p.m. That was a rough-enough start. Things got worse when Billy quickly picked Dewey as "a snob." Plus—a silly thing, this: Dewey had a strange high-pitched laugh that set Billy on edge. And besides, more than any of that, something in his gut told him that Godfrey Dewey couldn't be trusted. And he was right. The truth was, Dewey didn't want Billy Fiske at his Olympics, and he didn't want Jay O'Brien or Clifford Gray there either. In his mind, Jay, Billy, and the others were arrogant out-of-towners who had come to steal the locals' glory. For the past two years, he had been plotting how to stop them.

It had all started back in 1930, when he first fell out with Jay O'Brien.

Dewey had staked so much on the Mount Van Hoevenberg bob run because he wanted to "establish a broad base of support" for the sport. He wanted the run to become the central attraction of the Lake Placid tourism business. He had fought Roosevelt to secure the money for it, the environmental lobby for the right to build it, and the Jewish lobby for the right to run it. It had cost, in the end, more than four times the amount he had quoted to the community, making it the single greatest expense of the Games—and all that, every single dollar spent, was on his head. He had poured still more resources into publicizing the run. He'd hired a firm for the purpose and given them a budget of fifty thousand dollars. They sent fifteen hundred posters, two hundred thousand booklets, and a quarter of a million stamps out around Europe, all of them advertising the new bob run. They gave out ninety thousand stickers to passengers on the New York Central Railroad. They sent salesmen out to department stores in New York, Cleveland, Boston, Philadelphia, and Montreal to install themed window displays. And around the Adirondacks they put up blue-and-white billboards reading, "This way for the thrills of a lifetime!" Even after all that, Dewey had one more ace up his sleeve. He had it planned that a local team was going to win the four-man bobsledding contest, the blue riband event of the Olympics. He wanted four hometown heroes, as payback for the community's investment and a promotional tool for his new winter sports resort.

The problem was, of course, that in the late 1920s there wasn't anyone in Lake Placid who had any real experience as a bobsledder. A few men had taken runs over the slopes in open fields, in the old American style. But no one, apart from Dewey himself, had ever ridden anything like the track at St. Moritz. Dewey had a solution. In 1929, when the architect Stanislaus Zentzytzki was over making his first survey of the land around Lake Placid, Dewey had him draw up designs for a simple, half-mile-long bobsled run at a site called Intervales, just outside the town.

Intervales was little more than a practice track, with seven curves built from sand and wood, but Dewey christened it the "first bobsled run in America." It served three purposes. The first was to whip up a little publicity and enthusiasm for the new sport—and right from the time the first sled set off down it, crowds came out to watch and ride. Second, it enabled Dewey to test-drive the new sleds he was designing. The third and most important purpose was that it would be the training ground for the local teams who wanted to compete in 1932.

Dewey soon found a few likely contenders. There were the Stevens brothers, all four of them, Paul, Hubert, Raymond, and Curtis. They were from an old Lake Placid family: their grandparents had been among the very first settlers in the town, back in the 1850s. They lived in their family's hotel, on a hill up on the other side of Mirror Lake from the club. They were all sportsmen, a little wild for Dewey's taste; and their mother was so scared about the risks they were taking in the sleds that she refused to let them all ride in the same one, just in case she lost all four in a single crash. So they couldn't make up a team together. Dewey had higher hopes for Henry "Hank" Homburger, from the neighboring town of Saranac Lake. He and Dewey were good friends. Dewey had even pulled a few strings on Hank's behalf to help secure an academic scholarship for a young friend of the Homburger family. Hank wasn't exactly blue-collar, but he was closer to it than any of the other bobsledders on the circuit. He had been practicing with a couple of other locals, Percy Bryant and Ed Horton, the town florist. They often took the eldest Stevens brother, Paul, along with them to make up a foursome. They called themselves the "Saranac Lake Red Devils."

Homburger was a good pilot. In February 1930, the Intervales run hosted its very first international bobsled race in North America when a team representing the United States took on another from Canada. On that occasion, Homburger was riding in the No. 4 spot, but he soon worked his way up to become a driver. When the Mount Van Hoevenberg course was up and running late in December 1930, he proved himself to be the best in the area. But then, he enjoyed one major advantage over everyone else: he had built the run. Homburger was an engineer by trade, and Dewey had hired him to supervise construction. At first he worked underneath Zentzytzki, but when the architect returned to Germany, Homburger took charge. While work was under way he was up on the mountain every day, and in the evenings he studied Zentzytzki's blueprints. By the time the job was done, he knew that course better than anyone else in the world, even the man who had designed it. He was familiar with every inch of every curve. If anyone knew the "perfect line" down the run, it was Hank Homburger.

Jay O'Brien wasn't impressed with the idea that an engineer who'd had twelve months' practice on a tin-pot slide could provide any real competition for the well-drilled team from St. Moritz. In November 1930, as the work at Mount Van Hoevenberg was being finished, Jay called in at the offices of the Amateur Athletic Union in New York. The AAU was, along with the United States Olympic Committee, in charge of Olympic selection. AAU secretary Dan Ferris told Jay about Dewey's plans. And as Ferris then told Dewey, Jay's response was to say that "he doubts we will be able to develop a team here fast enough to make any showing against foreign competition. He believes it will be necessary to bring over from St. Moritz two steerers and two brakes who have experience in racing." Dewey bit his lip and replied, tartly, "We know of at least two or three Americans who are planning to train bob teams here this winter in anticipation of the Olympics." He added, in another note, "we are much less dependant [sic] on the St. Moritz group than Jay O'Brien seems to think."

A month later, Dewey had hardened his attitude. He wrote to Ferris again, to complain once more about O'Brien's position as the American representative at the International Bobsledding and Tobogganing Federation. He reminded Ferris of Jay's "gross discourtesy," his "deliberate disregard" and "defiance of explicit instructions" given him by Dewey for the International Federation congress in February 1930. He told Ferris to "make it unmistakably clear" to Jay that "if his St. Moritz teams expect to represent the United States in the III Olympic Winter Games, they will have to qualify by showing superiority here on the

Olympic run." In other words, just because Billy Fiske won the gold in 1928, it didn't mean he would make the team in 1932. Conditions in St. Moritz, Dewey thought, were so "altogether different from the modern type of run" at Mount Van Hoevenberg that past performances there didn't reckon in selection.

He had a point. Mount Van Hoevenberg was different. Zentzytzki had designed a new type of run. The curves had a steeper gradient than the rest of the track, so the sleds were still plummeting downward even as they came round the turns. In Europe until that point, bob runs had been built with flat corners. The change meant that Mount Van Hoevenberg had undoubtedly the quickest bob run that had ever been built.

On February 7, 1931, it was finally ready for its grand opening. The occasion would be the very first North American national bobsled championship. Dewey organized a special train up from New York to carry a posse of forty politicians who had helped him drive the bill appropriating state funds through the legislature. Dewey planned to ride in the two-man competition himself. He still imagined he could make a good pilot. He actually crashed in a practice run, tipping over coming round a corner. He fractured his ankle and spent the rest of the championship hobbling around in a plaster cast. To his credit, he still managed to compete the following week. No doubt he was brave enough; it was just his driving that wasn't up to much. Homburger, though, was an ace. The Red Devils, dressed in blue and scarlet, led through every single one of the four heats. They finished their final run in 1:52. It wasn't just a track record, carving four seconds off a mark they had set earlier that same day; it was a new world speed record. No one, at St. Moritz or anywhere else, had ever traveled as fast in a bobsled as Homburger did down Mount Van Hoevenberg that day. They clocked a top speed of just under 70 mph. The nearest competition was eight and a half seconds back—a long gap in any sport, and an age in bobsledding. Godfrey Dewey had found his hero. Hank Homburger, he decided, would be the face of the Games, the man whose image they put in the booklets and up on the billboards.

That December, two months out from the start of the Olympics, Billy Fiske booked his ticket to travel over on the SS *Europa*. He was coming with his old friend Jack Heaton. Jay had even arranged for their bobsleds to be sent up from St. Moritz so that Billy and Jack could bring them over in the hold. Many of the competitors decided, as Billy and the current world champion Werner Zahn both did, to bring their own sleds with them, despite the fact that Dewey had promised they could use the new sleds specially designed for the Mount Van Hoevenberg course. A couple of years earlier, he had arranged to have Zahn send over several sleds from Germany, which Dewey tested on the run at Intervales. He found that they kept breaking because they couldn't handle the steep drops on the corners. So he drew up plans for a "fundamentally different" bob, one that, he said, "clings to the run more closely, steers with a minimum of skidding, and rides and controls much more smoothly than any bob I have ever driven." Zahn was distinctly unimpressed. The sleds, he said, didn't matter so much; it was the drivers who won the races.

When Dewey learned that Billy and Jack Heaton were on their way, he sent another round of letters to the AAU's Olympic bobsled committee. Jay O'Brien, of course, was chairman of that committee. He was the one member Dewey didn't write to. The others—Gustavus Kirby, Dan Ferris, and Major Philip Fleming—all heard from him. "I have no doubt that O'Brien has virtually promist them both places on the American team, regardless of their showing in the try-outs," Dewey wrote. "If so, this will have to be handled somewhat tactfully. Don't lose sight of the fact that while three teams may be chosen, only two teams may actually compete."

Jay came to Lake Placid in early January 1932. The Olympic publicity department welcomed him with a press release announcing the arrival of the "internationally known polo player and sportsman." Godfrey Dewey sent out yet another round of letters. This time he targeted Gus Kirby, who had been the United States Olympic Committee's delegate at St. Moritz in 1928; he was on the bobsled committee for 1932 too. "It appears," Dewey wrote, "that Jay O'Brien is to be himself a member of one of the bob teams competing for the American Olympic team . . . Naturally, and I think properly, this situation is vigorously questioned by the other contenders. It seems to me a decided danger and impropriety, even if the chairman in question were more suitable." Again, he had a point. Jay would be both picking the team and competing on it. But then, he had been in the same position in St. Moritz in 1928, when he had managed the squad that won both the gold and the silver. And Dewey had often done the same thing during the National Championship competitions at Mount Van Hoevenberg. Still, he suggested that Kirby should arrange to have Jay replaced as chairman of the selection committee to "guarantee for greater fairness." Jay's conflict of interests was, Dewey said, "an urgent and serious situation for both the quality and still more the morale of one of the most important American Olympic teams."

Kirby's reply can be condensed into two words: nothing doing. But Dewey had already won one battle: selection for the US Olympic squad would be based on results in a series of pre-Olympics trial races on the Mount Van Hoevenberg run. After all the fuss, Olympic qualification would be a simple business. Anyone who wanted to make the team would need to finish in the top two in the tryouts, which were due to be held on January 15 and 16. That meant the odds were already stacked in favor of the local riders, especially Homburger. They may have had only a year or two of experience, but almost all of it was on that one track. Billy, Jay, and the outsiders, on the other hand, had never even seen the run before, let alone ridden it. And Billy himself hadn't been able to practice much in recent months: he had broken his ankle in the autumn and only just come off crutches. The injury meant he had couldn't compete in the 1931 World Championship in St. Moritz, which had been won, in his absence, by Werner Zahn. In fact, Billy hadn't ridden a sled in almost a year. He was so rusty that when he set off on his very first run down Mount Van Hoevenberg, riding a two-man sled with Jay working the brake, he didn't even make it round the first corner. The sled slipped into a skid as it climbed the bank and toppled over onto its side, spilling Billy and Jay out onto the ice. "So this," Homburger thought, "is the great Billy Fiske."

For the next fortnight, Billy and Jay found themselves bound up in bureaucratic red tape. It was impossible then, and now, to prove that this was Dewey's doing. But it certainly suited his purposes. On January 11 the referee for the Olympic trials, George W. Martin, who happened to be the sporting director of the Lake Placid Club, announced that he had decided to limit practice on the run to "properly entered teams and contestants who have been entered in writing." Jay didn't have his paperwork in order, so his team couldn't get back on the run until he did. It cost them precious practice time. But he and Billy got lucky. When the weekend of the trials came around, the weather was too warm for the track to be used. So the trials were postponed. It was decided that the National Championship, due to be held on January 28 and 29, would double up as the Olympic tryouts. Billy and his team would have two badly needed weeks in which to practice—if, that was, the race officials would let them on the track. Jay and his committee would need to pick a squad of fifteen men before the National Championship, as the date for final entries was January 21; the trials would be used to decide which eight of those fifteen actually got to race in the Games and which men would be left in the reserves.

It was then that Dewey declared his hand—though he had kept it at best only half hidden—in a five-page letter to Gustavus Kirby. He had, he said, "conferred with all the best bob drivers" and found "a surprising and encouraging unanimity in their judgments." Billy, Jay, Clifford, and Eddie, he said, should not be selected for the team. "In the absolutely unanimous judgment of every driver who has watcht their preliminary work on the run, they have not the slightest chances of qualifying for the final team." In fact, Dewey continued, one of the local drivers—he wouldn't say who—had easily raised five thousand dollars to bet that Billy and his team wouldn't finish in the top three at the trials. It is a large-enough sum today; back then it was six months' earnings for the average American household. "I fully recognize the impracticability of eliminating without trial the men who are identified in the public mind with the brilliant St. Moritz victory," Dewey continued, but he didn't recognize it enough to stop him from suggesting that they do exactly that. "Billy Fiske drove the winning sled at St. Moritz, and deserves utmost credit for a brilliant win against keen competition, altho not so keen as will be shown here. The conditions, however, were entirely different." And so they were. At St. Moritz, the teams had been five-strong rather than four. At St. Moritz, they had raced ventre à terre; here they would be sitting up. At St. Moritz, they had used old European-style sleds rather than the new ones Dewey had designed. And then there were the runs themselves, which were, as Dewey noted, incomparable in both their speed and their difficulty. "With the best of good will, not one of the experienst drivers here concedes them an outside chance in any event this year."

Dewey said that he, personally, would select Hank Homburger, since his "world record calls for no comment," and Hubert Stevens to lead two teams of local drivers. Stevens, he pointed out, had "built to order this year a personal bob including all the distinctive features of our Olympic design with a few slight further refinements which quite possibly make it the fastest bob in the world today."

To press his point, Dewey argued that it wasn't only the bobsledding medals that were at stake, but the United States' overall position in the final medal table. "I feel keenly that the American chance of winning the III OWG . . . stands or falls with securing the bob sports points to offset the inevitable leadership of the Scandinavians in skiing."

The bobsled committee decided to meet on the morning of January 21—the latest date possible—to make its final selections. They planned to wire the teams over to Lake Placid as soon as they had finished talking. Godfrey Dewey made one final attack. He objected again to Jay's "dual position" as both a contender for a team and the chairman of the selection committee, as well as to Jay's position as a delegate of the International Bobsledding and Tobogganing Federation, even going so far as to dig into the small print of "rule 2, section 3," which stated, "Contestants are ineligible for any official function." He trashed Billy on the grounds that he insisted on racing with his own crew of Jay, Clifford, and Eddie, whereas other drivers were happier for the selectors to pick and mix teams from across the squad. "If Fiske would show the same sportsmanship which has been displayed by all the rest of the drivers," Dewey complained, "the way would be open to pick the strongest possible American representation."

By now, Kirby, Ferris, and the rest were thoroughly sick of Dewey's meddling. At noon on January 21 they sent a telegram to Lake Placid listing the fifteen men they had selected for the Olympic squad. Homburger was on it, along with all three of his Red Devils and the other three Stevens brothers. So were Billy, Jay, Clifford, and Eddie. Dewey had lost his battle. But he still had plans for the war.

The National Championship was postponed again because the weather was still too warm to race. This time, however, the Olympics were so close that they could put the competition back only two days. On Friday the 29th, two days before the big race, Jay O'Brien was called into the office of a man named Ralph J. Ury, chairman of the Adirondack branch of the Amateur Athletics Union. Ury was in charge of registrations for the National Championship. "Sorry to say it," Ury told O'Brien, "but I'm going to have to ban you and your team from the championship."

It was a paperwork problem. Ury pointed out that Jay, Billy, Clifford, and Eddie did not have the necessary AAU traveling permits. The document was designed to authorize athletes and officials to claim AAU expenses. If they didn't get the right papers to Ury before the races started on Sunday, they wouldn't be allowed to compete. Publicly, Dewey was indignant on behalf of the banned athletes. "We deeply regret that this unwarranted action should have been given out," he told the *New York Times*. Ury, however, was an old friend of his. The two of them had worked together for years organizing sports in and around Lake Placid. The *Boston Herald* didn't buy Dewey's line. "Behind the entire move," the paper reported, "was seen open evidence of the discomfiture of local bob sleighers over the manner of choosing the United States bob team." The journalist Westbrook Pegler agreed. This, Pegler said in his column, was a "cruel class war" between the blue collars and the blue bloods. The Associated Press's Edward Neil described how "the natives sniffed and hawed as the bobsledders put on a running fight all over town." AAU secretary Dan Ferris declared it all "a tempest in a teacup" and arranged to have the correct papers sent up that same night.

Edward Neil was a canny man. He ended his AP report by pointing out that Dewey, Jay, and everyone else at Lake Placid would soon have much bigger worries. "Unless brisk weather appears almost immediately there seems little hope that the event can be sandwiched in before the start of the Olympics next Thursday." And he was right, if for the wrong reasons. It wasn't the weather that stopped them but the German and Swiss teams, who felt the Americans were trying to cheat them by staging their National Championship so close to the Olympics. They argued, at first, that they should be allowed to enter as well. Dewey duly offended them again by demanding that they pay a registration fee for the event. Irked, the Germans dug an obscure rule out of the IOC's small print. It stipulated that no races were allowed to be held on the bob run in the eight days before the Olympics were due to start. So the National Championship was postponed yet again, until after the Olympics. There would be no trials. Instead, the decision about which two teams would compete in the Olympics would be made by Jay O'Brien and his fellow committee members. They picked Billy, Jay, Clifford, and Eddie to ride the United States' No. 1 sled. The second team would be Hank Homburger's Red Devils, whose record on the run was too good to ignore.

In his final report to the USOC, Jay wrote that the selection committee "had a very hard task," but "thanks to the experience of the members of my committee in the athletic world, they exercised rare good judgment in the policy and action that they took in the final selections. I feel that I would be very ungrateful if I did not mention the unswerving support that Major Philip B. Fleming, Gustavus T. Kirby, and Daniel J. Ferris, gave your chairman in all matters pertaining to these selections. When I state the term 'unswerving support' it is not a phrase lightly used, as there was tremendous opposition to the committee from several sources in their selections, and the committee was caused ceaseless annoyances by the advice and suggestions from outside parties who did not know the requirements of this sport as well as did your committee." Being Jay, he was too polite to mention any names. He could afford at least a little magnanimity since he had gotten his way. Godfrey Dewey, after all his Machiavellian machinations, had not.

The very same week that the final selection decision was made, the fourteen trustees of the Lake Placid Club Foundation met to discuss the issue of who should succeed Melvil Dewey, who had passed away in December, as president. They resolved to postpone the full election till July, when the Olympics would be long over. In the meantime they would appoint a temporary president. Since Godfrey was a candidate, he left the room while the remaining trustees discussed the issue. The candidacy of Emily Dewey, Godfrey's stepmother, was swiftly dismissed. Godfrey's candidacy was voted down twelve to one. Instead, another man, from outside the family, was elected. It was an extraordinary show of ingratitude, considering all that Dewey had done for the club and the town. It was proof, too, of just how unpopular his high-handed manner had made him with his peers.

So he had been defeated, again. But he still had some hope. The final decision on the succession would be made at the club's annual conference in July. The weight of opinion among the trustees was stacked against him, but if the Olympics were a success, well, perhaps that could turn it around. All he needed was a cold snap. And on January 30, Dewey finally got what he wanted. The weather broke. When he woke that morning, it was blowing a blizzard. There was a storm coming.

Left picture: The Swiss team take Shady Corner, Lake Placid, 1932.

Right picture: The wreckage of the sled, Lake Placid, 1932.

CHAPTER 10

THE SUICIDE CLUB

The sled hurtled down the mountain, 60 mph and still accelerating. There was a rattle from the metal frame, and a sharp rasping hiss from the runners as they cut through the ice. The wind whipped the sounds away from the ears of the four riders. Up front the driver was hunched over the wheel. He squinted through the early morning mist. He was thinking three corners ahead of the sled, trying always to urge it onto the right racing line. He had so little time. At that speed, as soon as he saw a corner, he was into it. And as soon as he felt a problem, it was too late. The sled moved almost as fast as his thoughts. Behind him, three riders were huddled together, with the first of them pressed right up against his back. They clung to the leather straps attached to the metal. Centrifugal force bowed them down, bent their necks, and pressed their heads toward their feet. But their stomachs shot back and up. Made them feel like they'd left their guts somewhere back up the track. They tried to lean together, as they had practiced, as the sled shot into and around the big white banks at the corners. Each one jolted the sled. *Whump . . . whump . . . whump.* One after another. The corners kept coming. They bounced the sled around, tipped it almost upside down, over and around, which is why the riders had to lean, until the course snapped them back up straight. They were like four coins in a tin can rolling down a flight of steps.

They counted every one of those corners. One, two, three. Eyrie, a dogleg kink from left to right that snapped their heads from side to side. On around five, six, seven, eight, nine. Then Whiteface, a sweeping hairpin, the biggest curve on the track, around a 30-foot-tall wall of snow. They passed the first grandstand. Out of that, then eleven, twelve, thirteen. Next, Cliffside, where the course ran right up against the rocky wall of the mountain. Fifteen, sixteen, a dogleg right at seventeen, and then four hundred feet of straight. The pine trees flashed by in fast-forward. Sixty miles per hour. Sixty-five. Seventy. As fast as a man could travel without a motor. And then Shady, a 28-foot-tall bank, almost straight up, with only a hint of a concave curve, which spun the bob around 160 degrees in the space of 150 feet. And that was where it happened. The sled slid up the wall, pulled higher all the time, up and up, passing perilously close to the lip. The riders leaned in, the driver stuck to his line, fixed the wheel in his hands to hold the front runners straight. A mistake. Too late. The sled crested the top lip of the wall and shot over the top. It was airborne for almost a full second before it hit the branches of a tree and crashed into the rocks and scrub in the ravine below.

The journalist Edward J. Neil was at the foot of the run, by the finish line, working on a story for the Associated Press. It was two days before the 1932 Winter Olympics were due to start in Lake Placid, and the bobsledders were the best story in town. He had just taken a run down the mountain himself for a feature piece. His editor thought it would be a good idea to give the readers a firsthand report of this strange new sport that had been in the headlines all week. He had been a passenger in a sled driven by Hank Homburger, the local boy, and one of the fastest sled pilots in the world. They had traveled with the brake on the whole way, moving so slowly that the brakeman told him afterward, "I wish I'd bought my gun, I saw a rabbit we could have shot on the way." They had covered the mile-and-a-half course in a shade under two minutes. It was plenty fast enough for Neil. It gave him, he said, "enough thrills to last a lifetime." He'd only just finished drinking the coffee they gave him to steady his nerves. He remembered how he saw it shimmer in the cup, spill out onto his shoes. That was when he realized how much his hands were shaking.

Neil and his crew were walking back up the track alongside the slide when the public address system burst into life. Through the static they heard the split times of the sled coming down the run. They leaped over to the lip and "peered through the snow up the twisted ice ribbon" toward Shady Corner. They saw the sled run out of control up the incline and smash through the top, scattering snow and rubble, "four bodies hurled through the air into the deep ravine below." Neil and Homburger raced on up toward the crash, pumping their legs as they ran through the powder snow. The wreckage of the sled was quite a way down the slope, wrapped around a tall pine. The snow around the trunk was dyed red. There were three "battered, blood-soaked forms" on the ground. It was the No. 2 German team: Fritz Grau, Helmut Hopmann, Rudolf Krotki, and Albert Brehme. Neil's mind shot back twenty minutes in time. He remembered how jovial Grau had been at the top of the run, how he had shaken Neil's hand and slapped his back before he set off on Homburger's sled.

The ambulance pulled to a stop a hundred yards away, up on the road at the far side of the track. Neil and the others carried the men back up. Three of them were unconscious, deadweights. The fourth, Krotki, was the lucky one. He was awake and could walk, so long as he had someone to lean on. He shouldn't even have been on the sled. He was the team's masseur and medical officer. He had only been riding as a favor, filling in for an absent member. Like all the crews, the Germans had been wearing protective gear—leather helmets, elbow pads, knee pads. But that didn't offer them protection against a crash like this. The driver, Grau, had fractured his shoulder and his hip and had internal bleeding, skin lacerations, and a severe concussion. His brakeman, Brehme, had a fractured skull, a broken arm, and contusion of the spine. The third, Hopmann, was a mess. His calf muscles had been ripped away from his right leg. Brehme and Grau would be in a critical condition for almost a week.

Of course, back at the track, Neil didn't know any of this yet. He was horrified by the "picture of sudden death and destruction," aghast at the idea that the same fate "might well have come to me from less capable hands." As the medics shut the doors of the ambulance, Homburger turned to Neil, sighed, and said, "That's the way it goes."

A mile away, up at the top of the mountain, a telephone rang. The shrill trill of the bell cut right through the cold air, across all the laughter and chatter, and carried right around the little plateau at the top of the bob run. An official answered it, spoke for a moment, and then raised a red flag into the air. The polyglot conversations of the assembled athletes—Swiss, Italian, French, Belgian, Romanian, German, Austrian, American—fell quiet one by one. "There has been a crash."

"It's Grau."

"They've gone through the bank at Shady."

It was the sixth crash of the week. The ice was too sheer. The run too fast. The risks too great. And they all knew it. But no one dared mention it. Not, at least, in earshot of one another. That was their code. You didn't discuss the dangers. The knowledge of it was already there, always there, in the backs of their minds. And that was where it stayed.

Twenty minutes later, another call came through. The ambulance had gone and the debris had been swept clear. The official lowered his red flag. "Track clear!" he said. "To the mark!"

The next crew swapped handshakes with the riders around them. A solemn ritual, and one performed before every run. "They act," Neil wrote, "as if they never expect to see each other again." They picked up their sled, five hundred pounds of steel and oak, and heaved it over toward the ice chute at the start of the run. The driver took his place at the wheel; the No. 3 man took his seat behind; and the other two, No. 2 and No. 4, crouched down on either side of the sled, ready to make their running start. They rocked back and forth, from their heels to their toes, then set off at a sprint. The two runners leaped on as the sled shot into the mouth of the run and raced away down the mountain, a bullet along the barrel.

Damon Runyon called it "the Suicide Club." There were fifty-two men in it—more if you counted all the reserves. The little town of Lake Placid had never seen their like. Billy, Jay, and the American blue bloods had nothing on this lot. From Italy, there was Count Rossi, the millionaire heir to the Martini and Rossi fortune, "whose vermouth," as Neil wrote, "is famous wherever they have cocktail hours." Rossi was Italy's national powerboat racing champion. From Romania, Alexandru Papană, a stunt pilot famous for the dazzling aerobatics he performed in air shows. From Belgium, Louis van Hege, a star striker for AC Milan and a gold medalist with the Belgian football team from the 1920 Olympics in Antwerp. Werner Zahn from Germany had been a fighter ace in the First World War, a onetime wingman of the Red Baron. The son of the hotel owner where Zahn and his team stayed always remembered their arrival: "These enormous men in long overcoats, they came in one at a time, bowed to my mother, clicked their heels the way Germans did then." The family of Barbara Tyrell Kelly took in the Swiss team. Their driver was Reto Capadrutt, a handsome "little hop-of-my-thumb," as Runyon called him, "with laughing eyes and coal-black hair." He had barely settled in before he struck up a relationship with Kelly's godmother, Betty Hood, a wealthy widow whose family ran Tammany Hall through the 1920s and into the 1930s. Capadrutt told the press that he couldn't speak English because he didn't want to have to give interviews, but he was fluent enough in it to woo Betty. Kelly still has copies of the love letters he sent her. They were such an exotic lot. "It felt," Kelly said, "as though the world had come to us."

The Suicide Club had met for the first time on the last day of January, four days before the opening ceremony of the Olympics. Mirror Lake had finally frozen over. Up in the shade on the northern slope of Mount Van Hoevenberg, the surface of the bob run had become a mile and a half of solid ice, without a lick of snow to slow the sleds. Even the officials felt intimidated. They argued that they needed at least four days of freezing weather before the run would be ready for use, to allow time for the ice to even out and a layer of snow to form on top. But the bobsledders themselves were sick of waiting, bored stiff after a week in which they had barely managed a full day's practice. There had already been dark mutterings among them about American gamesmanship. The foreign teams felt they were being denied the chance to get familiar with the run. The officials simply couldn't afford to wait for four days and agreed to open the track. They were swayed by the size of the crowd. Six thousand people came out to watch the first full day of practice.

And even then the officials thought twice about letting anyone take a run. It was Werner Zahn who snapped them into action. Zahn had come to Lake Placid to add an Olympic gold medal to the world championship title he'd won in St. Moritz the previous year. He was a proud and stubborn man. It was Zahn who had told Dewey that it was "the driver who won the race, not the sled"—a clear dig at the inexperience of the local riders. Which was a little disingenuous of him, given the machine he had brought with him to Lake Placid. It was named the Fram III, in honor of the ship Roald Amundsen had used to explore the South Pole. The ship, the original Fram, had been designed to float on top of the polar ice, just as Zahn's bobsled had been designed to float over the run. Zahn had built it himself, with the help of the engineers at the manufacturing firm he ran in Brunswick. No one had ever seen anything quite like it before. The Fram III had a streamlined hull, with a nose like a bullet that enveloped the driver's legs. It made a joke of Dewey's assertion that the sled owned by Hubert Stevens was "the fastest bob in the world today." The Fram III, which preempted the aerodynamic designs of the late 1940s and 1950s, traveled like lightning. Zahn was itching to get it out on the track. And now the bureaucrats were trying to tell him the conditions were too dangerous to allow him out?

Zahn knew all about the risks. He had pulled out of the 1928 Olympics when his brakeman, Werner Schroder, died in a crash during the trials. The idea that Homburger, a civil engineer who had been bobsledding for a year, could handle the conditions, but he, the world champion, couldn't . . . well, he considered that an insult. "We are being treated like little children," he said. "What are we supposed to do if the slide is this fast on the days of the Olympics? Automatically default to the unadmitted superiority of the Americans? They are our necks, to break as we want to."

Billy Fiske had no desire to get involved in a petty squabble, but he knew, too, how dangerous and difficult the course was. He'd already crashed on it once. He suggested a compromise.

"Werner," Billy said, "you know this run is quite different from the ones we ride in Europe. Why don't your team let me drive you down the run, to give you a chance to get accustomed to it?"

"Thank you," Zahn responded, "but there is nothing we can learn from the American team."

It sounds brusque. And it was. Zahn was an arrogant man, and he didn't appreciate being patronized, however well Billy meant it.

"Well then, at least let me tell you this," Billy continued. "You'll be going about seventy miles an hour into Shady corner, and your drivers will lose consciousness for a second or two in the turn. They'll come out of it when the pressure releases in the outlet, but be sure going into Shady that you take it early and come off it early, so you can straighten out for Zig-Zag."

Zahn smiled. "Germany," he said, "needs no help, Herr Fiske."

The German team carried the Fram III over to the start chute. They were actually a man short—their No. 3 had fallen ill—so they had recruited Charles Devine, whose family owned the hotel they were staying in. Devine had done a little bobsledding over the last year, and would do a lot more in the years to come. He would, in fact, end up as a member of the team that won the American National Championship in 1932. But that ride with Zahn was one he never forgot. "Zahn was such a stubborn man," Devine said, years later, "and so proud of the fact that he was world champion at the time. From the very start he took the run wide open—he didn't feel his way at all, and he never once called for the brakes."

Anger can be a useful fuel in some sports. But not bobsledding. As Steve Holcomb, the 2010 Olympic champion, explains, "At the start the best drivers are just sitting there. They're not stressed, they're not panicked, they're not pacing back and forth. They are calm at the starting line, relaxed, ready." And then they have to flick a switch. In 1932 they were using sprint starts for the first time at the Olympic Games. Three seconds of fury. Pump the legs, pound the snow, push the sled. Jump in, then switch off again. "You flick that switch right back again," says Holcomb. "Calm down. Slip right back into that mind-set you had three seconds ago, be relaxed and passive, because here comes the track." You don't fight the g-force. You can't. Instead you go with it. The driver lets it pull the sled up, around, and down, all the time making the tiny adjustments to the steering, urging the runners on to that perfect line, not for the corner ahead—it's coming too fast—but the one four, five, six bends down the line.

Zahn was running hot. He had designed the Fram III to cut through snow. But there wasn't any snow on Mount Van Hoevenberg, only ice. The sleds designed by Dewey had long, flat, flexible runners that held contact with the run right along their length. The blades on the Fram III were short and curved in bows; only the middle inches were in contact with the ice. They were quick because there was no traction. Which also meant there was no control. "It was the wildest ride I've ever been on," Devine said. "I knew from the first moment that the sled was out of control, that we wouldn't make it."

The Fram III shot along, stopping the split-clocks as it went. The announcer called out the times through a public address over the grandstands. A new record as they sped through Cliffside. A new record as they swept through Shady. They were running at about 75 mph as they came into the wicked chicane at Zig-Zag. The Fram III started to fishtail wildly as it approached the first curve. Its rear end swung from side to side, heaving the riders first one way, then the other. Zahn shot low into the Zag, and the sled traveled on up the wall. "We went straight up," said Devine, "and straight up and straight up, higher than the treetops, and planed through the air." The sled flew over a hundred feet. "Remarkably, we all stayed on the sled until the impact," Devine remembered. And then they hit a tree. The four of them scattered like shrapnel from an explosion. Devine was lucky: he landed flat on top of the No. 2 rider, Heinrich Rossner, who weighed three hundred pounds. "He saved me. His great size cushioned the impact." Rossner, on the other hand, was battered black and blue. Zahn shattered his left arm.

Ed Neil was a mile away when word reached him. The press had set up office in the high school on Main Street, their typewriters set out on rows of trestle tables in the hall. They had a PA wired up, so they could listen to broadcasts of events happening around the town, and a wire service run by a team of young ladies. When one of them read out a snap line about the crash at Mount Van Hoevenberg, the pack split for the bob track. But Neil picked up his hat and made for Lake Placid General Hospital. He figured he'd find the story there, if anywhere. And he was right. Charles Devine and the brake, Hans Melhorn, had both been discharged that same afternoon, after the doctors had checked them over, but Zahn was still being treated. Neil sneaked in to see him in his hospital bed. The crash made news across the country, from San Diego to Seattle, Boston to Biloxi, and Ed Neil was the one man who had an interview. He scribbled it down on his pad, put it out on the wires as a first-person account of the crash "dictated exclusively for AP" by "the ace of the European drivers and the most serious foreign threat to the Americans."

"My sail of 110 feet through the air after cracking up on the Zig-Zag turn was the greatest thrill of my career," Zahn said. "During my 20 years of bobsledding I have been in five accidents, not a bad average for a sport. But I never before took an airplane ride in my bob. You know we really should have been killed. Take a man and throw him through the air for 110 feet and then drop him 45 feet more into a thicket of trees, stumps, and rocks, and you expect to find him dead. I sometimes feel like a cat with nine lives." Instead, he had escaped with a broken arm. "The injury is nothing at all, as soon as it gets better I am going to get right back to bobsledding. It is insignificant compared to the fact that our team will be unable to shoulder its responsibility to Germany during the Olympic Games." Zahn paused. "Every member of my team is keen to get back into the game. I guess that is what this sport does to you. You take hold of it and you can't let it drop—at least until it drops you."

Back at the mountain, the bobsledding hadn't stopped. Two hours after Zahn's disaster the run was open again, though by now it was blowing a blizzard. Hank Homburger and Hubert Stevens took runs from the top. Despite being local men well used to the track, both had trouble making it down. They told the race officials that they "nearly went over the embankments on several occasions" and that "the course was too fast for the prevailing conditions." There were more protests. Jay O'Brien, for one, was convinced that the Lake Placid teams were trying to screw their opposition, and even their American teammates, out of the chance to practice. He argued that if the organizers didn't let the athletes run now, they could find themselves "racing for the first time over a strange course" come the Olympic competition. The officials relented, reluctantly. They allowed each team to take a single run from the top, with the proviso that they "had to brake all the way," which was only a little better than nothing.

As soon as the teams were done, the officials had workmen shovel fresh snow into the run, to slow it down and "minimize the chances of an accident." A fat lot of good it did too. The next morning, the first day of February, the bobsledders had company on the mountain. The press were out in force, eager for more, as Neil put it, of this "spectacular ballyhoo." And they got it. The Austrian two-man team toppled over at Shady, spilling the two riders out onto the track. The driver was fine, save for the cuts and grazes he suffered as he skidded along the ice. His brake, Count Baptist Gudenus, twisted his leg underneath the sled. It wasn't the only close scrape. The Swiss four-man bob, driven by the dashing Reto Capadrutt, snapped an axle midway down the run. It was, Daley wrote, "miraculous" that Capadrutt still managed to steer his team down the mountain. "By a freak of fate the two parted ends caught in the supporting structure underneath the sled and it was not until the bottom was reached that the break was discovered. Veteran bobsleighers paled at the sight of the broken part and could not conceive how the Swiss managed to go the full distance without being upset and hurt."

Dewey was faced with a dilemma. He had promised the crowds that bobsledding would provide them with "the thrills of a lifetime." And no doubt the run had delivered in that regard. But at the same time, he was determined to establish bobsledding as a mass-participation sport. He was planning to start running competitions for schoolchildren and novices as soon as the Olympics were over. He even encouraged his own daughter, Katharine, to take up the sport.

While "the promise of contusions and abrasions or worse has appealed strongly to the buzzard instinct" in the spectators, as Westbrook Pegler put it, the crashes had received so much publicity "that the businessmen of Lake Placid, who are businessmen after all, with investments at stake, were afraid the bob run would receive a bad name with prospective customers who might wish to recapture the spirit of childhood's happy hours by sliding down hill on sleds." Dewey had no great sympathy for the injured athletes. He felt the drivers themselves were "chiefly responsible for these accidents, for they would accept advice from no one, either as regards the bobs or the run itself." But he decided to pile more snow on the run to slow it down.

He also came up with the odd idea of strapping four sandbags to a sled and sending it down the mountain, to demonstrate the safety of the run to the press. He wanted them to understand that it was the drivers who were at fault rather than the run. The sandbags, Pegler wrote, were named "Eenie, Meenie, Minie, and Moe," although, he added in his inimitably acid style, "the head of the Lake Placid sports objected to the name of the last sandbag and suggested it be rechristened some Nordic name." The sandbag team, Pegler continued, made easy work of the run. "This was all very embarrassing to the Olympic bobbers, as it seemed to indicate that a staff of sandbags presented just the correct degree of skill and intelligence for bob-bob-bob-bobbing downhill on a sled."

Insulted, the bobsledders broke out in open revolt. That simmering spat between Jay O'Brien and Godfrey Dewey finally boiled over. Jay spoke out against the "high-handed" running of the track in the press. He and the other competitors drew up a list of demands, which Jay then presented to Dewey. The bobsledders asked that the running of the course should be handed over to two officials from the International Federation and that each team should be allowed to take a minimum of two runs each morning. Faced with the threat of a full strike, Dewey gave way. The bobsledders were given their head. And so the run didn't get any safer, or any slower.

The Germans, having lost almost half their team before the Olympics even started, received special permission to recruit a new crew at late notice. And so the Suicide Club gained a new member, the "Champagne King," Baron Walther von Mumm. He was perhaps the most remarkable of the lot. He had four scars on his chest, one for each of the bullets that had hit him in his life: The first two were a parting gift from his mistress, who shot him when he told her he was breaking off their affair; another he suffered while fighting on the Eastern Front. And the last was so fresh it had only just begun to heal. Mumm's friends liked to say that he had one scar for each of the four fortunes he had lost. The first went when the French confiscated his family's vineyards in the war; the second when the collapse of the German economy crippled his investments there; the third when prohibition ruined his attempts to launch the Mumm brand in the United States; and the fourth when he lost the little he had left in the Wall Street crash. By 1930 he was living in a boardinghouse, paying ten dollars in rent a month, and working in a brokerage. He was so depressed by his situation that he tried to shoot himself in the heart. He missed. That was in October 1931, just four months before the Olympics. He came up to Lake Placid to recuperate.

Mumm was a pilot, really, rather than a bobber. He used to race balloons. But he had done a little bobsledding, and when his country called, he was happy to join the squad. He roped in three extras, none of them with a scrap of bob-sledding experience. One was a baron, another a Bismarck. The other was Georg Gyssling, the German consul in New York and a card-carrying member of the Nazi Party. He wasn't the only one in the Suicide Club. The Swiss driver René Fonjallaz became one of the Nazi Party's leading propagandists in Switzerland.

Fonjallaz was the next to crash. He was riding a two-man sled with his cousin Gustav when they wiped out at Whiteface. René was left unconscious for five minutes, flat on his back at the bottom of the bank. Capadrutt crashed at the top of Shady, knocking a ten-foot-long slab of ice off the wall at the top of the bank. It was beginning to feel like Dewey had built a $227,000 death trap. And the upshot was, as Neil wrote, that "the bobsledders have stolen the show from a couple of hundred serious-minded competitors in other sports because of those breathtaking smashes on the most dangerous curves in all of bobsled-dom. If the thrills and terrors of the bobsledders continue through the Olympic Games, there seems little chance of getting it out of the limelight. Bob running, almost unknown until a few weeks ago, is king, the breath-taker of all the Olympic sports."

The Olympics started on February 4. Franklin Roosevelt arrived in town, ready to give a speech at the opening ceremony; President Herbert Hoover had declined the invitation. Roosevelt called in at the general hospital to visit Zahn.

"Mr. Roosevelt," Zahn said, "I'll race even with a broken arm."

Roosevelt told the press, "Bravo, this Zahn is a brave fellow."

Roosevelt was less impressed with his wife, Eleanor, who decided that she wanted to ride on the track "that had put so many contestants in the hospital." Dewey gladly fixed it for her, thinking it would be good PR. He had Hank Homburger drive her down the final half mile of the course, with the brakes on all the way as a concession to her husband's "evident anxiety."

The day before the opening ceremony, in his grand eve-of-Olympics preview, Neil laid it out like this: "Almost every team of the 21 two-man combinations and the 15 four-man teams that have practiced here have been in one accident or another on the slide. Only the American ace, Harry Homburger, Saranac Lake, and his rivals, Hubert and Curtis Stevens, seem immune through knowledge of the course."

As for Billy Fiske, well, no one gave him much of a chance. He was on the team, most reckoned, only because the chairman of the committee happened to be doubling up as his brakeman. And for all his feats four years before in St. Moritz, he had shown nothing on the track in Lake Placid that suggested he could get anywhere close to winning the gold. With the world champion Werner Zahn out of the running, everyone agreed that the title should be Homburger's for the taking.

The Olympic program owned by
Billy Fiske's young cousin, Newell. Lake Placid, 1932.

CHAPTER 11

THE FINAL

Thursday, February 4, dawned bright and cool. Most woke early; some never went to sleep. Workmen had been up all night making the final preparations for the opening ceremony, fixing flags and sprigs of evergreen up around the bleachers and the grandstands at the stadium. They had flooded the skating track, and the ice had set hard, with neither a scratch nor a blemish. It caught in the sun and shone steel blue.

On the far side of Mirror Lake, in his room at the Lake Placid Club, Billy Fiske lay awake in his bed. He had a lot on his mind. Gus Kirby, the man from the United States Olympic Committee, had asked him to carry the US flag in the parade at the opening ceremony. Billy didn't much care for ceremonies but of course he had agreed, not least because he wanted to spite Godfrey Dewey, who thought the honor should go to a local man. Billy's team uniform was laid out on a chair on the other side of the room. Red socks, blue woolen trousers, and a sweater of the same hue, but with a red polo-neck. Then a white Hudson Bay blanket jacket with red buttons, and a white cap. Billy looked good in it. He had a breakfast of coffee and eggs. Or "cofi" and "egs" as the menu insisted on calling them.

The stadium was full by 9:30 a.m. The tickets for the opening ceremony were the most expensive of the Games: five dollars for a seat in the grandstands, three dollars for the bleachers, and two dollars for anyone who wanted to stand. By five to the hour, Governor Roosevelt had taken his spot on the stage. The band welcomed him with "The Stars and Stripes Forever." As with all Roosevelt's public appearances, it was intricately orchestrated to ensure that as few people as possible saw the extent of his disability. He wore his leg braces beneath his trousers, and when he walked into the stadium, he came with his cane in one hand and his other clasped tight to the arm of his press secretary. The photographers had been told they weren't allowed to take pictures while he was making his way to the stands, so they were waiting for him in the stadium, along with the newsreel cameramen and radio and print journalists. At 10 a.m., he was in his place, and the athletes started to file in through the gates.

First came the Austrians in red and white, then the Belgians in blue ski suits, and then the Canadians in red and white, "red maple leaves standing out strikingly against their white coats." Czechoslovakia was next, followed by Finland, France, and Germany, all in red. In the middle of the pack was Werner Zahn, his arm in a bright white sling. They had asked him to carry the flag, but he had only just got out of his hospital bed and wasn't strong enough. Then came the four female figure skaters from Great Britain, all in long fur coats: Joan Dix, Megan Taylor, Mollie Phillips, and Cecilia Colledge, only eleven and the youngest athlete at the Games. Phillips walked at the front, the first woman in Olympic history to carry her country's flag at an opening ceremony. Next in the parade were the Italians, the Japanese, and the Norwegians in royal blue, except for the figure skater Sonja Henie, already famous from her feats at St. Moritz: she was wearing a bright burnt-orange coat. The Poles, in maroon, and the Swedes and Swiss, both in blue and yellow, followed them, and then, at last, Billy Fiske appeared at the head of the American team, a column ninety-six strong. They marched with a precision that betrayed the fact that many of them had once served in the military.

Billy led the team round, then paused in front of Roosevelt's box, to dip the flag in his honor. He stayed in that spot as Godfrey Dewey rose to give a speech in that odd, squeaky voice of his.

"Four years ago," he began, "Lake Placid was studying the II Olympic Winter Games at St. Moritz. Three years ago Lake Placid was organizing the necessary co-operation of state and county with town and village and with the whole Adirondack region to secure the award of the III Olympic Winter Games. Since the award of the Games to Lake Placid by the International Olympic Committee in April 1929, this indispensable co-operation has been splendidly manifested in the face of the most difficult conditions, both national and international, in the whole history of the modern Olympic Games. Today Lake Placid in the Adirondacks in New York state stands ready as a worthy host to the most distinguisht winter sportsmen of the whole world."

Billy stood there, on ceremony, holding the US flag, staring up at Dewey. The speech irritated him. Everything about the man irritated him. It seemed to him that Dewey had done every damn thing to stop him from defending his Olympic title. He had stopped him from practicing, banned him from the trials, and warned the bobsled committee over and again that they shouldn't pick him. "America, the country of sportsmen!" Billy wrote in his diary. "What rot."

Dewey prosed on some more, all in praise of his own efforts, before, eventually, he ceded the podium to Roosevelt, who rose uneasily to his feet, cleared his throat, and then welcomed the athletes on behalf of the United States. It was a short speech—shorter, for sure, than Dewey's introduction had been. "It is an evidence of the age of our modern civilization that the Olympics date back nearly 2,800 years," Roosevelt said, "and although in those early days they did not have the Winter Games, we in these later days, through the Winter Games, are trying to carry out the ideals of sport that were instituted in the Olympiads. Throughout the history of these Games, athletes have come to participate in them, seeking no recognition other than the honor received in simple medals. But that medal has come to typify the very best athlete in all nations in honor as well as in health." He paused, then came to his point. "I wish in these later days that the Olympic ideals of 2,800 years ago could have been carried out in one further part. In those days it was the custom every four years, no matter what war was in progress, to cease all obligations of armies during the period of the Games. Can those early Olympic ideals be revived throughout the world so we can contribute in larger measure?" Admirable as his words were, they stirred some controversy. The Olympic rostrum wasn't supposed to be a place for political statements. The *New York Times* ran his speech in full, under the headline "Roosevelt Invokes an Olympic Peace."

"And so," Roosevelt finished, "we are glad to welcome to this nation, our sister nations, as guests of the American people and of the State of New York, and I proclaim open the III Olympic Winter Games."

A bugle blew, a cannon fired, and a great white Olympic flag with its five rings was pulled to the top of the tallest flagpole, where it immediately snapped straight out in the stiff breeze blowing down from the mountains. The Games were open.

Within half an hour, the first event was under way: the 500-meter speed skating sprint on the ice rink. A canny piece of scheduling, this, since the favorite was a local boy, Jack Shea, whose family ran the grocery market on Main Street. Shea had learned to skate on Mirror Lake, "only a little time after he had learned to walk," as the local paper put it. He won in 43.4 seconds, just a lick shy of the world record. Billy stayed at the rink to watch the second event, too, since it involved Irv Jaffee, his old friend from St. Moritz. This time round, to Jaffee's relief, the speed skating was being done in the American style, with all the riders starting in a bunch and racing each other rather than the clock. The Europeans were as unhappy about the unfamiliar rules as the Americans had been four years earlier. Just as he had back then, Jaffee won the race with a late sprint, starting from fifth place on the final bend and finishing in first. This time, no one took his gold medal away from him.

With two gold medals won on the very first day, the American team—athletes and journalists—had plenty to celebrate. Question was, where to do it? The Lake Placid Club was as arid as the desert. But Jay O'Brien knew the way to the nearest oasis. On Saranac Avenue, a short way out of town, stood the Hotel Belmont, a grand old three-story building. Until now it had only ever been open in the summer. But the owner, John Schatz, had just had it done up for the Olympics. The chief new feature was the speakeasy he'd built in the basement.

Westbrook Pegler christened it the "Cellar Athletic Club" since, from that first night on, it was where you'd find most of the athletes. Except for Billy. He was in no mood for drinking. Hubert Stevens remembered that "Billy was a very quiet man. He didn't party much. After practice was over each day he would just go back to his room at the Lake Placid Club." But what Stevens didn't know was just why Billy was keeping to himself. He was tired of the press, who, he said, were making his life "a perfect hell" with all their "ballyhoo" over the bobsledding. He was sick of Dewey, his hypocrisy and pedantry. And he was wary of Hank Homburger and the other local drivers. He had heard about the five thousand dollars that the local riders had suggested they bet on Billy's head, wagering that he wouldn't finish in the top three. They looked on him and Jay as just a couple of expatriate playboys. And on top of all that, he was serious about winning the gold. That, he figured, would be the way to show the locals, and to stick it to Dewey. So yes, early to bed. There would be time to drink and dance when it was all over. Till then, he had more important business to attend to. As he put it in his diary, "He who laughs last . . ."

So Billy holed up at the Lake Placid Club in the evenings. He wasn't alone. He spent a lot of time talking with a new friend, Jimmy Walker, the mayor of New York. Walker was a friend of Jay's from way back in their Broadway days, when they had both run with "Ace" Rothstein. They were both from old Irish-American stock. And Walker had a reputation as a playboy. The press called him "Beau James" and teased him for swanning around town in a top hat and swallowtail coat. Walker had been a songwriter once, but these days he was, as *New York* magazine put it much later, "the public servant who favored short workdays and long afternoons at Yankee Stadium, who was loath to miss a big prizefight or a Broadway premiere, who left his wife and Greenwich Village apartment for a chorus girl and a suite at the Ritz-Carlton."

Walker had his own private booth in the secret cellar at the 21 Club, the most famous of the New York speakeasies. The 21 had a "disappearing" bar, which, at the flick of a switch, would tip all the liquor into a chute that ran down into sewers, just in case the prohibition agents came calling. Walker was once stuck in the cellar there for five hours while a raid went on up above. He grew so sick of the inconvenience that he got on a telephone, called the city police, and had them ticket and tow away all the federal vehicles. As popular as acts like that made him with a certain section of the electorate, he was also, at that particular time, fighting for his political career. He had been on the make ever since he first came to office, in 1926. In the early years no one minded. He was a popular mayor, not least because he legalized boxing and allowed theaters to open on Sundays. It was only after the crash that his career collapsed. He was denounced by the archbishop of New York, who suggested that the Depression was divine retribution for Walker's immoral mayoralty. He also became ensnared in the Hofstadter Committee investigations into corruption in the New York police department and court circuit. Long story short, when one of the chief witnesses, Vivian Gordon, was murdered, her body dumped in a park, public pressure grew so great that Roosevelt decided Walker would have to answer to Samuel Seabury, the Hofstadter Committee's presiding judge.

Billy took to Jimmy right away. "What I like about him is the fact that he is a fighting Irishman," Billy wrote. "A more charming, amusing, or really nice man it would be hard to find." He admitted, however, that his family was "disgusted" at their close acquaintance. In the evenings, when everyone else was out at the Cellar Athletic Club, Billy and Jimmy would be back at the Lake Placid Club. They listened to Seabury's speeches on the radio and heard the judge call out Walker for his corruption and rail against Tammany Hall. "Jimmy kept up a running commentary," Billy wrote. "And with the facts he made Seabury look the biggest fool in the world. 'Let him make a few more speeches like that and he'll condemn himself,' said Jimmy." Walker told Billy that he planned to run as vice president on the Democratic ticket in 1933, "depending on his health, and his adversaries." As it turned out, Walker would be drummed out of office within six months.

Billy lost himself talking politics with his new friend to take his mind off that mile and a half of mountainside on the edge of town. Because the more he thought about the run, the more it scared him. He had made the mistake of reading one of Pegler's articles. The bobsledders, Pegler wrote, "are that rare kind who know nothing about fear. They cannot understand it any better than a cat understands loyalty." But of course Billy knew fear. They all did. Even Jay was starting to crack. Practice on the bob track had continued in the days following the opening ceremony, and there had been another crash on Saturday. The Belgian four-man sled tipped over on Whiteface after the front right runner had caught on the rim of the curve. The driver, Max Houben, had managed to wrench the sled back into the bowl of the corner, where it capsized. Now he and the brake, Louis van Hege, were with the others in the hospital. Jay had said then that "the course is too fast to be safe." They had called off practice for the day. Anyone, Billy thought, who says he doesn't feel fear is either a fool or a liar.

The first bobsledding competition was scheduled for the first Sunday of the Games. But that morning a blizzard hit. Snow fell for twelve hours straight. In those conditions, the only athletes able to compete were the ice hockey players, who now had a roof over their heads, and the dog-sled racers, who went out whatever the weather. The Suicide Club took the day off. Or rather all but four of them did. Billy gathered his team together at the club and took them out to the mountain. He had realized that Dewey was right about one thing. The style they were using at Lake Placid, where all four riders were sitting up, was a lot different than the one they had used at St. Moritz, where the riders were lying down. With the crews sitting up, the sled had a higher center of gravity. A single mistake, one man leaning the wrong way at the wrong time, wouldn't just slow the sled but could also throw the whole thing over. The crew had to be trained, to be of any use.

In three weeks of practice, Billy and his crew hadn't once broken the two-minute mark on the Mount Van Hoevenberg run. Homburger's course record stood at 1:52. If they couldn't get near that, there was no chance they would win gold. So Billy had an idea, a trick he had used back in St. Moritz. The four of them carried their sled out of the shed and set it up on four big wooden blocks underneath an awning. Billy and Clifford took their seats, and Eddie and Jay stood by the stationary sled. Billy flicked the switch on the stopwatch he was holding, and shouted, "START!" Eddie and Jay sprinted on the spot, then leaped into their seats. Then Billy cried again: "Eyrie, LEFT!" All four of them leaned over to that side. "Whiteface, HARD RIGHT!" They threw themselves down flat on their backs whenever they entered the straights. "Cliffside, LEFT!" They threw themselves forward again, bobbing back and forth as they came into the corners. "Shady, HARD LEFT!" They rocked from side to side as Billy called the turns. "Zig LEFT! Zag RIGHT! . . . FINISH!" He stopped the clock. Two minutes. Not good enough. So they began again. They practiced. And practiced. Until the clock stopped at 1:51. And then they kept practicing.

The four of them broke up after noon. Jay went into town to take in a hockey game with his wife, Dolly, and Jimmy Walker. He asked Billy if he wanted to come, but Billy still had some work to attend to. He had hired a tractor driver, and the two of them loaded the sled up on a trailer and drove it through the snow to the Ames garage over on Saranac Avenue. He had told Walt Morrison, the garage mechanic, to expect him. The three men unloaded the sled, hauled it into the workshop, and set to it. "All I want is more speed," Billy told Walt. He had learned from watching the Fram III in action. He decided to insert a series of wedges into the joinery around the runners, to make them curve upward like those on the German sled. Then he and Walt carved a series of notches into the sections of the runners that would be in contact with the track, the better to grip the ice. By the time they were done, it was dark out. Billy, exhausted, went back to his room to think things through.

As for Eddie and Clifford, they had a little business of their own to deal with. Ever since he had been in Lake Placid, Clifford had been going by his nickname, Tippy. But his cover had been blown. Damon Runyon had revealed—in what he described, tongue in cheek, as an "exclusive exposé"—that Tippy Gray, "the solid meat of Jay O'Brien's American bobsled bunch," had enjoyed "a former career as a movie juvenile" but was "trying to keep his past buried." So Eddie, who knew Runyon from way back in his days on the Colorado boxing beat, popped round to the journalist's quarters to put him straight.

"Damon," Eddie said, "I'd like to take you for a ride."

"A ride?" Runyon replied.

"On a bobsled."

"Your correspondent scarcely believed his ears," Runyon wrote the next day. "Now up to this moment, your correspondent had always esteemed Eagan as a kindly, open-faced youth, of many high-attainments. Your correspondent had followed with deep interest Eddie Eagan's career as an Oxford student and an amateur light heavyweight champion, rejoicing in Eagan's many triumphs, for were we not from the same neck of the woods—fellow Coloradans, no less? Your correspondent had even watched with friendly orb, Eddie Eagan's progress in his new career as a bobber, though feeling somewhat regretful that Eagan had tired of existence at such an early age. Now the fellow stood revealed in his true character. For the first time your correspondent noted the murderous gleam in Eddie Eagan's hitherto innocent eye. Your correspondent observed the blood-thirsty set of Eagan's jaw. Your correspondent turned and took to his rubber heels, issuing such yelps of dismay that the citizens of this Adirondack village thought that one of the pooch teams in the dogsled derby was making a hot finish."

The three of them made it up in the Cellar later that night. "Unless you are an ale hound there isn't much to do in Lake Placid at night," Runyon wrote. "Except go to bed. And I must say the sleeping here is first class. I hear the same thing of the ale, which comes down from Canada."

Runyon wasn't the only one who had been telling stories about the speak-easies. Someone slipped word to the local Prohibition Bureau. Five agents stopped by at the Cellar and took the owner, John Schatz, out for a walk in the night air. As Westbrook Pegler observed, Schatz "undoubtedly had an agree-ment permitting him to conduct his AC in return for certain considerations, and when these conditions were met he was allowed to continue his business." Since the price of beer stayed fixed at one dollar a quart all evening, Pegler could only assume that those "considerations" hadn't been "too excessive." Thirty minutes later, Schatz was back behind his bar and the bobsledders "were beating the tables with their ale glasses again."

These were strange days for the Suicide Club. Their competition had been postponed for two days in a row now, while the storm swept through and the officials worried over the state of the track. The competitors were starting to suffer from both boredom and nerves. So they blew it out in the bar. They seemed to "train on ale," wrote Pegler. Every night in the barroom of the Cellar Athletic Club "the bobbers of many nations would sit at adjoining tables," drink-ing, bragging, singing. Werner Zahn was there, "hoisting strong Canadian beers and beating the time of robust German stein songs on the table top with his one good hand." Zahn told anyone who would listen that it had been "a puff of snow" that caused him to crash. It hit him in the face and blinded him for an instant, "so I was a tenth of a second late when I started to come down." A tenth of a second too late. That was all the margin of error the Mount Van Hoevenberg run allowed. The other riders didn't buy it. Zahn, one told Pegler, "was game, but a bad driver, because he crashed too often."

That was typical. The bobsledders were a band of brothers, bound tight by the risks they shared, and the sport they loved. But for all the camaraderie, there was also real rivalry between them. "The bobsledders," remembered another local rider, Paul Dupree, "were a breed of cat that didn't usually have too much good to say about each other. They were always in combat over something." They loved to bet. When Sonja Henie came in one night, just after she had won her second gold medal on the figure skating rink, they ran a contest to see who could sweet-talk her into accepting a drink. Not one of them managed to get by her parents, who had wisely decided to come along to act as chaperones.

That was nothing next to the screwball wager between the columnist Henry McLemore and Paul Stevens, the brother riding with Homburger and the Red Devils. Stevens, McLemore said, was "the maddest of the mad, mad Stevens boys." He kept, no joke, a black bear as a pet. He had domesticated it when it was still a cub. He called it Tobias. Now, Paul's two brothers, Hubert and Curtis, were due to compete in the two-man bob competition for the United States. McLemore made the mistake of asking which of the brothers was the best bob-ber in the family. "I am," Paul Stevens replied. In fact, he explained, he was planning to enter a team in the National Championship, which had, of course, been postponed until the Olympics were over. At which point . . . well, while offering no guarantees as to the veracity of his story, it's best, perhaps, simply to hand it over to McLemore himself. Bear in mind that the two men had been, as McLemore put it, "quaffing great beakers of orange juice in the club all evening." This is how he told it:

"Well, who are you going to get to ride with you?" McLemore asked.

"My bear," Stevens replied. "My great black bear, Tobias. I'll drive, and Tobias will ride along as brake ballast. I figure we'd win without any trouble. You know weight is what counts in a bobsled race, and me and Tobias will pack plenty. I weigh 250, I guess, and Tobias, despite his refusal to eat since he went into hibernation last December, figures to weigh in the neighborhood of 500."

"Has Tobias got enough sense to work the brake?"

"Has Tobias got enough sense to brake? Listen, that bear is nine years old. He is simply overloaded with brains. He's been doing the heavy work around the house for four years now. And the only thing he has broken is a piano he was moving. But even if he wasn't smart, he'd be quite all right as a brakeman. For, after all, who wants the brakes on when you're trying to get somewhere in a hurry? Besides, braking isn't safe; when you are traveling 75 or 80 miles an hour it's bad business to have somebody monkeying with the brakes."

The tale grew in the telling. In later years, McLemore insisted that at dawn the next morning the two of them drove by Paul's house, picked up Tobias, and headed on out to Mount Van Hoevenberg.

"I stood at the finish line with a stop-watch. Paul shouted from the top and he and the bear took off. On the first turn, the bear fell off the back. And Paul kept zipping down the course in the bobsled, now without a brakeman. And the bear kept zipping along the course in quick pursuit, not in the bobsled, and howling all the way. At the finish I clocked Stevens at two tenths of a second under the world record. And the bear, missing a big patch of fur on his backside, tied the world record."

Even Paul Stevens and his bear might have had a shot in the two-man competition, which finally started on Tuesday, February 9, five days after the opening ceremony. The snow was so thick that the run was slower than ever. The two-man course record stood at 2:03. Most teams clocked something in the range of two minutes and the high teens. Even the Stevens brothers were ten seconds back from their best time. The only man who got anywhere near the record was Reto Capadrutt, whom the *New York Times* reckoned to be the "most daring driver in the Olympics." He took risks that caused "several uneasy moments," but then, the *Times* added, he could afford to, since "the two-man bobs are much safer than the bobsleds, and recklessness is not penalized as greatly as in the four-man event, where even the slightest slip may mean serious injury and possible death." Which was true. The boblets, as they were known, were smaller, slower, and safer. After the first two heats, Capadrutt had a combined time of 4:13.09, good enough for a four-second lead over the Stevens brothers. Billy Fiske's old pal Jack Heaton was way back in third.

The two-man teams returned to the mountain the next day. They each had two runs left. The four times would be combined, and whoever had the lowest would win gold. The Stevens brothers, Hubert and Curtis, had come up with a cunning plan. In the minutes before the race, they took a blowtorch to their runners, heated them till they were white-hot. Swept of snow, the course was already running fast. Capadrutt clocked his best time yet. But the Stevens brothers, on their burning blades, were quicker still. They cut across the ice in 1:59.69, and on their last run in 1:57.68. This was a new course record, a new world speed record, and easily good enough for the gold. Capadrutt, two seconds back, took silver, and Heaton the bronze.

Godfrey Dewey was delighted. He had been proved right; the local riders were quicker than the crews from 1928. Heaton was almost fifteen seconds shy of the Stevenses' winning time. And it looked like it was going to work out that way in the four-man competition too. The track had been opened for practice again on the Wednesday, right after the boblet contest was over. The conditions were as good as they had been at any point in the last six weeks, and the riders, accustomed to the conditions, were quicker than ever. Hans Kilian, Germany's lead driver now that Zahn and Grau were out, had gotten his team down in 1:51.3. That was seven-tenths inside the Red Devils' track record. That time was then beaten by Billy Fiske and his crew, finely honed and freshly drilled. They finished in 1:48, four seconds inside the Red Devils' time—their best run yet. Records set in practice didn't go down in the books, only those made in competitions. But the bragging rights were worth plenty. Not that Billy got to keep them for long: the Red Devils set another unofficial course record, lowering it to 1:47.2. Billy had closed the gap, but not by enough. And he was fast running out of time. The final was just eighteen hours away, due to start at dawn the next day.

Every hotel in town was already full, but another 1,200 spectators had arrived that morning on a special express from Manhattan just to watch the finals of the four-man bobsledding. "For days now," Neil wrote, "the bobsleds have been the lure that brought the incoming throngs into town." And then the rains came. On the morning of the 11th, the streets of Lake Placid were awash. The ice columns on Main Street, festooned with evergreen sprigs and sparkling lights, dwindled and sagged, the ski jump turned into a water shoot, the skating oval a shallow pond, and the bob run was a river of meltwater. It rained right through Thursday, and all the while the bobsledders grew more anxious, and more impatient. They were almost out of time. Saturday the 13th was the ninth and final day of the Olympics. The closing ceremony was scheduled to start that evening. All that money, all that time, all that effort—it was starting to look as though it would all be for nothing. It was all the more frustrating because the bobsledders were convinced that if the temperature would only drop to the freezing point again, the course would be faster than ever. All that water would turn to ice, and there wouldn't be a lick of snow to slow it. Homburger told the *New York Times* that if the track froze again, he expected the sleds to cover the run in 1:40—a full seven seconds up on the record he had set only a couple of days earlier. But the freeze didn't come. On Saturday morning, the run was just so much slush. The rain had stopped the night before but the weather remained mild. The Winter Olympics ended later that afternoon.

The ceremony was a simple affair. It took place right after the ice hockey final, a 2–2 tie between Canada and the United States settled, in the end, on the results the teams had achieved earlier in the tournament. The Canadians won. When they were done, they joined the other athletes in the outdoor arena, where the opening ceremony had been held. It was only then, at the very end, that the medals were given out. A podium had been erected in front of the main grandstand, and the winning athletes from each event were called forward, one by one, and presented with their medals while the flags were run up the poles and the band played the national anthems. Sonja Henie got a gold. So did Hubert and Curtis Stevens. Jack Heaton got his bronze. But there was no four-man bob champion.

When the ceremony was over and the last medal had been handed out, Count de Baillet-Latour declared the Games closed. And as he spoke, his breath caught in front of him, condensed in the air, hung like smoke. Then snowflakes started to fall, each one illuminated by the bright spotlights shining on the flags. The athletes started to stamp their feet: the slush had begun to freeze. The cold weather was back.

The IOC's regulations allowed the organizers a single day's grace. After the closing ceremony there was a twenty-four-hour window to finish any events that had been left uncompleted. It didn't take the bobsled committee long to make their decision. The race was on. Word soon spread: the next morning, Sunday, February 14, they would run all four heats of the race back to back. Dewey panicked. He was terrified that after all the rain, the run would be nothing but glare ice, too fast to be safe, too dangerous to sell. The last thing he wanted now that the Games were over was another crash, and the ensuing rash of bad publicity for the run. If they were going to race after all, it would be on his terms. The organizing committee sent a party of 150 volunteers out to the mountain that evening. They were up all night working to get the course ready, "searching for snow," Ed Neil wrote, "as though they were hunting rabbits." They waded through the woods and shoveled snow into lorries, which drove over to the run. There it was unloaded and packed into the straights.

That night the atmosphere in the Cellar Athletic Club was a little different. A tension was in the air. The good spirits the sledders had shown earlier in the week were gone. Westbrook Pegler sat down for a drink with Eddie Eagan. For once, the writer wasn't feeling sarcastic. He liked Eddie. Admired him even. And he just couldn't understand what such a man, "a collector of degrees, more or less settled down to practice as a criminal lawyer," was doing risking his neck in a sport like this. "Young Mr. Eagan has spent years educating himself at Yale, Harvard, and Oxford, he has honors galore, money, a family and position, and yet he has been taking these risks for weeks in practice," Pegler wrote. "Why?"

The answer, Eddie said, was glory. "Our team is going to win this race. When that race starts, there will be no such thing as caution. We will forget the brake. It won't be touched. We are going to bob together on every turn to drive the sled through. Everything will depend on the steering. But we have confidence in Billy Fiske. If he loses the sled, we all take our chances. People say 'you might be crippled.' But if we come through we will win that race. That would be worth it."

"Bobsledding in the Olympic style never will be a sport of the masses anywhere," Pegler wrote, skewering Dewey's dream in the space of a single sentence (and he was right). "However, the Lake Placid people, with much money invested in their bob run, now deplore the very publicity which drew more attendance to their show than any other single attraction." It was possible, he continued, to bob conservatively, to run with brakes on, kicking up showers of shaved ice all the way and landing safe at the finish. But Eddie scoffed at that. "Bobbing with brakes?" he said. "I'd just as soon go for a street car ride." What was going to happen on Mount Van Hoevenberg that Sunday morning was something else altogether. Something more serious, more deadly than the safety-first version Dewey was peddling to the public. The bobsledders, Pegler wrote, would be "slick, fast, and perilous"; they "were supposed to forget everything," to "forget the brakes and bob their bodies in unison going into curves to make momentum in a race for hundredths of seconds."

Their conversation was "honeyed with jests," but neither Pegler nor Eagan were in any doubt about the risks. "What if you are killed?" Eddie said at one point. "You go one way or another." And at the end of the night, Pegler said, "The bobbers stood up. Nobody got sick. Nobody was called home unexpectedly. Nobody overslept."

No one had ever seen anything quite like the scenes at Mount Van Hoevenberg that Sunday morning, not at a bobsled race. There must have been a thousand cars in the parking lot at the bottom of the mountain. Anyone who came late had to park a mile away and walk the rest, and anyone who couldn't drive or catch a lift came by foot, bus, or carriage. The traffic was so thick that it took two hours to travel the short distance from the town to the mountain. The bobsledding final was the only show in town, and everyone had come to watch. The best estimates reckoned there were twenty-five thousand there, spilling out of the grandstands, crowding onto the hummocks of high ground that overlooked the corners, standing on the road that ran up alongside the course. They were lined five or six deep from the foot of the run right up to the very top. The public address continually had to ask people to stand back from the track so they would be safe from harm.

But the run itself was in a sorry state. The ice was worn so thin that the wooden boards were showing through on some of the banks. At Eyrie, a stream of water seeped through the ledge and puddled up on the bottom of the track. The rain had eaten away at the rims of the run, and the ice walls had jagged edges, like the teeth of a saw. And then, in the straights, Dewey's teams of volunteers had packed so much snow into the run the previous night that the sleds almost stopped dead as they passed through them, "as if," the *New York Times* reported, "the brakeman had applied all his strength to the steel prongs." In conditions like that, who knew what the perfect racing line was? The run was a fluid thing, and the shape it had taken in this weather was unfamiliar even to Homburger, who knew it better than anyone. The drivers would need to sense all those slow spots on the track, the puddles and piles of snow, and then steer around them. So much for practice. This would be a test of instinct.

Three weeks earlier, thirteen teams had been entered for the event. Since then, six had fallen away. The last withdrawal happened that very morning, when the first Swiss team, led by Donald Unger, pulled out because they simply didn't believe the course was safe to ride. So there were only seven teams left, the survivors "seven reckless, iron-nerved pilots" and their crews. There were the Romanians, led by the stunt pilot Lieutenant Alexei Papan; the Italians, led by Count Rossi; and the Swiss, a late entry, led by Reto Capadrutt, keen to exact revenge for his defeat in the two-man competition. Capadrutt was the only driver in the field who insisted on using a sled steered by rope pulleys rather than a wheel, which meant he was handicapped from the start. Then there was Walther von Mumm's screwball group, only recently recruited to the sport. Most reckoned it would be a miracle if they could just get down without breaking their necks. Finally, the contenders, the three favorites in the betting: Germany's

Hans Kilian and the two American sleds, No. 1 driven by Billy Fiske and No. 2 by Hank Homburger.

From the moment the first sled set off, it was obvious that the times were going to be slow. Capadrutt finished in 2:06. Papan and Rossi were slower still. Mumm, of course, was well back, in 2:11—over twenty seconds slower than the times the top teams had achieved earlier in the week. Then came Kilian, his team bobbing together to try to wring every little drop of extra forward momentum they could from the sled. Even he could make only 2:03.11. Next up, the Red Devils. There were, the *Times* said, "involuntary exclamations of awe from the crowd as Homburger swept past each point." The Red Devils were kitted out in extraordinary leather helmets, which covered their entire faces. "They looked like automatons rushing down the course." The times came over the PA as the sled traveled. They were 1:46 coming out of Zig-Zag into the home straight, and then they hit a thick patch of snow. It stripped them of all their speed. When they broke the thread attached to the electronic clock at the bottom of the course, the timer stopped at 2:01.77—the quickest of the day but still slow by Homburger's standards. Billy's team was last to go. They reached Zig-Zag in 1:47—a little slower. But he brought the sled right around the thickest part of the same patch of snow and stopped the clock at 2:00.52. He had the lead.

While Billy was steering, he was charting the course in the back of his mind. It took four runs to win the title, not one, and he knew better than to blow it all out on this first run. He used this first trip for reconnaissance. He made mental notes about the slush puddles and snow piles, plotted a quicker route for his next run. And it showed. On the second run, Kilian got his time down to just under 2:02. Homburger was a little quicker, just outside 2:01. But Billy, Eddie, Clifford, and Jay broke the two-minute barrier. 1:59.16. With two runs to go, they led the Red Devils by a little more than three seconds.

When Billy hit the ramp at the bottom of that second run, there was a gaggle of athletes and officials waiting. He could see right away that something was up, since the first teams should have already been back at the top of the mountain, ready to make their third descent. He climbed off the sled and walked into an almighty row. The Red Devils were in the thick of it, along with officials from the organizing committee and the International Bobsledding and Tobogganing Federation, surrounded on all sides by eager onlookers and journalists with their notebooks out. He could hear shouting. It was Paul Stevens. He had buttonholed Erwin Hachmann, the man in charge of the course that day. "If you insist on making us race in these conditions," Stevens said, "you'll go on without us. We're through racing today. It's a travesty on bob-racing. We came down so slow I had time to get off at Shady and fetch myself a drink."

Stevens was on strike. He had had enough of Dewey's meddling. Control of the track had been handed over to the European members of the International Federation, but they were just as keen as Dewey to keep the track running slow, since it suited the European drivers. They'd done their work so well that the American riders considered the slowness of the course an insult to the sport. Soon, Henry McLemore wrote, it was a mutiny. The rest of the Red Devils joined in with Stevens, and then Hans Kilian declared that he, too, was going to pull out of the race unless something was done to speed the course up. "The snow had slowed the course to a sluggish descent that would hardly baffle a kid," Neil wrote. "The crowd of 25,000 was starting to wonder who started those stories about the thrills of bobsledding as they watched sleds plow through several inches of snow, slowing down almost to stopping at some points."

As for Billy and Jay, they kept their thoughts to themselves. They were in first place, after all. But when it became clear which way the weight of opinion was falling, they, too, nodded their assent to the strike. There would be little satisfaction to be had, Billy realized, in beating the Red Devils if they had a ready-made excuse. All right then. He'd beaten them twice on a slow track, he could beat them twice more on a quick track. Whichever way they wanted it.

"The officials stomped their feet in rage," McLemore wrote. "The officials coaxed and teased. The officials threatened all manner of dire things. But the bobsledders stood firm." Eventually, after an hour's argument, the officials caved in. They called the races off for the day, even though that meant they would now take place after the IOC's twenty-four-hour window had shut. They didn't like it. But they didn't have any choice. That night, the volunteer workforce was out again, undoing all the work they'd done the night before. They raked away all the snow they'd shoveled onto the course a day earlier and sprayed it with water until it glistened in the moonlight. At last the sledders had gotten the kind of track they'd wanted all along. "This," wrote Neil, "is now a course for Americans, with American speed."

The Suicide Club met for the final time early on the morning of Monday the 15th. The Olympics had been over for two days already, but twenty-eight athletes had business to settle on the mountain. The crowds had already split up and quit town, even Billy's own family. There were only around seven thousand fans left. The grandstands weren't even full. It was a bitterly cold morning. And the run, Neil wrote, was "a huge open conduit of twisted, burned silver," one long ribbon of ice winding down the mountain. It looked quick. And it was. Capadrutt and Papan both cut their times down to a shade over two minutes flat. Kilian broke the barrier, finishing in 1:58.19, which was quicker even than Homburger, who clocked 1:58.56. And then there was Billy Fiske. Fastest again. As he had been in all three rounds. His time was 1:57.41. That meant he had a lead of 4.33 seconds going into the final run. But Homburger, at his quickest, had done the run in 1:47, ten seconds faster than the time Billy had just set. Homburger was sure he could find four or five seconds in a single run if he needed to. And he needed to now.

There is a second line that all bobsledders have to keep in mind. The first, we know, is the fastest path down the mountain, the racing route, high into one corner, low out of another, high into the next. The second line is in the mind. It's the one that marks that outer limit. Cross it, and you crash. Because when you reach the far side, that's when the sled flips over and you wind up unconscious on the track like René Fonjallaz, or the sled flies off track and you finish up in hospital with a broken arm, back, or skull, like Zahn, Grau, and Brehme. "The best drivers in the world," says Steve Holcomb, "are the drivers who know exactly where that edge is." They can push their sled right up to it, to the point where the runners are shrieking, and voices inside the riders' minds are screaming, and then they hold it there. Right on the line. "You go over that edge, and you will crash," says Holcomb. "And if you hang back from it, you will lose. Because every single guy out on that track is pushing it as far and as hard as they can. Right to the edge. So that's where you have to take it. And that's where you have to hold it." And that was the line Billy hit on his fourth and final run.

The sled hurtled down the mountain, 60 mph and still accelerating. There was a rattle from the metal frame, and a sharp rasping hiss from the runners as they cut through the ice. The wind whipped the sounds away from the ears of the four riders. Up front Billy Fiske was hunched over the wheel. He squinted through the early morning mist. He was thinking three corners ahead of the sled, trying always to urge it onto the right racing line. Behind him, Eddie, Clifford, and Jay were huddled together, with Eddie pressed right up against Billy's back.

They counted every one of those corners. One, two, three. Eyrie, a dogleg kink from left to right that snapped their heads from side to side. On around five, six, seven, eight, nine. Then Whiteface, where Max Houben had crashed. They passed the first grandstand. Out of that, then eleven, twelve, thirteen. Next, Cliffside, where the course ran right up against the rocky wall of the mountain. Fifteen, sixteen, a dogleg right at seventeen, and then four hundred feet of straight. The pine trees flashed by in fast-forward. The sled was really racing now. Sixty miles per hour. Sixty-five. Seventy. As fast as a man could travel without a motor. And then Shady, where Grau had flown over the lip. The sled slid up the wall, pulled higher all the time, up and up, passing perilously close to the lip. Eddie remembered looking down, seeing the rim inches from the runner. He saw a picture in his mind of "a steel comet with four riders hurtling through the air." And then the sled spat down and around, swept on toward Zig-Zag, where Zahn had lost control. Snap, snap, this way and that. Then the home straight.

In 1:56.59. The fastest run of the Olympics.

But there was one team still to come. If Hank Homburger and his Red Devils were going to beat Billy to the gold, they would need to match the world record set on this same course in the National Championship the previous year. Billy, Eddie, Clifford, and Jay climbed out from their sled and stood by the finish line. There was nothing they could do now but wait, watch, and listen to Homburger's times come over the PA.

"Twenty-nine seconds at Eyrie!" That was quick. Quicker than Billy.

"Fifty seconds at Whiteface!" World-record pace.

"One minute five seconds at Cliffside!"

Billy bit his lip. He could hear the roars rolling down the mountainside. The crowd was howling in excitement. Homburger was going to do it.

"One minute twenty-four at Shady!"

Homburger had done it. "It was a spectacular effort," wrote Neil. "He was riding the curves high and taking every chance."

Then he hit Zig-Zag. He took his sled so high on each bank of the chicane that the spectators thought, just for a moment, that he was going to fly over the top. Homburger had crossed the line. He was going to crash. He wrenched the wheel, hauled the sled away from the brink and back into the center of the track. It hit a bad patch of ice, rutted and torn from all the previous runs, and swerved around, almost turning sideways. The sled slowed. The thread broke. The clock stopped at 1:54.28. Billy Fiske was Olympic champion by all of 2.02 seconds.

Billy turned to Eddie, Jay, and Clifford. "Fellas," he said, "I think I'm going to go check myself into a sanatorium. I think I've earned it."

Just like 1928, there was no great ceremony. No band. No national anthem. No flags. Not even a podium. Just the bobsledders, gathered at the bottom of the run, in celebration this time rather than in protest. Hans Kilian won the bronze, Hank Homburger the silver. Billy, of course, got the gold. "He had nerves of steel," McLemore wrote. "But what a modest kid, all he did was smile and shrug his shoulders."

The sweetest part of it? Godfrey Dewey was there to present the medals. He called Billy, Eddie, Clifford, and Jay forward from the pack. Billy made sure to look him right in the eye. "That two-faced, pedantic, hypocritical Dr. Dewey," Billy wrote in his diary that night. "Thank God I managed to win that absurd event, otherwise his filthy, cackling laugh would have haunted me to my grave."

After that they stopped to pose for a few photos, some with Jimmy Walker, others with Werner Zahn, his arm still in a sling. He presented them with the fine silver cup, the Martineau Trophy, which he had won at the World Championship the previous autumn. It seemed right, he said, that they should have it, since they were now the quickest men in the world. The papers carried a picture of the four of them kneeling around their sled, each flashing a broad grin, while Zahn, the old World War I fighter ace, handed Billy the trophy. Eddie Eagan had just become the first athlete in history to win a gold medal at both the Summer and Winter Olympics. Jay, at the age of forty-eight, had just become the oldest Winter Olympics champion in history. And Billy, only twenty, was the youngest male athlete ever to win a second Winter Olympics gold.

Billy, Eddie, Clifford, and Jay never rode a sled together again. The National Championship was due to start at Mount Van Hoevenberg the very next day, and several of the overseas teams were going to stick around so they could take part as guests. Billy and his team turned the invitation down flat. They caught the first train back to Manhattan together with Jimmy Walker and Jack Heaton; picked up with Irv Jaffee, Peggy Eagan, and Dolly O'Brien; and went on a weeklong spree, from Delmonico's to the Silver Slipper to El Morocco and, of course, the 21 Club. "We certainly broke down our bodies well in New York that week," Billy wrote, "just as well as we had built them up for the Placid campaign."

A fortnight later, when life in the small town of Lake Placid had returned to normal, a letter arrived at the Lake Placid Club lodge. It was to Godfrey Dewey from Gus Kirby. He was a scholarly old soul, a lawyer by trade, and a man who put great store in the amateur code. He was also an old friend of both Jay's and Billy's.

My dear Godfrey Dewey,

Being but human, I can't help but take considerable satisfaction in that we won the bob-sleigh events at the III Olympic Winter Games, and particularly, in that I am confident that even you will now admit that those "experienced drivers here" who did not concede Billy Fiske and his team "an outside chance in any event" were either dumb or prejudiced, and that those who offered "to raise $5,000" to bet that the St. Moritz group would not place either first, second, or third in the eliminations should rejoice in that they had not realized their money. And further that the drivers whose opinions you quoted when you said that "Fiske and Heaton and their crews, in the absolutely unanimous judgment of every driver who has watched their preliminary work on the run have not the slightest chance of qualifying for the teams" didn't really know what they were talking about. After all, it is not practice, but racing that counts, and that was the position taken by the bob-sleigh committee—and the results here have justified our conclusion.

Perhaps somewhat maliciously, but none the less sincerely yours,
Gustavus T. Kirby.

Godfrey Dewey, so far as anyone knows, never replied.

PART THREE

I wish now I'd never relaxed or looked back—but said at the end of "The Great Gatsby" I've found my line—from now on this comes first. This is my immediate duty—without this I am nothing.

—F. Scott Fitzgerald, in a letter to his daughter, Frances, June 12, 1940

Rose Bingham at El Morocco, New York, 1937.

CHAPTER 12

THE NEXT BIG THING

Looking back from the stern, the ship's wake seemed to stretch all the way to San Francisco. Billy breathed in the sea air; held it, let it out in one long, slow puff. He felt some of the tension slip away. It was only now that he realized how much those couple of months in the United States had taken out of him. After the Olympics, the bobsled team went their separate ways. Jay traveled down to Palm Beach. He had his eye on a house down there. Eddie was supposed to get back to work, but he was full of big talk about getting back in the boxing ring. As for Tippy, he had some half-baked idea about signing up as a crewman on a yacht for a race across the Atlantic. And Billy? He just wanted to get far away from it all—from Lake Placid, from bobsledding, from Godfrey Dewey. One morning in New York he picked up a copy of the *Times* and saw a picture of Hank Homburger and his crew in the sports section. "The Saranac Red Devils," read the caption underneath, "who retained their North American bobsled title yesterday." Billy thought about the gold medal on his bedside table. The national title? Hank was welcome to it.

Billy was twenty, had two Olympic titles, a degree from Cambridge, an allowance of five thousand dollars a year, and a one-way ticket to the South Seas with his friend Jack Heaton. The two of them cut out for the West Coast. Their plan had been to hole up at a friend's ranch just outside San Francisco for a little rest and relaxation. But the city turned out to be just too tempting. "Without doubt the most charming city in America," Billy wrote in his diary. "They still have that old pioneer hospitality and good will." Their last night there had been one of the wildest yet. They'd been drinking in a speakeasy run by an old Basque chap. He had invited them along to a party at the local police station. They'd thought it was a joke, but went along anyway, and an hour later they were knocking back beers in a back room of the district headquarters with the local lieutenant and a couple of his sergeants. They'd even taken their guests for a tour of the cells. "They were full of drunks and hop-heads," Billy wrote, "ordinary humans who have had the bad luck to exaggerate a bit and be caught." Then they'd gone on to the morgue. It had seemed like a swell idea until the moment they got there. The corpses had smelled like stale fish. "I guess," Billy said, "God doesn't think too much of us after we're dead." It had sobered them up sharp enough.

"America," Billy thought to himself as he walked up to the bow. "What a swell country. So law-abiding!" His thoughts turned again to Godfrey Dewey. "I never knew such human beings existed on this civilized earth," he wrote in his diary that night. "I insist it is over-civilization that has taught humans to be so damned crooked." And, ah, well, imagine caring. Billy and Jack were on their way now, and all that was well behind them, back beyond San Francisco.

They were sailing on a ship named the *Monowai*—"the ugly duckling," her crew called her. There were twenty-five passengers, made up, in Billy's words, of "pansies, would-be-businessmen, nondescripts, and two very ugly girls." He was putting all his thoughts down on a typewriter, a decrepit old thing he'd picked up in San Francisco. He thought that a regular supply of letters would go some way toward assuaging his parent's worries about his whereabouts. Or, as he put it in a letter to his sister, Peggy, "the only reason I bought the damn thing was to enable me to write a little more balls for the family." He spent so much time at it that he was suffering "from writer's cramp and sore nuts." He was actually trying to write a little poetry. His first efforts had proved to be . . . well, they hadn't worked out quite as he had hoped:

> The din of America behind
> The dreams of youth ahead
> And drivel in between

NEW TITLE—Two Boys Set Out

Twas close of day,
The fog, dull, damp, cold,
Came rolling slowly down the bay
A ship enveloped in its fold.
Twas dawn next day,
Hot sun, trade winds, the sea a sapphire blue,
The course Sou'west by South, to islands far away.
Could it be, their dreams came true?

Billy, Jack pointed out after he had read it though, was a man with many talents. Poetry wasn't one of them. That was one career he could cross off the list.

His father, of course, wanted him to come to work at the bank under Clarence Dillon. But Billy wasn't sure that bank work was quite his speed. He'd sold this trip to his father on the grounds that it would give him a little time to make up his mind about what he wanted to do with his life. Some of those "would-be businessmen" on board had twigged that Billy was looking for openings. One of them tried to persuade him to invest in a "new system of teaching piano by training the ear," the theory being, Billy explained, "that the ear is the mechanical outlet to the soul in music." The man was planning to open a series of music schools and "guaranteed that with two lessons a week for six months anyone with any ear at all will be able to play music moderately well." Another huckster tried to convince him that the Kenyan coffee trade was the thing. Billy passed on both. The only idea that had stuck with him so far was the silly one he'd had when the *Monowai* was sailing past the American fleet outside San Francisco. "Passed a lot of battleships of the American Atlantic Fleet today, out here for battle-practice," he wrote that night. "Great sight—always makes me want to join the airforce just so I could drop bombs on 'em."

On March 26, they made their first stop in Tahiti. They landed in Papeete, which Billy had imagined as a land of blue seas and skies, with white beaches sprinkled with coconut palms, but found it to actually be a "tawdry, ramshackle, dirty sea-port." It was all black cinder streets and matchbox buildings, filled with men who "would rob their grandmothers' pants," and women who would "sleep with Vincent Astor one night and the third engineer on the cargo boat the next." The worst by far, he thought, were the expatriates, who could be found gathered around at one of the town's three hangouts. There was Tony's Cabaret, "which boasts an old and tinny piano"; Quinn's bar, "the toughest spot this side of Barcelona and woe betide the fellow who tries stealing the stoker's gal"; and the Tahiti Yacht Club, "the meeting place of the town's elite, and a more annoying spot I can't imagine."

So Billy and Jack didn't linger there long. Driven on by Billy's "weakness," as he called it, "for doing things and going places nobody else had gone," they headed down the coast to Punaauia, country rather more like the images they'd had in their heads before they arrived. They rented a house on a stretch of white beach backing onto the mountains and in front of a lagoon sealed off by a coral reef, with a gap just big enough for a canoe to pass through. They spent their days diving for fish, which terrified Billy in a way bobsledding had never done. "In the water one can go on indefinitely thinking about all the things that can hurt one," he wrote. "I was swimming inside the reef a few days ago and I dove to about 15 feet when a scurry of small fish came out from behind the coral about 20 feet away. I started to swim under water in their direction, harpoon clutched firmly, when suddenly a 'small' swordfish about 8ft long came out in pursuit. I took one jump from the bottom of the ocean and landed in the boat."

Other times they were off exploring the interior, hunting boar with local guides. It was there, up in the hill country, that Billy found the peace he had been looking for. In a camp, with a belly full of fish and shrimp they'd just fetched from a river, "the boys got together and had a little chorus around the fire. The moon, nearly full, was just coming over the Arohena mountains, and the last purple glows of the sunset lit the western skies; the stars seemed to grow brighter and brighter by the minute; the stream rattled along on its journey down the valley and the three coconut palms stood like sentinels on a nearby hilltop, outlined against the sky. And the boys seemed to be inspired by it all because their songs blended so perfectly with this marvelous scene. I thought then of how much those poor old fools, who labored their lives away worrying about New York Central dropping two points, were missing."

He was happy here, among the "pure-spirited Tahitians," and besotted with the women. "Their eyes! Great big long lashes that look as though they had been painted on a piece of china. They can say more with their eyes than any race I have ever come across . . . Now cross, now fascinating, now quizzical, now hurt, now amorous, now happy, now tearful. Yes, the Tahitian eyes are a thing that one seldom forgets, and the same is true of their skin. Like the most marvelous silk, it's so smooth one is scared to touch it for fear of scratching it."

These observations were drawn from intimate experience, though in his letters home he cloaked in generalizations the details of his affair. But Billy's sister found a photo tucked into the back of his diary with the words "Billy's Tahitian girl" scribbled across the back. They met, he said, in the most peculiar way. "If a girl takes a liking to some man at a party where they happen to be singing, she will stand up and command attention and then start singing an ode to the man's sexual organs! It is an old Tahitian custom and the man doesn't feel the slightest bit embarrassed. How natural and how unspoilt by all the plots and intrigues that it takes to win a European girl!"

Soon, they were living together in his shack on the beach. Billy was bewitched. "In the presence of strangers the girls, especially, are inclined to be very introspective and will remain absolutely silent for some days. It takes a great deal of patience and forbearance to draw them out, but when they feel at ease they are always giggling and happy and can talk far more intelligently at the same time than many white girls. Likewise they are extremely clever in their treatment of men. They make him feel he is entirely their lord and master, and of course by doing so they usually get away with nothing short of murder. For what man on earth is not a sucker to a woman's flattery, especially if she is good-looking!"

They stayed three months, longer than they had planned. Billy made it a habit to move on before he grew too attached. "I hate to be sorry to leave a place or person." He broke the rule for her, and for Tahiti. "Never," he wrote, "was departure so painful. As we sailed away, and the last rays of the sun made a kaleidoscope of colors over the island, and then the lights began to twinkle all along the coast from Arué to Papieri. I made a solemn vow, to nobody in particular, that some day I should return. And then suddenly the whole beach on which our house stood, and from which we had taken a tearful farewell a few hours before, was lit up by colossal bonfires, the flames leaping high into the air. Our neighbors, the inhabitants of Punaauia who had made us love that place so much were signaling us a last farewell. Gradually, the light faded away in the distance and all was darkness."

Jack was sure that they would find the cure for Billy's broken heart in the Cook Islands. No such luck. "We made a complete tour of the island," Billy wrote, "and didn't see a single pretty girl." At first, he thought that it was just bad luck. Especially when he was told that the island's most "exquisite" women would be at a big dance that same night. "I arrived on the scene of the party, shoes polished and full of hope, but the minute I entered the room my ardor was thoroughly soaked. If I had tried my best to collect all the ugliest female under-graduates of Newnham and Girton, I could not have done better."

From there they traveled to New Zealand, then on to Australia, where Jack insisted that they get back to more civilized pursuits, and they spent their time at a club in Rose Bay, playing golf and tennis. Billy, too, was soon back in his old ways. "I was constantly impressed by the extraordinary beauty and healthy good-looks of the girls," he wrote. "Their dress is a little loud and eccentric—the Australians call it 'individual'—but then as most of life is spent in bathing suits, it really doesn't matter." They went on up around the coast to Brisbane, traveling on a tired old ship with a permanent list to port, the SS *Marella*. She carried a cargo of "ministers, miners, and dyspeptics," who spent their evenings arguing about the Aboriginal question. Billy was minded to agree with the missionary who argued that "the whites were inclined greatly to underestimate the Aborig-inals' intelligence" and who "claimed they are a race who have been and still are grossly mistreated and misunderstood."

Darwin on Australia's northern coast was "conspicuous only owing to its state of decaying uselessness," so they were happy to reach, at last, the Dutch East Indies, where they spent their time and money gambling on horses, on kite fights, and in casinos, "where the Chinese foregather with anyone else who can stand a good skimming." Billy saw one Chinese businessman lose "five sugar refineries, six beautiful new cars, and about $100,000 in cash on one poker hand." Which was a little fast, even for him. In Bali, he was back on the "beautiful women" again, these ones "working in the sugar refineries, so damn good looking I nearly fell into a vat myself." He especially admired their eyes. "They not only have beautiful eyes, but they also have the art of using them. For what good is a magnificent pair of eyes if they are not properly manipu-lated?"

They had to cut out of Manila quick sharp when, in a story Billy kept from his diary but shared with his friends, he became, as one of his pals put it, "in-volved with a lady whose husband was an oriental diplomat." The husband had been recalled to his home country but "very quickly heard about Billy and the affair with his wife and sent some countrymen to pay him a visit. Subsequently, Billy and Jack decided it was in Billy's best interest to depart Manila sooner than planned."

They fetched up in Hong Kong. By now, Billy's travel trunk weighed around four hundred pounds. He'd stuffed it full of presents for his family and friends: vases for Peggy from a shop in Canton; a sacred idol for his father, "full of stories, magic and poison, which I am sure he won't appreciate"; a diamond ring that "really looked worth a million in the suppressed light of the pawn shop" and which he'd imagined "selling to Cartiers at a thousand percent profit"—which had turned out, of course, once seen in the light of day, to be quite worthless. He also had a duffel bag stuffed with gifts, so many of them he was still handing them out a year later.

Billy's letters home also dwelled on his other great preoccupation, politics. The League of Nations had just published the Lytton report, an investigation into the causes of the recent Japanese invasion of Manchuria. "It has caused much of a stir, as everyone seems to feel the absolute futility of it," Billy wrote in a letter to Peggy. He returned again to one of his favorite topics—the ineptitude of American politicians. "Christ they make me sick . . . They are the goddamnest fools I have ever seen. They sit back for a century with their goddamn [isolationist] Monroe doctrine and let the rest of the world make suckers out of them and then they jump in all of a sudden at the only spot where it is entirely contrary to their interests." Japan, Billy thought, "is entirely run on American capital," and so it was in the United States' best interest to let Japan have Manchuria. Instead, they were siding with the Chinese. Peggy was convinced that Billy was planning a career in politics. Certainly he had a passion for it. "He cared far more about ideas and ideals than money," she said. "And he had a keen sense of what he thought was the 'right' thing to do."

At that time in his life, though, Billy had other ideas. In fact, later that very same day he had *the* idea. "Must stop now," he signed off his letter. "I am going to play golf in the Amateur Championship of China with Douglas Fairbanks, who is arriving out here in a couple of days, what a laugh! So long Snooks, Bill."

Fairbanks, an old family friend from St. Moritz, had just been featured in Howard Hawks's *The Dawn Patrol* and Warner Bros.' smash gangster flick *Little Caesar*. His star had never burned brighter. He hadn't come to Shanghai just to play golf. He was planning an ambitious new film project, "a colorful history of China from Confucius to the present day." Fairbanks figured his picture could be an international epic. It never happened. But while he was in the city, he spent plenty of time shooting the breeze with his old friends from St. Moritz. And that was when it dawned on Billy. Where was the one place a young, handsome man like him could go to make a lot of money and have a little fun? He was amazed he hadn't thought of it sooner.

Screenland Magazine, May 1934

WHEN GILDED YOUTH GOES CELLULOID!

And here is another American "Golden Spoon" youth, with the irresistible urge to do something with motion pictures! He is William Fiske, 3rd, the son of an American banker in Paris who was brought up abroad with the idea of following his father's footsteps in business. Instead he has decided to desert the counting room to count for something in the movies!

They called it Seven Seas Productions. Billy was the president. He'd earned the job since he'd sunk most of his money into the company. He was its public face too. The idea, as the smitten interviewer from *Screenland* explained, was to "make pictures with Garbo players in authentic settings." They planned to travel "all over the world in interesting spots, with a small unit of Hollywood players, technicians, directors, and supplemented by native casts." It was all inspired by Billy's time in Tahiti. He explained "quietly, but with bright eyes" that "in every country there are tales and superstitions based on fabulous characters that have at some time lived there. There are heroic figures living today in difficult and remote countries, doing great things unheard of in civilized centers." At the same time, he admitted, they would be open to the idea of a movie made "on the spot in Monte Carlo," since that would be "authentic" too.

In the end, they decided that their first picture would be set in Hawaii. A writer named Jim Bodrero was hawking a script about a romance set on the sugar plantations out there. Better yet, because Bodrero's grandparents owned one of those same plantations, he could help them fix up the locations. And that was what mattered to Billy. He wanted to make an authentic movie, one shot on location, not in a studio.

White Heat, as it was eventually titled, is the story of a young socialite named Lucille who marries William, the foreman on her father's Hawaiian sugar plantation. William is really in love with his housekeeper, Leilani, but he can't be with her because she's a native. Cooped up all alone in the house, Lucille starts to go gaga. When her former fiancé, Chandler, arrives for a visit, she succumbs to his advances. William finds out and is furious. Then, in the grand set-piece finish, Lucille, utterly potty by this point, sets fire to the crops and runs off with Chandler. William falls from his horse trying to fight the fire, but, just as he's about to be consumed, Leilani arrives to rescue him. All the extramarital love stuff was an old Hollywood theme. But an interracial affair was a new one.

They hired Lois Weber as director, a cheap and inspired choice. Weber had been Hollywood's first great female director, but she hadn't made a movie since *The Angel of Broadway*, for Cecil B. DeMille back in 1927. Only six years ago, but it was also in the silent era and a bomb besides.

Mona Maris, who was Argentine and spoke English with an utterly unintelligible accent, played the Hawaiian housekeeper. They had David Newell, a young up-and-comer, as the lead man. Hardie Albright, an old vaudeville ham, was Chandler. For Lucille, Billy wanted Virginia Cherrill, the pretty blonde twenty-something who had played the blind flower girl in Charlie Chaplin's hit *City Lights*. And he got her, even though she was contracted to Twentieth Century Fox.

Cherrill came with baggage. Chaplin, another old friend of the Fiskes from St. Moritz, warned Billy that he had fired her from *City Lights* because she had walked off the set to get her hair done. Worse still, she had a wildly possessive fiancé, who hated the idea of her being away working with Billy in Hawaii for however many months. The fiancé's name? Cary Grant. At the time, Grant was at a particularly low ebb. He'd just finished work on what he described as "a grotesque version of Alice in Wonderland," in which he'd played the mock turtle.

He had spent the entire shoot encased in a suffocatingly hot papier-mâché shell, topped off with a large head with little false eyes. He wasn't feeling great about the place his career was in. And Billy, well, as his friend Patsy Ward wrote, "In those roving years, wherever he went and among whomever he moved his gaiety, warm-heartedness, and quick intelligence won him instant popularity; his natural ability to excel in whatever form of sport he tried his hand at, his complete lack of arrogance, and his unfailing sense of humor brought him not only admiration but love among many different classes of people in many different lands." His pal Neil Cleaver was a little more to the point: "Billy, was short, 5ft 8in," said Cleaver, "but the women found him wildly attractive."

Cherrill always denied that there had been anything between the two of them. "After a day's shooting in the heat and the dust, we returned to the ranch exhausted," she told her biographer. "I had a long bath and then my supper and retired early for the next day's shooting. Billy and his co-producer would sit and talk about the next day's shooting. Those few times I was involved in after-dinner talk, Billy would tell the most amusing stories." That was her story, and she stuck with it. Even if she changed the details a little over the years. "Virginia remembers both the unpleasantness of the film-making and the intensity of Cary's jealousy," wrote a biographer of Grant's. "She had to work day after day on a sugar plantation, covered with red dust blown by a savage wind. At night, she would return to the boarding house to be scrubbed by a housemaid in an effort to remove the dust from her hair, pores, and nails. Fiske, accompanied by his co-producer, would disappear to a local brothel; the director went to her room; and Virginia was left completely alone."

Grant didn't buy it. "He hated the fact that he couldn't keep an eye on her during the many weeks of shooting. He would telephone her in Kauai, or try to check up on her with the switchboard at her Japanese boarding house, a difficult task in those days of comparatively primitive telephone services. He was maddened by an unfounded belief that she was having an affair." Grant got to be so paranoid about it all that even after shooting was over and Cherrill had moved to the Beverly Hills Hotel, he bribed the switchboard operators there to eavesdrop on any calls between Billy and her.

Cherrill's recollections of life on set, all "red dust blown by a savage wind," didn't exactly tally with everyone else's. But then, she was the star. The two things everyone remembered about the production were how much fun it was and how little work they got done. Progress was slow because so many of the crew were injured, cut, bruised, and sprained playing a game Billy had invented. There was a spot where the sugar cutters worked, a plateau high above the plain. From up there, they delivered the cane down to the lowlands by bundling it up and tossing it into two small streams, separated by a foot or so, which ran side by side down to the bottom of the hill. Billy thought it would be a sport to stand, one foot on each bundle, and water-ski down the slope. "It was dangerous and difficult," wrote Patsy Ward, "and he excelled at it."

It turned out they had a lot more fun making the movie than anyone did watching it. *White Heat*, as it was now called, had its premiere in New York on June 14, 1934. The reviews were awful. "White Heat is a humorless account of the amorous difficulties of a young sugar planter," began the *New York Times*. It got worse. The themes, the paper conceded, were "by no means trivial," but the film cheapened them by "resorting to rotten and predictable clichés." Worse, its critic found the grand finale of the fire in the cane fields to be a "completely foolish episode." Whispers were that Billy had spent $400,000 on it and made only $125,000 back. Certainly all plans for their next film, *Moro*, set in the Philippines, were quietly shelved. As for Weber, she never worked again.

Ah, well. Billy's career as a producer was a bust, but he was still having a high time in Hollywood. And as Peggy said, he never cared too much about money. He had a house on Lookout Mountain Avenue, off Laurel Canyon. He lived there with an old pal from his Cambridge days, Paddy Green. The two of them used to run around town with David Niven, who lived just around the corner. Niven was still working bit parts then, looking for his big break. Billy and Paddy even took flying lessons together out at Burbank. They'd been inspired to sign up after going to see *The China Clipper*, the latest Warner Bros. picture—starring, in a supporting role, a new player by the name of Humphrey Bogart. It was all about a man's obsession with building a flying boat capable of crossing the Pacific. And Billy could still dream of those fighters he saw over the US fleet on his way to Tahiti.

In those days, Billy was dating Alice Faye, a platinum blonde with a singing voice so sweet that Rudy Vallee signed her up as the vocalist on his hit radio show after hearing her perform at a party. (Vallee's wife thought there was a little more to it than that, and named Faye as a co-respondent when she sued for divorce in 1934.) Faye was tougher than she looked in her china doll makeup. She had grown up in Manhattan's Hell's Kitchen and quit school when she was thirteen to try to join the Follies. She had a hard edge, which appealed to Billy. And to Darryl F. Zanuck too: he gave her the lead in the 1934 film *George White's Scandals*, then cast her opposite Spencer Tracy in *Now I'll Tell*. She soon shot to the top of the bill, and dropped Billy on her way up.

While Billy was pining after Faye, he fell in with another hell-raiser, the actor William Boyd, a man who drank a lot, and gambled more. In 1935, Boyd was offered a six-picture deal for a series of Westerns based on hit pulp stories about Hopalong Cassidy. Boyd persuaded Billy that the series would be a good investment. Billy agreed, and became the vice president of Western Pictures Corp. Boyd retooled the character, took the hard-drinking hell-raiser described in the books and turned him into a teetotaler who didn't smoke or swear. "He was part philosopher, part doctor, part minister," reckoned Boyd. "He was everything." Everything that Boyd was not. So that was one of the few deals Billy struck in Hollywood that worked out well. Though by the time the Hopalong films got really big—by 1938 Boyd was one of the best-paid actors in Hollywood—Billy's involvement was already over. He only ever made piecemeal change from the early films in the series. So he continued to look for the next big thing, an investment that would give him a better return on his money than Hollywood had done.

───────────

Early in 1936, he found it. The way T. J. Flynn tells it, it all started at a cocktail party in Pasadena. T.J. was from Aspen, Colorado. In the thirties, Aspen was a one-horse town, and the horse was dead. The mining boom was long since over, and the population had slumped from a peak of twelve thousand to just seven hundred in the space of three decades. With a background like that, T.J. didn't have much to say about polo, which seemed to be all anyone at the party wanted to chat about. Apart from this one guy, off on his own, evidently equally bored with the small talk.

"Are you more interested in any sport than polo?" Billy asked.

"Yes," T.J. replied, "I like horseback riding in the mountains."

Billy lit up. "What mountains?"

"The High Rockies," T.J. told him. "Back where I grew up."

"Do they have skiing out there?"

"They do."

And from then on, Flynn said, "Billy became more and more interested, and plied me with more and more questions about the mountains."

Well, T. J. Flynn always did like a good story. Another of Billy's friends, Ted Ryan, remembered it a little differently. T.J. was out in Los Angeles trying to find someone to invest in a silver mine back in Colorado. "And he kept trying to sell it to Billy. And Billy was just not at all impressed." But he insisted on sending over some photos of the mine's location, high in the Rockies. Billy saw then "the terrain, the heights, the altitude." He had no idea such country existed in America. Billy called T.J. back, told him that maybe he wanted to invest in Aspen after all. T.J. was delighted, said, "I told you so." And Billy replied, "But it's not the mine I'm interested in, T.J. It's the mountains."

Later that summer, Billy, Paddy Green, and a third friend, Robert Rowan, a renowned real estate developer, took a trip out to Aspen. Billy's brother-in-law, Jennison Heaton, flew them out there in his little four-seater monoplane. Flynn met them, just as soon as he could find them, in his truck. He took them up past the Midnight mine to Richmond Hill, where they got out to walk. Billy and Paddy were so excited to be there that they broke into a sprint for the final five hundred yards of the climb to the peak, racing against each other like a couple of kids. Rowan and Flynn followed them up in their own sweet time, found them both wheezing at the top, doubled over, a couple of husks. When they'd got their wind back, they stood up and saw the summer snows on the fields of Mount Hayden, the Swiss meadows running down to the junction of the two creeks, Castle and Conundrum.

"This," Billy said, "is the place."

His dream, so very similar to the one Godfrey Dewey had once held for Lake Placid, was to turn the sleepy little town of Aspen into America's leading winter sports resort. Perhaps, for Billy, the fact that they would be competing with Dewey's resort was part of the appeal. Certainly Billy threw himself into the work. "Without Bill Fiske, the whole skiing area would probably be as hopeless today as it was in 1936," said Ted Ryan in a 1965 interview. "Bill came through without question." He coughed up the first lump sum of money. His contacts were even more valuable. "Billy," Ryan said, "knew just about everybody." He persuaded Robert Benchley, once a key member of the now defunct Algonquin Round Table, to write them a promotional pamphlet. Harold Ross, Benchley's editor at the *New Yorker*, was actually from Aspen, though, according to Ryan, Ross never cared to admit it if he could help it. He was amazed when he saw the brochure. "However did you get into this, Benchley?" Ross asked. The answer was, of course, that Billy had charmed him into it.

The little lodge they built on their new land was designed by a friend of his from Pasadena, G. B. Kaufman, who had designed the grand old Jockey Club at the Santa Anita racetrack. And it was decorated by his pal Jimmy Bodrero, the man who wrote *White Heat*. Bodrero had given up screenwriting and turned, instead, to drawing and painting. He was a lot better at it too: he was working as one of the chief artists over at the new Walt Disney studio at Burbank. The lodge was only a little place, but Billy wanted it to make a big impression, since the idea was that they would be bringing potential investors out to stay there for a week. There was a pump house, a ski room, a barn, and a hayloft that housed a team of horses and a sleigh. There were two bunkrooms, which, the adverts promised, housed "beds fitted with box spring mattresses, down pillows, patch quilts" and built on—a Billy Fiske touch, this—"frames constructed from Philippine mahogany."

Aside from swish bed frames, what they needed were a couple of real winter sports experts, men who could chart the weather, mark the trails, and map the mountains, men who really understood the work that would need to be done to turn the empty slopes into a first-class skiing resort. They couldn't think of anyone in their circle in the United States with the necessary experience or qualifications. But Billy knew just where to look. The same place he'd first come up with this wild idea of building a ski resort—St. Moritz. Billy recruited Swiss mountaineer Andre Roch and the Italian Gunther Langes, the man who had laid out the fastest downhill ski piste in Europe, at Marmolada. Billy was so committed to the Aspen plan that he paid Roch's and Langes' wages, $125 a month, out of his own money. They got to work the following winter, once the log cabin had been built.

Roch had mixed news. The land at Aspen Mountain, around the old Little Annie Mine, was good and could provide, he said, some of the best skiing in the United States. But there was another spot, at Ashcroft, six miles up Castle Creek, that could well be the finest ski site in the whole world. They were, Roch reckoned, building in the wrong place. They were going to need more time and more money. So Billy hadn't found his path yet—but wherever he was heading next, he wouldn't be representing his country in any more winter sports. Since he had won the gold medal in '32, so many new doors had opened for him, but that one had been firmly shut.

Tryouts for the 1936 Winter Olympics had been held at Lake Placid back in February of 1935. Billy had had no desire to go back to Godfrey Dewey's little patch, and besides, he'd never been too interested in racing for tin-pot titles anyway. Hank Homburger had retired, and in Billy's absence, the trials had been won by a new crew led by, of all people, an undertaker from the Bronx named John Donna Fox; second place had gone to Hubert Stevens, and third to Frank Tyler, who was a policeman from Lake Placid. Dewey, in a way, had achieved his aim of making bobsledding a popular activity, insomuch as the track at Mount Van Hoevenberg was open to all, so there were now plenty of blue-collar crews, men who raced for weekend kicks when their work was done. You didn't need to be rich to be a bobsledder anymore. But Billy was still a two-time Olympic champion. The USOC knew what he could do. If they wanted him, they could just go ahead and pick him.

And they did. Jay O'Brien was still in charge of selection at the time. He'd named a fifteen-man squad that included fourteen who had raced in the trials at Lake Placid, plus Billy. But Jay had been stood down soon after, since he was too busy socializing in Palm Springs to make it over to Germany for the 1936 Games. He'd been replaced as head of the bobsled committee by Jack Garren, a Lake Placid local, and the only contact Garren had with Billy was a letter forwarded from Avery Brundage, the president of the USOC. In it, Fiske explained that he was planning to make his own way to Europe that winter, sailing from California for Germany via the Pacific. He'd signed off with "See you there." And that was the last they'd heard.

On the day before the US Olympic team sailed from New York, Clifford

Gray turned up at the Olympic Committee's bustling office on the twenty-seventh floor of the Woolworth Building. The committee had been trying to contact him for weeks now, to check on his availability, and they hadn't heard anything back. Now he had turned up out of the blue, and with a proposition. He had made his mind up the night before. He was willing to pay his own way to the Games, just so long as the USOC would add him to the official bobsled squad list.

It just so happened that at that precise moment, Clifford was caught up in an especially lurid scandal and had been in the papers far more than he cared for. He'd had a fling with an actress—at least, that was what she called herself—the previous November. Her name was Ruby Lockhart. He'd made some rash promises to her in the heat of the moment, and when he hadn't come through, she'd threatened to sue him. Her lawyers were demanding ten thousand dollars on her behalf. They called it a "heart balm." It seemed like a good time to go to Europe.

Garren was delighted. The bobsledders they'd selected, off the back of the trials at Lake Placid, were a raw lot. "And by the way," Tippy told them as he was on his way out, "Eddie says he'll be happy to come too, on the same terms, of course, so you should expect a call from him sometime soon."

Gray was right. Half an hour later, the phone rang. It was Eddie Eagan. He told Garren that he, too, would be traveling to the Winter Olympics in Garmisch-Partenkirchen, in the German Alps, so they should add him to the squad list as well.

Now that Eagan and Gray had turned up, Garren made plans to put the three of them in a sled together and to fill out the final seat with another squad member. Then they could race against Fox and Stevens to see who got to compete in the Olympics proper.

It turned out that the track at Garmisch-Partenkirchen, the site of the '36 Games, wasn't ready for use. If the bobsledders wanted to get any practice in before the Olympics, they would need to up sticks and move the 120 miles west across the Alps to St. Moritz. But, without Jay's money behind them, they couldn't even afford the train fare. The manager of the team had to send a telegram back to the USOC office in New York pleading for extra funds. He promised that the team "would travel third class and sleep in a barn" to keep costs down. The USOC agreed, so they all set off for Switzerland. And, well, guess who was waiting for them at the other end? "The mystery concerning Billy Fiske has been solved," reported the *Times* on January 18. "It was thought he was in California. Yesterday it was learned that Fiske was already in St. Moritz, ready for training, and would meet his American teammates there."

For Billy, St. Moritz had always felt like home. It had been almost a decade since he'd first seen the town, and the more things had changed in the years since, the more they seemed to stay just as they were. If anything had changed, it was him. He was older, of course, twenty-four now, and had seen more of the world than most of his age. But it was those two Olympic medals that marked him out, as well as the manner in which he handled all the success he'd had. "He was a gentleman," remembered Paul Dupree, another American bobber of that era, "what a fine man. He took all his glory in his stride. And he was very well respected by the Europeans, who were a tight little circle. He certainly had the respect of his fellow man, which was unique among bobsledders. They looked up to Billy as though he was an idol." Some of the officials, on the other hand, couldn't stand him. Especially Brundage, who ran the USOC much as the Dewey family had the Lake Placid Club. Brundage was irked by the offhand way in which Billy had skipped the trials and then refused to respond to his selection for the 1936 Games, and his attitude trickled down to the men on the ground, team managers Fred Rubien and Dr. Joel Henry Hildebrand. As soon as they arrived in St. Moritz, a row broke out.

Billy's position hadn't changed. If the USOC wanted him in the team, they should go ahead and pick him, but he had three conditions. The first two were that he wanted to drive the United States' No. 1 sled, and without being made to win his place in a trial. The third was that he wanted final say on the makeup of his team, as he'd had at Lake Placid, so he could be sure he would be riding with Eddie and Clifford. The officials quibbled. They insisted that Billy would have to win a series of qualifying races to get the No. 1 spot, and said that they couldn't promise him the right to pick his own team, since the other eight men in the squad deserved their shot—despite the fact that Billy had won the last two Olympic competitions and was the only pilot there who had ever driven on the snow-covered European tracks. So they cut him. They were mindful, just as Dewey had been, of "the impracticability of eliminating without trial the men who are identified in the public mind" with brilliant victories, so they made sure to make it look as though Billy was to blame. The Associated Press reported that Billy had "notified the officials that he would compete if appointed captain with full authority and if he could drive both the four and two-man teams. His offer was not accepted." Even the *New York Times* quoted Billy, secondhand, as saying, "I have two gold medals and several other championships. I've everything to gain and nothing to lose by staying out. So if I drive I'll be the driver of the No. 1 sled. I won't compete in the elimination trials. I'll also choose my own team. The rest of you will be at liberty to compete for bobsled No. 2. Take it or leave it."

Jim Bickford, a member of that Olympic team in 1936, remembered it all a little differently. "Billy was a quiet, calm type of fellow, liked by all the sportsmen. I never saw him be demanding or disruptive." Bickford couldn't imagine that Billy would ever say anything like the quotes attributed to him by the USOC. "There were," Bickford recalled, "a lot of politics that I didn't go along with, even though I was from Lake Placid and had grown up there. Things were all screwed up." As Bickford remembered it, Brundage and the USOC told Billy that he could be a reserve, but wouldn't be allowed to drive because he hadn't competed in the trials. "But Billy didn't want any part of that, he wanted to compete." For Billy, no doubt, all this was an unwelcome reminder of the nonsense he'd had to put up with before the Lake Placid Games. He decided he was happy enough without it. With Billy out, Eddie and Clifford also stepped down. Tippy stayed on in St. Moritz; Eddie never even left New York. The US team went ahead and competed without them. Neither of its two four-man teams managed to win a medal.

There was, and still is, another theory about why Billy decided not to compete in 1936. It was put about by Billy's old pal Irv Jaffee, who insisted, "Billy just didn't want to go to Germany. Way back in 1932 after the Lake Placid Games, Billy was talking to me about his hatred for Adolf Hitler. Almost every day he would tell me how important it was that he won at Lake Placid because it would be his last Olympics. He didn't want to compete in front of Hitler. When the USOC insisted that he enter the trials, Billy had a graceful way of saying "nothing doing." This is certainly possible. Jaffee is the only one of Billy's friends and family members who went on record with the story, though Virginia Cherrill recalled that "Billy often spoke about Hitler coming to power, and how there would be another European war" when the two of them were working on *White Heat* together. According to Peggy, her brother's antipathy toward Nazi Germany came about a little later in his life, in 1938, when the two of them went to watch England play soccer against Germany in Berlin. The match is infamous now, for the Nazi salute made by the English team before the kickoff, under orders from their ambassador, as a token of respect. Peggy remembered how "amazed and distressed" Billy had been by the "aggressive militarism of the young children, their uniforms, their marching, and their grim faces."

Jaffee, proudly Jewish, certainly decided early on that he wouldn't attend the Games. He was one of thousands who believed that the US should boycott the Nazi Olympics. The movement was led by Jeremiah Mahoney, former New York supreme justice and head of the Amateur Athletic Union. He had serious support, from the likes of New York mayor Fiorello La Guardia and the governors of both New York and Massachusetts. Newspapers and magazines, too, lined up behind him. Mahoney, an enlightened man, argued, "There is no room for discrimination on grounds of race, color, or creed in the Olympics." On his watch, the AAU had voted, back in 1933, to attend the 1936 Games only if Germany pledged that there would be no discrimination against Jewish athletes.

Avery Brundage, to his eternal discredit, had satisfied himself that there would be no anti-Semitic prejudice at the Olympics when he made a six-day tour of Germany in August 1934. He was chaperoned by two members of the Nazi Party for the duration of his stay. The Olympics, Brundage said, "must be kept free from outside interference or entanglements, racial, religious, or political." He even suggested that the Jewish lobby was trying to hijack the Olympic movement. "Certain Jews must understand that that they cannot use these Games as a weapon in their boycott against the Nazis." His line of argument seemed absurd and offensive at the time. Decades later, it appears downright disgusting. But the USOC stuck to it. Charles Hitchcock Sherrill, a US member of the IOC, even argued that a boycott would be harmful to the Jewish cause, since "we are almost certain to have a wave of anti-Semitism among those who never before gave it a thought and who may consider that 5,000,000 Jews in this country are using 120,000,000 Americans to pull their chestnuts out of the fire." Sherrill, incredibly, accused the Jews of "over-playing their cards" and declared their attitude was, in fact, the start "of the whole trouble in Germany."

Despite Brundage's best efforts to suggest otherwise, the boycott lobby included men and women from all walks. The *Commonweal*, the weekly Catholic newspaper, had come out in support of it. So had the *Christian Century*, a leading Protestant publication; the *Nation*, the flagship magazine of the left; and the *New York Amsterdam News*, the oldest African-American weekly in the United States. Assorted church groups, labor unions, and student bodies signed up to the campaign. But Brundage stood his ground, even after the Nuremberg Laws were passed, which the Nazis used to strip citizenship from Jews and "Gypsies, Negroes, or their bastard offspring" and to prohibit sexual relations between Aryans and non-Aryans. Still, though, the German government maintained the pretense that their Olympic team would be open to all. They even made a great song-and-dance about the fact that they had, at Sherrill's behest, already selected two Jewish athletes. Though, to be eligible, athletes needed to be members of registered sports clubs, and most of those clubs had rules that barred Jews from entry; at the same time, the Jews' own clubs had been disbanded on the grounds that they were all Zionist fronts. Brundage won the argument, regardless, and Mahoney resigned.

Was Billy Fiske among the ranks of the boycotters? Sadly, we can't simply take Jaffee at his word, though his explanation of Billy's behavior fits better than the one provided by the USOC, which insisted that he pulled out in a fit of pique. At the same time, while Billy was certainly firm friends with Jaffee, he was no great philo-Semite. In his travel journal, which he wrote when he was twenty, he unthinkingly used the Jewish race as the butt of some unsavory jokes—which was a young man's foolishness. What he did have, indisputably, was that keen sense of "courage and justice" that his father had installed in him as a child.

But then, Fiske Sr. had a complicated relationship with the Nazis himself. He was still living in Paris, and still working as the head of Dillon, Read & Co.'s European operation. The bank had parlayed the early returns on their German transactions in the 1920s into further investments in the country. Dillon Read was now doing more business in Germany than any other bank on Wall Street. That had, after all, been Clarence Dillon's plan from the outset. In 1926 they underwrote the creation of the United Steelworks, which soon became Germany's single-largest industrial corporation. They invested elsewhere, too, so much so that Dillon Read employee Ferdinand Eberstadt was able to boast of the firm's work in Germany, "We have the iron, steel, and coal industry, in the electrical industry we have Siemens, and in the banking industry we have Disconto and Deutsche Bank." After Hitler came to power, Dillon Read retained its investments in Siemens and in United Steelworks. Dillon loaned more than seventy million dollars to United Steelworks, and by 1938 that same firm was producing 95 percent of all German explosives.

Clarence Dillon, and Billy's father, worked especially closely with steel magnate Fritz Thyssen, who was not only a member of the Nazi Party but also provided it with a million reichsmarks in personal donations, as well as loans from his family bank. Thyssen welcomed the Nazi suppression of the Communist Party and of the trade unions. He acceded, too, to the demand that he fire all Jewish employees from his factories. There was no doubt that Clarence Dillon, famously well informed about every little detail of his operations, knew all this, and knew, too, that the steel being produced in those same factories was being used to build munitions. Dillon was a Polish Jew himself, remember, who had changed his name from Lapowski. Despite that, he thought the investment worth the return. As for Thyssen, he realized the errors he had made too late. He quit the Nazi Party early in 1939, after being shocked into action by Kristall-nacht, the horrific night in November 1938 when Jewish businesses, homes, and synagogues in Germany and Austria were attacked, leaving the streets littered with broken glass. "My conscience is clean," he told Hitler in a letter. "My sole mistake is to have believed in you, our leader, Adolf Hitler, and in the movement initiated by you—to have believed with the enthusiasm of a passionate lover of my native Germany."

After the war, Dillon, Read & Co. escaped punishment, but not censure. James Stewart Martin, chief of the Decartelization Branch set up after the war to investigate German industry, called out Dillon Read for the firm's role in it all. "Their loans for reconstruction," he wrote, referring back to the Dawes Plan, "became a vehicle for arrangements that did more to promote World War II than to establish peace after World War I." Dillon Read itself was "intimately related to the growth of Nazi industry," since Germany's military production "was from capacity built" by the bank's loans.

In St. Moritz in January 1936, it seemed Billy was a world away from such issues. One of the lines attributed to him, in the *New York Times*, was that "he wasn't interested in bobsledding just now." There was a measure of truth in that, at least. Billy had turned his attention, instead, to the other great sport of St. Moritz: the Cresta Run, a headfirst sled ride down one of the most famous stretches of ice on earth. Three-quarters of a mile, a drop of 514 feet, and a gradient, at its steepest point, of one in three.

The Cresta had grown up right alongside the St. Moritz bob run. Billy had first tried it as a boy back in 1928, when he had won the Novices Cup, run from the starting point at Junction, midway down the course. He turned to it in earnest in the winter of 1935, when he won three more trophies. In 1936, though, fueled by the anger he felt after his arguments with the USOC, he attacked the Cresta in a way that had never been seen before, and has seldom been seen since. He won five trophies in the space of just eleven days, including the most glorious of all, the Grand National. On January 30 he broke the record for the quickest time in the run's history, 56.9 seconds. The feat was all the sweeter because the old mark, of 58 seconds flat, had been set seven years earlier by his old friend Jack Heaton. No one had ever seen riding like it. "As a Cresta stylist," wrote historian

Michael Seth-Smith, "he was a joy to watch, taking the banks at the highest speed in perfect curves without the trace of a skid, without risking a fall." One of Billy's great rivals on the run in those days was the Swiss Christian Fischbacher. "Once Billy mastered the technique of riding his toboggan," Fischbacher said, "he became the unbeatable challenge for all his competitors. He seemed to enjoy a total sense of balance and body co-ordination, besides being an excellent all-round sportsman." Even today, Seth-Smith wrote, "it is impossible to discuss the Cresta without him."

Riding the Cresta, Billy worked alone. It was just him, the sled, the ice, and the clock. A solitary business. It suited him. For a driver that fast, a crew was almost a burden, even one as skilled as the team of Eddie, Tippy, and Jay. Each error they made slowed him down, forced him to check the sled to compensate. Racing alone on the Cresta, traveling face-first, inches above the ice, Billy achieved a kind of perfection. Astonishingly, he never once fell off—which meant he was ineligible for the Shuttlecock Club: the only qualification for membership was that you had to have crashed, just once, at the infamous low, raking left-hand bank. In the end they had to make Billy an honorary member. Even today, the best riders reckon on crashing at least once for every twelve times they make the Cresta Run. There are ten corners, and the best riders cover them in less than a minute. In Billy's mind, the race seemed to last so much longer than that. His mind had grown so attuned to speed that life seemed almost to slow down as he traveled the run. He had all the time he needed, and more, to steer his sled along that "perfect line" down the mountain. "Billy," one of his rivals once asked him, "how the hell do you manage to beat us all so easily?" Billy thought for a second. "I'll tell you what I think it is," he replied. "You all seem to be in such a hell of a hurry getting through the banks. I seem to have more leisure and more time than you."

By night, he was the same old Billy. It is said that after one nightlong tear, he even rode the run at dawn in his tuxedo. Sounds unlikely, until you learn that there was money at stake.

That winter, Billy was hung up on Paulette Poniatowski. Or, to give her her full name, Doña Paulette Amor, Princess Poniatowski. "One of Billy's rather more serious girlfriends," said his friend Neil Cleaver. The trouble was, the princess, who was Mexican, was married to a Polish prince, with whom she had three little children. Billy was so smitten that he insisted Cleaver drive him the 280 miles down and across the Italian border to Sestrieres to visit her. "I didn't want to," Cleaver said, "because we—the English—had put sanctions on Mussolini over the war in Abyssinia, and we were pretty unpopular in Italy just then. But as usual Billy talked me into it."

The fling didn't last long. At the end of the season, Billy traveled back to California. Soon after that he met T. J. Flynn and turned his attention to the Aspen project. By the summer, Paulette was another distant memory. Not because he was so engrossed with plans for the skiing resort. But because Billy had met someone else, someone new.

The papers called her the Countess of Warwick. To everyone who knew her, she was Rose. Billy had never met anyone with a name so apt, not even his old flame Doña Amor. She was startlingly beautiful. She was a brunette, and wore her hair short and pinned up in curls around her neck. Her face was broad, with sharp cheekbones and long slim eyebrows, which curved over her round brown eyes, alive with energy. Her lips seemed to be set with the hint of a wry smile, which suggested, somehow, that she was always laughing at a joke she hadn't shared with anyone else. She was a couple of years younger than Billy, born in 1913.

Rose's father had been a lieutenant in the Coldstream Guards. She never knew him: he died fighting at Aisne on the Western Front in September 1914. Her mother, Lady Rosabelle Brand, raised Rose alone, an only child, at a house in Beddingham in Sussex, an hour or so south of London, and not far from the coast. It was a traditional-enough upbringing. Rose was even presented at court as a debutante in 1931, when the press pronounced her "one of the most popular and most beautiful of the younger members of society." But she wasn't a traditional girl. She loved to smoke, through a dapper little cigarette holder, and liked to drink, and, as she grew older, could swear like a sailor when the mood took her. She was, in the language of her day, "a modern woman." But she made an old-fashioned match. In 1933, when she was still nineteen, she got engaged to Charles Greville, the Earl of Warwick. He was the most eligible bachelor about town, a handsome man who had ascended to one of the most prestigious peerages in the country when he was nineteen. He and Rose seemed a perfect fit. They were married in July 1933, in the East Sussex village of Glynde, in a church decorated for the day with masses of roses, yellow and white and pink and scarlet. Several hundred villagers, all dressed in their finest Sunday outfits, were there to cheer them along. They even had policemen to hold the crowds back.

It would be easy to say the marriage was an unhappy one. But life is seldom so simple. They had happy moments, certainly, and a child together, a boy, David, in 1934. But they certainly never settled into life together, for all that the papers tried to portray them as a pair of joyful childhood sweethearts. There were rumors, even in the year of their wedding, that the earl was also in love with an American actress, Sally Blane. Hollywood was certainly where he wanted to be. In the summer of 1936 he signed a five-year deal with MGM, for $300 a year, plus a paid-for valet and secretary. Irving Thalberg, the boy wonder in charge of production at the studio, was convinced they could launch him as a film star, playing, as he told the press, "romantic roles—dark complexioned, he-mannish, of a strictly English type." Warwick and Rose came over to Hollywood together, but by then it was already an open secret that their marriage had fallen apart. She was dating a man named Roger Bailey, and he, as the print scuttle-butts delighted in telling their readers, had been seen out and about with Greta Garbo. Who was, of course, also on the books at MGM.

It was David Niven who first introduced Rose to Billy. Niven was living with Errol Flynn at that time, in a bachelor pad on North Linden Drive, which Flynn's ex-wife had nicknamed "Cirrhosis-by-the-Sea." Billy and Paddy had moved to Santa Barbara. They had a nickname for their house too: the "Rat and Weasel mansion." Niven's parties were worth coming into town for. They knew Flynn as well. He was an old friend of Eddie's. In the late twenties. Flynn had entertained lunatic ideas about becoming a heavyweight boxer and had asked Eddie to teach him the ropes. "I cracked him with blows that would drop an ox," Flynn said. "But he wasn't an ox." He abandoned his fledgling career as a fighter soon after. Niven was still playing supporting roles, but he was very much the ringmaster of the "Hollywood Raj," which was what the yellow press called the British ex-pat scene. It was only natural that he should invite the earl and the countess over to get acquainted. "Rose, I'd like you to meet my old neighbor, Billy . . ."

Billy and Rose took a trip down to Baja California together, along with Douglas Fairbanks, Jr., and his wife. But Billy was just one in a queue of suitors, and after three years in a failed marriage, Rose was in no hurry to commit to any of them. But she liked life in the United States, and decided to stay on, even though she was apart from Warwick. She moved to New York and took a job as a secretary in a travel agency run by a man named Bill Taylor. "She took the calls, made travel arrangements, things like that," Taylor said. "She never said anything about her being a Countess. She wasn't that kind of girl. She enjoyed the work. She was happy." Rose, Taylor said, was "one of my favorites, one of the most delightful girls I ever knew. She was always in high humor, gay and happy.

And whenever things got dull, she livened them up." For those few months in 1937, Rose was, as Taylor put it, "free-lancing" her love life.

As for Billy, he was beginning to feel, for the first time in his young life, as though he was in a hole. His career "making B-movies," as Rose called it, had stalled. And while the Aspen project was a sound one, Roch's survey had made it clear there was a lot of work to be done, and a long wait to be endured, before the resort was earning them any kind of return on their outlay.

At the age of twenty-five he had decided, at last, to give in and become, as he put it when he was in Tahiti, one of "those poor old fools, who labored their lives away worrying about New York Central dropping two points." He took up a post at Dillon, Read & Co., which gave him a job as a bond salesman at the New York office. Ted Ryan, Billy's partner out in Aspen, remembered how much the decision pained his pal. "The one thing Billy had a love for was mountains, and outdoor sport. I think, in fact, he was rather sad when the exigencies of life pulled him back and set him to work with Dillon Read in New York. He loathed Wall Street." Rose, typically, was altogether more to the point: "He hated it."

The one upside to it all was that he got to be near her. Billy wasn't all that interested in business, and he certainly didn't care to set the details down. The important thing for him, that year, was that he and Rose grew closer and closer as it slipped by while he, for the first time in his life, was working a nine-to-five job. The earl had filed for divorce, citing Rose's infidelity with Roger Bailey in 1936. Rose was waiting for the decree nisi to come through. That winter, she and Billy both traveled back to Europe to spend Christmas with their families. They agreed to meet in St. Moritz in the New Year. And it was there, away from New York, on the slopes, that they fell for each other.

Billy's sister, Peggy, once asked him exactly what it was that he liked about Rose. He thought for a while, then replied, "She always has the right answers." And that, for him, was it. Of course she was beautiful, and witty, and great fun. But Billy had known plenty of women who had been all those things. Rose, though, seemed so wise. Billy, who had spent years wandering from one thing to the next, always wondering what to do, had found an anchor. He was happy to stop and settle. As for Rose, she couldn't but be charmed by him. "He was one of the most popular people I ever met," she wrote. "To the extent of almost giving me an inferiority complex. No matter what country, with whom, or what, everyone loved him, and admired him."

Billy even took her for a ride in his bobsled. That winter of 1937–38 he won a series of startling contests on the Cresta, racing against Fischbacher and an Australian, Freddie McEvoy, nicknamed "Suicide" Freddie because of the obscene risks he took. Freddie was too foolish for the Cresta. As another rider, Owen Francis, said, "The Cresta is no good for youngsters who behave like fearless Fred. You have got to be frightened before you understand the thing at all. You have got to damn well convince yourself that you have to take risks. You have got to be prepared to have a go." By now, Billy was well acquainted with the risks, and he knew how to master his fear. When Fischbacher broke Billy's Cresta record, the mark stood for all of an hour before Billy took it back again. His new time, 56.7 seconds, stood for almost twenty years. His fellow riders were so enthralled by his performance that they hoisted him into the air and carried him back to the Palace on their shoulders. The celebrations lasted until dawn.

That winter, Billy and Rose fell in with a group of Englishmen, all skiers and all old friends of his pal Paddy Green. There was Neil "Mouse" Cleaver, his old friend from the playboy days—he and Billy had once taken a golfing tour across France, during which they'd stayed only in brothels; Willie Rhodes-Moorhouse, absurdly rich, even by their standards, whose father had won the first Victoria Cross ever awarded for gallantry in the air back in World War One; Roger Bushell, a barrister, flamboyant, dashing and acutely intelligent, fluent in four languages and able to swear in many more; Billy Clyde; and Max Aitken, the eldest son of Lord Beaverbrook, the first baron of Fleet Street, who held a string of records flying transport planes owned by his father. They all knew "Rosie," as they called her, from London. "She was very down-to-earth," said Clyde. "A woman who knew what was what, forthright and worldly."

Rose thought that Billy was especially drawn toward the Englishmen because he was still sore with the way he'd been treated in 1932 and 1936 by the United States Olympic Committee. "He did not like America very much," she wrote. "He had a brush with his compatriots in the 1932 Olympics and found them not only unsporting but underhand and cheats." He found the English to be easy company. They were all in their twenties, and had a lot in common. "Like him," wrote Rose's friend Patsy Ward, "they all loved any form of sport in which speed was a ruling factor." Rhodes-Moorhouse was a superb downhill skier; so was Bushell. Billy Clyde was perhaps the best of the bunch, a regular on the British ski team. But their first love was flying. Rhodes-Moorhouse had his pilot's license by the time he was seventeen, and all four of them were members of the RAF's 601 Auxiliary Reserve, based at Northolt, just outside London.

In those days, 601 was a social club as much as a flying squadron. It had been founded in 1925 by Lord Edward Grosvenor, youngest son of the Duke of Westminster. They were known as the Millionaires' Mob. Grosvenor, so the story goes, drew his first recruits exclusively from the membership of White's, the oldest and most prestigious of the many gentlemen's clubs in St. James's. According to 601's official history, written by Tom Moulson, "Recruitment under Grosvenor involved a trial by alcohol to see if candidates could still behave like gentlemen when drunk. They were apparently required to consume a large port, and gin and tonics would follow back at the club." And while the squadron's membership criteria may have loosened a little over the following decade, it still adhered to Grosvenor's ideal that the pilots should be "of sufficient presence not to be overawed by him and of sufficient means not to be excluded from his favorite pastimes, eating, drinking and White's." They were the only squadron in the RAF that divided its flights into light and dark blue, according to whether the pilots had gone to Oxford or Cambridge.

When it came to flying, Billy was just a novice. He'd had a few lessons with Paddy Green when they were living in LA, but no more than that. But he would sit up with them all the same, talking, as Ward wrote, "of airplanes and aerial warfare." He was so taken with it all that he decided to sign up for more flying lessons as soon as he could.

As fun as it all was, the atmosphere in St. Moritz wasn't as carefree as it had once been. Nazism cast shadows, even in the neutral territory of the Engadine. Billy's friends and rivals, his fellow members of the Suicide Club of '32, were already being pulled in opposing directions. There were rumors that the Swiss rider René Fonjallaz was now working as an agent for the Gestapo. Georg Gyssling, one of the scratch German crew from 1932, had spent the past six years working as the Nazi's foreign consul in Los Angeles, lobbying the Hollywood studios to keep anti-Nazi sentiments out of their movies. And then there was Werner Zahn, still on the scene, and as arrogant as ever. Zahn's manufacturing company, the same firm that had built his sled Fram III, was now making helmets for the military. Hubert Martineau, still at the SMBC, remembered how Zahn had told him, in 1939, "Hubert, I want you to promise me one thing. When you leave here, pack up all your goods and chattels and take them to America. We made a mistake in the first war, but we shan't repeat it this time. So promise to do what I tell you." Martineau didn't take his advice.

In 1938, Zahn issued a challenge to the British members of the SMBC on behalf of the Luftwaffe. "We received a devious suggestion that we should, or rather 'must,' persuade the British team to compete against them in uniform," wrote Martineau. "The boys in gray-blue were convinced of their own invincibility in every sphere at that time, and considered a few pictures of them beating the RAF on the ground would make excellent propaganda at home and in neutral countries." Switzerland, however, had strict rules forbidding anyone from wearing foreign uniforms, "so their little scheme was punctured from the start."

In March that year came the Anschluss, the German annexation of Austria. By then, Billy and Rose had quit St. Moritz. Dillon Read had posted him to London for the year, and she stayed over too. The decree nisi on her divorce had come through. The earl kept custody of their boy, David, but she was officially single again. Billy, Rose wrote, "was never happier" than he was in London that summer. "And nor was I." The two of them had "quiet dinners together," and days out in the country around the upper reaches of the Thames in Oxfordshire, where he had once gone to school. Patsy Ward noted, "They attended all the gala parties together." And they met each other's families. Rose's mother took to Billy from the first. "One always felt with him a perfect sense of security and trust," she wrote. "Bill was everything in the world to Rose, and their life was so happy."

Good as his word, Billy started taking flying lessons at an airfield outside London. "I remember the big day when he was finally allowed to take me up in a two-seater," Rose wrote. She thought they were going for a flip around the airfield, but Billy had grander plans. He decided they should pop across the Channel and spend the weekend at Le Touquet. But things didn't go as planned. The plane sprang a leak, and oil splattered all across the windshield. "So visibility was non-existent," Rose wrote, "and so was the navigation." Twenty minutes passed. Then forty. Then sixty. And they were still circling around the Channel. "I must have bogged it," Billy shouted back over the engine. "We may have to come down in the sea, but don't worry, we're sure to float all right so just get ready to climb out on the wing." Rose was just trying to decide what to do with her handbag when she heard Billy whoop with joy. Land, at last. They were actually at Deauville, 150 miles to the south of the spot they'd been heading for. No matter. They spent a happy weekend there anyway.

"Wonderful," Rose said, "how foolhardy one was at that age!"

The decree absolute for Rose's divorce was announced on August 24. A fortnight later, she and Billy were married at the register office in Maidenhead, Berkshire. The ceremony was quiet and simple. No pomp, no cameras or press, no guests even. And when it was done, Billy went right back to work at the bank.

They took a short honeymoon, a week in France. Then, at the end of the month, the newlyweds prepared to sail to New York. Dillon, Read & Co. had decided that it needed Billy back in the United States. He had one last thing to do in England before he left: he put in an application to join the RAF as a volunteer. They turned him down, because they weren't accepting foreign citizens into the ranks. Roger, Willie, Max, and the rest of the 601 crew had a laugh about it at his expense. Ever since St. Moritz, Billy had been telling them he wanted to join up, even though he was a Yank. "If and when it breaks, I want to be in it with you—from the start," Billy said, over and again. "It had just become an ongoing joke between the lot of us," remembered Billy Clyde. "None of us took him seriously."

Billy Fiske in uniform, London, 1940.

CHAPTER 13

THE WAR BEGINS

Billy Fiske's Journal, Page One.

October 29, 1939

This is not meant to be a diary, less a book. It's simply an attempt to record in chronological order, if possible, some of the experiences and events brought about in my life as a result of Mr. Hitler's indiscretions. They are probably not very different from the things that are happening to hundreds of thousands of other individuals. There's really only one reason other than my own amusement why they may be worth recording, and that is the fact that I believe I can lay claim to being the first US citizen to join the RAF in England after the outbreak of hostilities. I don't say this with any particular pride, except that insofar as my conscience is clear, but only it probably has some bearing on the course of my career . . .

Now that I've started I might as well go right back and begin at the beginning, which was in the city of New York on the day of August 30, 1939, the Wednesday before war was declared. And a hectic day it was, too . . .

To begin at the beginning, we actually need to move back another couple of days. In the early morning of Monday, August 28, Billy blinked, rolled over on his side, and flicked on the light by his bedside. He took a quick look at the clock. Two a.m.? Who the hell was calling at that hour? Whoever it was, the phone had been ringing for so long that they must be drunk, or desperate. He resigned himself, at last, to the fact that he was going to have to get up and answer it.

"Hello?"

"Billy? It's Roger, Roger Bushell. Sorry if I woke you. Listen, is Little Bill there? It's urgent."

Little Bill was their nickname for Billy Clyde, who was, at that precise moment, sound asleep in the guest bedroom. Billy could hear him snoring from out in the hall. That man, he thought, could sleep through anything. "One minute, Roger," he said. And then he crept into Clyde's room and gave him a gleeful poke in the ribs.

Clyde's eyes shot open.

"Phone for you. It's Roger."

Billy slunk back into his bed. But he didn't go back to sleep. Instead he lay up, listening in to the muted conversation going on in the hall.

"I see," he heard Clyde say. "I see. Yes. All right. I'll come. Tell them I'll be back on the next boat."

He heard Clyde put the receiver down. There was a pause. And then a knock at the door.

"Billy?" Clyde said. "Roger says things are cranking up. He says they're going to mobilize the squadron. If I get back now, they'll save a spot for me. Otherwise I'll be back in the pilots' pool." If that happened, then it was likely Clyde would end up being assigned to another squadron, rather than 601, where all his friends were. "I suppose I had better call the girls and let them know."

"No, Bill," Billy replied. "It's late, best wait till the morning." Besides, he had some thinking to do.

When Billy came into the kitchen in the morning, Clyde was already up. The *New York Times* was on the table in front of him. Billy could read the headlines from where he stood in the doorway: "Hitler Tells Paris He Must Get Berlin and Corridor"; "Berlin Thinks Door Is Left Open to Peaceful Solution"; "British Answer Today to Insist on Rights of Poland." Over breakfast, Billy broke his news: he had decided to come back to England with Clyde, to join the RAF. By then, Little Bill knew better than to try to talk his friend out of it. He was too busy to spare the time, anyway. He needed to get a ticket on the next boat from New York to England. That was the *Aquitania*, which was due to sail in a little over forty-eight hours—little enough time to pack and wrap up his business at the firm.

Over the past eight months or so, the two of them had become close friends.

Clyde was working for Johnson & Johnson in Princeton. Billy, of course, was with Dillon, Read & Co., at its offices down on Nassau Street in Manhattan. Just as they were both called Bill, their wives were both Rose. The four of them had hired a house on Rhode Island for the summer, by the harbor at Watch Hill. The two women would stay there together during the week while their husbands went to work; the men would come up to join them on weekends. On the occasions when Clyde's work brought him into New York, he'd stay with Billy at the little flat he kept downtown, which was where he was that night. It had taken Bushell, who was over in London, some time to track Clyde down.

They'd had a lot of fun, the four of them. Billy had introduced them to his old pals Eddie, Tippy, and Jay, who came up from his mansion in Palm Springs—which he'd christened "the Garden of Eden"—just to meet Rose. They'd all gone to see the new singer Carmen Miranda perform at the Waldorf-Astoria. But hanging in the background, always, was the threat of war. And while everyone else discussed it as though it were a distant thing, for Clyde the conversations were always overshadowed by the knowledge that he might have to return to England to take up his place with his squadron.

Once Billy had spoken to Rose, the next thing he did was call his lawyer out in LA. There were a lot of loose ends to tie up, like the investments he was in the middle of, with the Lockheed Aircraft Corporation, and the Aspen business, and the film company, which, though he hardly ever had anything to do with it these days, was now producing newsreels and educational shorts. Bad news. The lawyer just didn't see how Billy could leave New York now. It would take three months, at least, to get his affairs in order. "Billy," Clyde said, "was so downhearted about it." But Clyde didn't have time to dwell on his friend's feelings. He had to get over to Princeton to clear out his desk.

The two Roses came down from Watch Hill later that evening. Clyde's wife would be staying on in the United States for a while and would join him in the UK when she could. She and Billy began to plan a farewell party. The *Aquitania* was due to sail at noon on Wednesday, so they decided it had better be an early luncheon that day. Real early. They started it just after midnight. By the following morning they were holed up in the 21 Club. It had only just opened for the day, and they were pretty much the only people in there other than the staff, who were all preparing for the lunch rush. At 11 a.m., Clyde cut out for the harbor. The *Aquitania* was moored at West 50th Street, six blocks over. He hated long goodbyes, so he left the three of them at the club and caught a taxi to the pier.

At the waterfront, everything was in chaos. Only the previous day, President Roosevelt had declared that the federal authorities would be searching all foreign ships in American harbors, under the 1925 Neutrality Act, to check whether they were carrying weapons or other war materials. The German liner *Bremen* had been stuck in New York for two days while customs officials conducted their search. Her crew spent their time running lifeboat drills in the harbor, in case they were bombed or torpedoed when they finally got to sea. Like all the other ships, each and every one of her windows and portholes had been blacked out so she'd be harder to spot.

Clyde had been on board the *Aquitania* for thirty minutes when the captain's voice came over the ship's address system. He explained that the sailing of the French liner *Normandie*, also due out that day, had been canceled because she was carrying so few passengers. Those who had tickets to sail with the *Normandie* were going to be transferred to the *Aquitania* instead. The *Aquitania*'s departure had therefore been put back; she would now be leaving at 7:30 that evening. Faced with an eight-hour wait at the docks, Clyde decided there must be better things to do with his final few hours in New York. So he walked back to 21, hoping the others would still be there. And they were. He walked up to the table and announced, in his cheeriest voice, "It's all over, I've won the war single-handed. Now, who'd like a drink to celebrate?"

"I sat down to tell them the real story," Clyde remembered. "And Billy got a very serious look on his face." Something in him had snapped in the short time since Clyde had left 21. Watching his friend go off to war, alone, without him, was more than he could take. "And he suddenly said, 'That's it, I'm going.'" Billy got up and walked away from the table. He had seven hours to get ready. He sent a telegram to a friend in Washington to double-check on whether his British visa was still valid, called his lawyer to give him instructions for tying up all those loose ends, then went to the head office of Dillon Read and handed in his notice. He decided to hold off from telling his family what he was up to. That, he thought, could wait. That night, he and Clyde boarded the *Aquitania* together. This time, both their wives came down to wave them off, neither sure when or if they would see their husbands again.

The *Aquitania* was at sea for eight days. The voyage took a little longer than usual because the ship, completely blacked out through the night, took a zigzag course, an evasive action designed to confound any lurking German U-boats. On the fifth day of the voyage, three days out from Southampton, war was declared.

———

Why did he do it? What made a man "blessed with all this world's goods" give it all up to volunteer to fight someone else's war? Billy's English friends didn't have either the time or the inclination to worry about it. "As regards Billy's reasons for coming over, what his inner personal feelings were I cannot know," wrote Mouse Cleaver many years later, "only surmise. He was a close friend of several of us, largely via the snow, [and] his wife was English. I might venture that he had become not so much English as more European. Maybe, maybe not. He was certainly not a rich kid looking for adventure. He knew exactly what he was doing, and the possible consequences."

Plenty have tried to reason why. Among them, the writers, historians, and journalists who have touched on Billy's life have come up with a range of answers, the most common of which was the one provided by Michael Seth-Smith, who put the decision down to the fact that "Billy disliked the influence of Nazism intensely." Billy stopped short of providing an explanation in his diary. "My reasons for joining in the fray are my own," he wrote, "and have no place here. Undoubtedly a great many people think I'm the original bloody fool, but again the object of this journal is not to discuss the pros and cons of a fait accompli." So no one has ever had the definitive answer.

Until now. On September 10, only days after he had arrived in London, Billy wrote a letter to his sister. Rose understood Billy's decision to volunteer. She had been prepared for it. His parents were startled by it, when he finally told them, but they soon came to accept it. But Peggy, who was living in San Mateo, California, safe with her family on the far side of the world, thought he was nuts.

> *Naturally, my coming over has been a shock to the family although I have tried to warn them I would do just that in case of war for the last two years. I want you to understand my reasons as you're the only sister I've got and I think we've always been closer than the average brother and sister. As you know, I've spent most of the formative years of my life here at school, Cambridge, etc, and most recently working here. I have far more friends here than in America. I have an English wife of whom I'm extremely fond, and altogether my roots are almost stronger here than any place I know. They've been damn good to me in good times so naturally I feel I ought to try and help out in bad if I can. There are absolutely no heroics in my motives, I'm probably twice as scared as the next man, but if anything happens to me I at least can feel I have done the right thing in*

*spite of the worry to my family—which I certainly couldn't feel if I was to
sit in New York making dough.*

Flash back through the years. "The two great characteristics to develop in
any child are *courage* and *justice*," Billy once wrote. "Broadly speaking, with
these well-developed a person can face the world and be successful." He came to
fight because his conscience told him that he should stand firm with his friends,
with his new family, for his adopted country. He had no better reason than that.
He didn't need one.

But before Billy could serve, he had to be accepted. At this point, the RAF's
Eagle Squadrons of American volunteers hadn't even been conceived, let alone
organized. The idea for them was still being thrashed out, in fact, by Billy's two
old friends the Sweeny brothers, Bobby and Charles, who had taken those run-
abouts around Nice, Cannes, and Monte Carlo with him in his Bentley back in
1930. Charles Sweeny soon set up a Home Guard unit for Americans who were
"deep-rooted in England." He wrote to his father and had him send over fifty
tommy guns for the unit to use. A little later, when he got permission to start
recruiting American volunteers for a fighter squadron, he sounded Billy out
about whether he would be interested in taking charge of it—a job that eventually went to Bill Taylor, Rose's boss from the travel agency in New York. As
Clyde remembered, "Billy insisted from the beginning that he would be posted
to 601 or else he wouldn't join the RAF."

If, that was, the RAF even wanted him. As soon as they had docked at
Southampton, Clyde had gone off to join up with 601. Billy had headed to London, to his club at Dover Street, where he discovered that only British citizens or
sons of British citizens were eligible to join the Air Force. They were actively
recruiting from around the empire, but it was felt, then, that taking in volunteers
from neutral countries, especially the United States, could be troublesome polit-
ically. The US ambassador, Joseph Kennedy, was actively discouraging Americans from getting involved. "As you love America," Kennedy had said, "don't let
anything that comes out of any country in the world make you believe you can
make a situation one whit better by getting into the war. There is no place in this
fight for us." But then Billy never could stand American politicians. He decided
"to pull every string" he could to get in.

The first thing he did was arrange to have dinner with Ben Bathurst, a
friend of his at the St. Moritz Tobogganing Club, which controlled the Cresta
Run. They met at the Savoy on Thursday evening, September 7. Bathurst was a

barrister, like Bushell, but he was a little older than the rest of Billy's St. Moritz crowd, and a little more influential too. His father was Viscount Bledisloe, who had been the governor-general of New Zealand. Ben had been an artillery officer in the First World War, and he was already in service again, as a squadron leader in the RAF. He promised to set up an interview between Billy and William Elliott, who was assistant secretary of the War Cabinet Secretariat, and Chief of Air Staff Cyril Newell. It was all fixed for that coming Sunday. The trouble was, the only paperwork Billy had with him was his passport, which was no good, since it showed he was a US citizen. So he and Bathurst concocted a story together. "I would have to make a very passable pretense at being Canadian and of Canadian parentage," Billy wrote. "I had to make up some very watertight answers for any questions they might be expected to ask me."

Billy spent most of Friday trying to think up his alibi. "I remember going out to Roehampton to play a little golf to try and get a healthy look on my face to survive the ordeal," he wrote. "Needless to say, for once I had a quiet Saturday night—I didn't want to have eyes looking like bloodshot oysters the next day." Looking back, he added, "It might appear that I rather over-emphasized the importance of me being accepted. Perhaps I did a bit. It was largely a matter of pride and the terrific desire to be doing something." He was desperately worried that he would be sent back to the US, humiliated. "I had walked out of my very good job on two hours' notice. So far as my family were concerned, I had disappeared completely."

In the end, the meeting passed easily enough. The main thing the officials seemed to want to know was whether it was true that Billy's former employer, Clarence Dillon, had really once signed a check for $150 million to buy General Motors. "Yes," Billy told them, "he did." They just couldn't quite seem to get their heads around the sum. He was accepted into the RAF that same day, on the lie that—as it says on his service record—he was born in Montreal. That evening he went to the Bath Club to celebrate. But first he sat down and penned that letter to Peggy, explaining what he had done and why he had done it. His feelings were so fervent that he even offered to help Peggy and Jennison volunteer too. "Please let me hear from you sometimes," he wrote. "Let me know if Jen wants to come over as I can fix it all right if he does. As I was the first volunteer American accepted I had to go and see the Chief of Air Staff who runs the whole show, so I know the ropes. Rose is forming an ambulance corps of 40 drivers and 20 ambulances so if you want something to do and could leave the house with the family, there is your chance."

The first step was basic training. It wasn't quite the glamorous life Billy had imagined when he was talking to the 601 lot back in St. Moritz. He was sent up to camp at Cambridge for six weeks. "I must admit that I never thought eight years ago I should be returning to Cambridge, going to lectures, and being told to be in by 10pm. Although I will admit the curriculum is a bit different," he wrote. He told Peggy, "I'm learning how to kill them instead of how to take their money—I don't know if there is much choice except one's slow and the other's quick." It was all drill and discipline, then ground training: "navigation, photography, gunnery, wireless, etc." He had been put in a flight along with "a lot of crazy continentals, from places as far afield as St. Helena, New Zealand, Africa, Ceylon, Seychelles Islands, Papua, and Canada. It was, he readily admitted, a tedious life. "We live on straw, high tea at 5.30pm, up at 6 in the morning. And it's bloody cold. But needless to say we've never been healthier." He hated the drills, the marching, and learning how to form fours. "I'd just got it right, when they go and decide that from now on we must only form threes." They had only been there a fortnight when they had their first deserter. "They brought him back today and he went straight off to the loony bin. Maybe he wasn't so crazy!"

Rose arrived in London in the middle of October. As Billy said, she had vague notions about starting a volunteer ambulance corps. But she soon found that the idea was wildly impracticable, because there were so many bureaucratic hoops to jump through. On top of which, of course, she hadn't the slightest shred of relevant experience. "To be an ambulance driver," she noted pithily, "is very much like putting one's son down for Eton, you have to do it the day he is born." And besides, only "a few wounded soldiers have come back, but most of those who have returned had some other illnesses, such as dysentery, skeptic [*sic*] wounds—nothing to do with actual fighting." All the other volunteer corps were, "as far as I can see, literally just sitting on their fannies doing nought." Worse still, those friends of hers who had signed up as volunteers had been promptly posted to the other end of England from wherever it was their husbands were stationed. "Another typically British habit. Not for me."

By now, Billy had been moved on to elementary flying training school at Yatesbury in Wiltshire. They were let up, at last, in Tiger Moths. He got leave each weekend and would always race up to see Rose at Claridge's, where she was staying.

Billy always had a couple of his new comrades in tow. They were, Rose said, "all 18 year olds from Australia, Canada and South Africa. Such babies. They all looked up to Billy, told him all their troubles, everything from their debts to their blind dates." Her plan, as explained in a letter, was this: "I am organizing my own Corps, called 'The SLOTTS'—"Sex Life of the Troops!" Actually, I am trying to arrange amusement and places to stay for poor unfortunate Colonials, who are training and are dependent on their pay, and do not know one solitary soul in England, and just sit at various training camps twiddling their thumbs—thumbs, I said. I shall most probably end up being 'the Madame' for the troops." She was as good as her word: she launched a volunteer corps with the rather more sober, and suitable, name the Western Counties RAF Hospitality League. *Tatler* even ran a feature on them. "As I say," Rose wrote, "a man can't do his best unless he's happy!"

Which Billy was, roving around the south of England in his Tiger Moth, practicing his barrel rolls and Immelmann turns, learning, in short, the difference between flying for fun and flying to fight. These were strange days in Britain, as her citizens endured the phony war, wondering when the fighting would start in earnest, and how long it would last when it did. In the autumn of 1939, Billy's biggest worry was that the war might be over before he'd even had a chance to get into the action. "It is quite plausible," he wrote, "that it will all be over before I am fit for anything. There seem to be very diversified opinions here although I think everyone feels it will either all be over by Xmas or go on for five years or so." Much as he would have liked to hold forth his own opinions, he couldn't, by letter at least, since "the censors and the head beak would have me in irons." He felt able only to hint that, as far as he could see, it all depended on the Russians. "Since their entry, I think mostly the 'longs' have it by a pretty safe margin, although many people qualify that by saying it will go on as long as the Russians want it to."

In the weeks while Billy was away, Rose whiled away the days in London. She and Billy had spent $10 on a car, "a 1930 Austen [*sic*] which looks very much like an antiquated London taxi," which they'd nicknamed Annie, so she could get down to see her mother in Glynde, back near the church where she had married Warwick all those years before. Otherwise, Rose was camped out at Claridge's. She wrote one long letter and had it copied out so she could send it on to her group of friends. It provides a fine portrait of life in the capital at the time.

Life goes on pretty much the same, except everyone is in the country.
And London looks awfully bare—so many of the houses are hermetically
sealed and boarded up. All the restaurants and night clubs are wide open

and packed jammed every night—women no longer have to dress, men of course nearly all in uniform. Every now and again one sees a man in a tail coat, and he looks positively incongruous! Bill has not got his uniform yet, but is about to be measured for one any minute—big excitement. The "black-outs" really are fantastic. Unless it's a pretty clear night, you literally cannot see your hand in front of your face.

Bond Street consists chiefly of sandbags on both pavements, so that walking there three abreast is out of the question, because one is perpetually catching a toe or heel on the corner of a sandbag, and I don't mind telling you, that a sandbag is as hard if not harder than a piece of concrete. All the shop windows have paper tape stuck all over them to avoid splintering etc. Some very chichi ones have their names written in the tape, or a picture of the type of things they sell inside!

I shall never know how taxi drivers know where the hell they are going, as honestly, if they used a torch they could see much more than with the regulation lights they have now, and of course one can never tell if it's a free cab or not, so that if one is trying to get one not off a rank, one is liable to become quite hoarse and worn out screaming at those already with fares.

Even in the country, one is only permitted to use either side-lights, or else a black metal contraption on the head lamp, with a hole a quarter of the size in the middle, and that pitiful ray of light is all one is allowed—so somehow I feel I won't be tearing around at night very frequently.

Down at my mother's house, in the depth of the country, where I stay during the week, all the curtains have been heavily interlined with black material, and not a crack of light is supposed to show from anywhere. We are not even allowed to put the light over the front door on, which, heaven knows, is no arc light, when anyone arrives. Bloody silly, I think . . .

The news we get is pretty sparse, but at least it's official and on the level. As far as the war in the air is concerned, I think we are doing pretty bloody well. The Germans, over the radio, are trying to make us believe it was the British who tried to blow Hitler up—whoever did try was a man of iron. About six times a day the Germans broadcast, one of the announcers is supposed to be a man called Baillie-Stewart, who went to jail here about three or four years ago for selling secret documents to the Germans, and apparently when he was released a few months ago, stamped out of prison, saying he would never see this country again, and

if there was any way he could do us down he would, and rushed back to
Germany: another announcer is known as "Lord Ha Ha," because he has
such a pompous voice. They are all English. They have such a ridiculous
way of putting over their propaganda, that even an infant in arms could
do nothing but rock with laughter. Every time any of our statesmen make
a speech, especially Winston Churchill, whom they loathe, the next day
that poor unfortunate individual really takes a beating. He's a liar, war
mongrel, and decadent illiterate. They don't care what they say, and if
they have nothing to pick on, they tell us what we all refer to as a bedtime
story, rather like an Aesop fable, with Chamberlain or someone as the fox
and piece of cheese, or one like it. It's too fantastic, I wouldn't miss
listening in for anything. It has almost made up for not having Charlie
McCarthy and Jack Benny.

Even our announcers on the BBC, who as you know are very prim
and circumspect, are making "digs" at them every so often. The
impatience of waiting for a German talk, after one of our men has been
speaking is terrific!

Gosh how I miss the central heating. I am permanently freezing cold,
and I have had to take to my woolen underwear! Horrors.

I don't think I can think of anything else. I know you would love to
hear something really worthwhile, but a) I don't know any and b) my
masterpiece of a letter would be thrown away by the censors. So you will
have to take what I can give.

We are both very well & Bill sends all love, so do I,
    Rose.

The novelty of it all—the blackout and the sandbags and the radio
broadcasts—wore off as winter wore on. The days dragged into weeks, then into
months. Christmas came and went. Soon those who had reckoned it would all
be over by the New Year lost their bets. The only thing Billy was fighting was
boredom. The winter was one of the coldest and most unpleasant he had ever
known. "Freak weather," he wrote, "I've never seen anything like it before." The
first week of February was all rain, but it was so cold the water froze before it
could run away. "Every single thing was covered by 2 to 3 inches of ice. That was
true down to each single blade of grass, wire fences, telephone wires, and of
course, all buildings. It was as though someone had wrapped everything in a
thick coat of cellophane." On the weekend of January 27–28 he had been up in

London as usual, with Rose, but it had taken him twelve hours to get back to Yatesbury, by road and rail. "And when I got back I found all the pipes had burst, no food was getting through, and practically no heat as coal couldn't get through on the roads." The weather was so bad that the pilots had been grounded. There was nothing to do other than indulge in that most English of pastimes, talking about the weather. "It's been the only and predominant factor in our lives since I last wrote to you," Billy told his parents.

What fighting there was seemed so remote, so far removed from his life. The first German bomber had been shot down by British forces, at Whitby, a few hundred miles away on the northeast coast. Billy was heartened by that. "They will soon begin to realize the nice hot reception waiting for them if they persist in poking their noses in unwelcome places!" And from the far side of Europe, where Russia had recently signed a nonaggression pact with the Nazis and then promptly invaded its neighbor Finland, came more news that made him feel optimistic: the Finns were finding the so-called winter war against the Russians to be "some of the finest shooting in the world, rather like a nice low-flying pheasant." "As for our own little war, it seems to be taking much clearer shape now and I still think it's going to be over well before the end of this year."

When he wasn't training, Billy spent his time reading, writing, and worrying. His parents were thinking about moving south, away from Paris to their house in Biarritz. He thought they'd be "safe as houses" down there. He even wanted Rose to move in with them, from London. "Although she'd be the last to admit it, I know she is feeling pretty run down and has very little resistance against colds, sore throats, etc," he wrote to his mother, and it would be "terribly sweet of you to offer to have her, and I wish you'd press the point again direct to her, as she really needs it."

It seems ludicrous, with hindsight, that Billy imagined his wife would be safer in the south of France than in England. But his mother's letters did make it sound idyllic. "The trees are coming out," she wrote. "The fruits are rampant, woods covered with violets, buttercups and wild daisy, and the birds singing their hearts out." Billy had even heard that Jack Heaton was knocking about that part of the world. Which made him envious. "Some day I'm going to retire to a little Basque farmhouse myself." It was only in early April 1940, when the Germans invaded Norway, that Billy, and his parents, began to feel uncertain about how safe the south of France was. Billy's mother was increasingly convinced that the United States would have to join the fighting. She had now made her peace with Billy's decision and wrote to Peggy, encouraging her to do the same. "The invasion makes me boil," she wrote. "And if you are not beginning to understand your brother now, you never will. My idea is that after the election of Mr. Roosevelt, possibly next spring, America will have to come in. Yes, it's a great pity. But it's going to take a lot to beat these b___s."

Rose, anyway, was having none of it. She wouldn't move until she knew exactly where Billy was going to be posted. Finally, at the end of March, he had finished at Yatesbury and was sent on to Brize Norton, in Oxfordshire, for advanced training. They rented what Rose described as "a darned nice furnished house, perched on a hill above the most adorable little village of Minster Lovell." It was so close to his camp that he was allowed to live off the base. The house wasn't far from where he had gone to school in Sutton Courtenay. It made him feel as though he had come full circle. "I go over to Sutton Courtenay quite often," he wrote. "It's about 13 miles away, and still looks much the same as it did 13 years ago. Christ that's a long time."

They weren't there long, only a couple of months, but it was a happy time, the last they had together. Bleak as the winter had been, it was a warm spring. Billy was able to fly in his shirtsleeves, through blue skies and great white puffs of cumulus clouds that he could skirt around as though they were mountain peaks. Rose's presence was, he wrote, "a great comfort." They had bought a second car—"another old crock," called Molly the Morris—so that he could commute into the airfield, and a dog, too, an Alsatian named Sinbad. While Billy was on duty, Rose would walk herself into a standstill trying to give Sinbad enough exercise. Or she would be out back, tending to their chickens. Billy was a little surprised to see how easily Rose took to the quiet life in the country. "I wish you could see our establishment," he wrote to his mother. "It's really pretty good and Rosie is the most efficient settler-inner and house-keeper I have ever seen. She works like a Trojan from dawn till dusk and is as happy as a clam. The country looks lovely now—and from the air the flowering bushes and trees show up for miles." He had to leave at 6:30 a.m. each morning six days a week, and was allowed only an extra hour's grace on Sundays. He was back home at six each evening, "which is swell." And then they would curl up by the fire and listen to music, "hot blues" most often, on their crackly old wireless set. On the odd occasions when he had twenty-four hours of leave, the two of them would shoot off to the nearby golf course at Frilford Heath and play a round together.

Bad news arrived early in April, in a letter from Billy's father. He'd had word from the United States. On Friday, April 5, Jay O'Brien died. He'd had a heart attack, while he was at home, in bed. Dolly was by his side. They had become pillars of Palm Beach high society. He'd actually spent the day with Joseph Kennedy, recently returned from his stint as ambassador to the UK. "The death of Jay O'Brien was quite a blow to Palm Beach," Kennedy wrote. It was a shock; he was only fifty-seven. He had seemed fine when they'd seen each other on the golf course in the afternoon, and again at the theater that same evening. Jay died after dinner that night. Dolly decided that he should be buried in New York, his spiritual if not his actual home. The *New York Times* gave his obituary a decent show, alongside a picture, in profile, which would have pleased him. There was no word from Clifford Gray—no one seemed to know exactly where he was. But Eddie Eagan was at the funeral.

For Billy, busy in wartime Britain, there wasn't time to mourn. "What a very sad thing about Jay," he wrote, when he learned of the news. "But on the other hand, he had a bloody good life and went full blast to the end so perhaps it's the best possible thing that could have happened. There's one thing about dying anyway, so many nice people have died in the last few years, one is assured of pleasant company on the other side of the pearly gates—and I'll bet they are laughing like buggery at us poor mortals."

The war was closing in. The Germans had invaded Belgium, and now that the fighting was in France, Billy's parents were finally making plans to move back to the United States. They were looking to buy a house in Hillsborough, California; Peggy and Jennison were handling the negotiations for them. They had hoped, and planned, to get across to London to visit Billy. But now they were cut off. It was time to get out of Europe, and the only way to do that was via a ship from Lisbon, in neutral Portugal.

On June 18, a fortnight after the retreat of the British Expeditionary Force from Dunkirk, Britain's new prime minister, Winston Churchill, addressed the House of Commons. Billy and Rose listened to the speech on their wireless set that night, never prouder, never more resolute, never more fearful.

> What General Weygand called the Battle of France is over. I expect that the Battle of Britain is about to begin. Upon this battle depends the survival of Christian civilization. Upon it depends our own British life, and the long continuity of our institutions and our Empire. The whole fury and might of the enemy must very soon be turned on us. Hitler knows that he will have to break us in this Island or lose the war. If we can stand up to him, all Europe may be free and the life of the world may move forward into broad, sunlit uplands. But if we fail, then the

whole world, including the United States, including all that we have known and cared for, will sink into the abyss of a new Dark Age made more sinister, and perhaps more protracted, by the lights of perverted science. Let us therefore brace ourselves to our duties, and so bear ourselves that, if the British Empire and its Commonwealth last for a thousand years, men will still say, "This was their finest hour."

Three weeks later, Billy finished his flying training and was awarded his pilot's wings. His final report noted, "Although average in ground subjects, his flying ability and officer qualifications were assessed as above average." The final verdict was that "he should make a sound squadron pilot." Of course, he and Rose headed for London for the night to celebrate. They met up with Ben Bathurst. He presented Billy with another pair of RAF wings to stitch onto his uniform. These ones were tattered and worn so that he wouldn't stand out as a greenhorn. It was a mark of respect, an acknowledgment of his commitment since they had met that night in the Savoy and first discussed how he could go about joining up.

Before Billy finished his training, he was sounded out by a man at the Air Ministry about whether he would consider going back to the United States to work for the RAF as a press and public relations man. He'd long since abandoned the pretense that he was Canadian, and they thought he could do good work on the propaganda side in Washington. There was an awareness, even then, within the British Foreign Office that, as the diplomat T. North Whitehead put it, "we are only likely to win this war if we obtain the whole-hearted co-operation of the United States."

Billy refused. "I've done nothing yet," he told them. "Why should they want to see me? Wait till I've shot down some Heinkels. Then, if you still want me, I'll go over." He hadn't spent the best part of a year in training just so he could go make pretty speeches and pose in photos for the American papers. "He is quite determined to go and join 601," wrote Rose. "The same squadron as Billy Clyde. They are all his friends, which would make it all infinitely more enjoyable than joining a squadron where he knew no-one."

"Billy had stayed in contact with us all during his training," remembered Mouse Cleaver, one of 601's pilots. "And on the 12th, he called up Archie Hope, the Commanding Officer of 'A' flight, my flight, and said that he had completed his training." Hope knew Fiske only a little, not nearly so well as Cleaver, Clyde, and the rest of the St. Moritz crowd. But he had heard good things about him.

"Archie told Billy to stay put, talk to no one about postings, and that we would fly up and get him." And they did. Cleaver went himself, in his Blenheim.

601 was based down at Tangmere, toward the coast sixty miles or so south of London, not far from the village where Rose had grown up. She spent the week calling around the area, looking for a house to rent. She found one in Chidham, ten miles down the road from Tangmere, an old farmhouse named Chidmere, on a pond, with an orchard. She "packed all our bits and bobs" into a van, and they "all moved in a body," her and the chickens and the dog.

That very same day, Hitler issued Führer Directive No. 16: "Since England, in spite of her hopeless military situation, shows no signs of being ready to come to an understanding, I have decided to prepare a landing operation against England, and, if necessary, to carry it out. The aim of this operation will be to eliminate the English homeland as a base for the prosecution of war against Germany, and, if necessary, to occupy it completely." The first step would be to win air superiority. "The English Air Force must be so reduced morally and physically that it is unable to deliver any significant attack against the German crossing."

Across the Channel at Calais, the German fleet began to assemble.

Billy Fiske, An American Citizen Who Died That England Might Live.
By Ronald Wong.

CHAPTER 14

THE LAST FLIGHT OF BILLY FISKE

T hey woke before dawn. Four o'clock, as often as not. Sometimes earlier. And always with the same routine. The *clang-clunk* of the door shutting, then a hand on the shoulder. The deep sleepers needed to be shaken awake. A cup of tea or cocoa to soften the blow. And then a pen, and a tatty Stationery Office notebook, which they had to sign by torchlight to prove that they'd received their wake-up call. Up, wash, shave, dress—last on was the leather Irvin jacket, its thick sheepskin lining a welcome buffer against the cold air outside. On the lawn, good-morning greetings with the other pilots, all equally blurry-eyed. The first wait of the day, for the truck to come and pick them up, then carry them over to the dispersal area by the runway. More hellos, with the fitters and riggers who were already up and at work, warming the engines, checking over the repairs, loading the guns. The petrol bowsers idled nearby, and once the ground crew were done, the tanks were filled with high-octane fuel. Over at dispersal, in the readiness huts, the flight commander rang through to Operations to announce that the men were "ready for business." And then, they waited. And waited.

Those who could stomach it would scoff breakfast. They had twenty minutes to eat, each group in turn. Some were wound up too tight to have any appetite. Billy didn't have that problem. "I live to eat," he wrote, "and I love it." Even powdered eggs. After that, some settled down with books and magazines—dog-eared copies of *Lilliput*, for the jokes and short stories, or the racier *Men Only*, for the pictures, according to taste. Others picked up games, darts, or shove ha'penny. In 601, they had a keen card school—poker, for high stakes. Time was when they'd played motorcycle polo, too, but they'd long since had to cut that out, since petrol was in such short supply. That said, 601 usually had enough to get by on. Willie Rhodes-Moorhouse had been appointed the squadron's "petrol officer," and he had decided that the simplest solution would be to buy a filling station. So they had enough to fuel their cars, at the day's end, for the short trip to the Ship in Bosham, or their other favorite watering hole, the Coal Hole bar in the cellar of the Spread Eagle Hotel in Midhurst. Even in wartime, 601 was still a cut above. "They were such wonderful guys in 601," Rose remembered. "They wore red linings in their tunics and mink linings in their overcoats. They were arrogant and they looked terrific, and probably the other squadrons hated their guts. But by God did they fight. Look at the records. None better. And they always did everything without any apparent effort. They had always been like that, all their lives."

By the time Billy and Rose arrived at Tangmere, in the middle of July 1940, 601 was just beginning to fray. The carefree atmosphere of the 1930s, which stretched right through into the phony war in the final year of the decade, had been dispelled during the fighting with the British Expeditionary Force in the battle of France. Two of 601's pilots had lost their lives. Billy's friend Roger Bushell had already been transferred, given charge of his own squadron, and then shot down over Dunkirk. He'd managed to force-land in a field and was promptly taken prisoner at pistol point by a passing German dispatch rider. Others were luckier. Billy's flight commander, Archie Hope, had been shot down twice, crash-landing on both occasions. The first time he'd managed to pinch a motorcycle from an abandoned military dump near Amiens and drive back to the base at Merville. The second time he came down on the beach at Calais and was evacuated back on a boat from Dunkirk. An RAF squadron was a small unit, including only twenty pilots. Each loss was acutely felt, and sapped a little more life and strength from the squadron. Especially as these early casualties were all old and firm friends, whereas the replacements were often strangers, fresh from flying school, with no combat experience.

In the air, pilots worked in teams. They flew in V formations, with two wingmen tucked on either side of the lead plane, so close that there was a constant risk they would crash. Each pilot kept one eye on the other two planes and the other eye on the surrounding skies. It was easier to believe in an old friend to do it right, someone you had flown and fought with, than it was to trust a man you'd only just met. Especially in 601. "There was a team feeling in 601 that the individuals wouldn't have had if they had been broken up and put in separate squadrons," wrote "Little Bill" Clyde. "They were older than most, and they'd been flying for several years."

Among the ground crew, and those pilots who didn't know him from St. Moritz, there was, at first, a measure of reservation about "this untried American adventurer," as Billy was described in the squadron's official history. There was a lot of gossip about the fact that he had once dated Alice Faye, who was in the cinemas at that very moment, starring in a new picture about the American singer Lillian Russell. But, as the history adds, "Billy Fiske arrived at Tangmere with no pretensions, and no illusions." He knew what it was to take on the responsibility for other men's lives. It was what he had always done on the bob run. He knew, too, how important it was to work as a team, which is why he had insisted on Eddie, Jay, and Clifford doing all those drills with him to learn the corners back in 1932. Besides, unlike some of the other new arrivals, he was already an old friend of the senior pilots. Max Aitken, Mouse Cleaver, Willie Rhodes-Moorhouse, and Little Bill Clyde all vouched for him.

The five old friends had a lot to catch up on. Billy let the others do most of the talking. They told him about a day trip to Paris they'd made at the end of May, escorting Winston Churchill to a meeting with the French premier. Churchill had decided to stay overnight, and the pilots had been released from duty until the morning. The prospect of a free night in Paris was too good to resist, and, though they had no cash or change of clothes, Hope managed to borrow a large sum from a friend at the British embassy. "And so," said Cleaver, "we set off for Lust and Laughter." They were back at the airfield the next morning, in pretty poor shape. But they made quite an impression on one of Churchill's aides, Sir Edward Spears, who wrote, "These men may have been naturally handsome, but that morning they were far more than that, creatures of an essence that was not of our world; their expressions of happy confidence as they got ready to ascend into their element, the sky, left me inspired, awed, and earthbound." Spears must have been a romantic sort, since Cleaver's recollections read a little differently. The assembly was, he said, "just about as hungover a crew of dirty, smelly, unshaven, unwashed fighter pilots as I doubt has ever been seen. Willie, if I remember rightly, was being sick behind his airplane when the Great Man arrived and expressed a desire to meet his escort. We must have appeared vaguely human at least, as he seemed to accept our appearance without comment."

After hearing his friends' war stories, Billy was more desperate to get into the action. But he had to wait just a little longer, while he learned how to handle his new plane. 601 flew Hawker Hurricanes; all Billy's training had been in old-fashioned Tiger Moths and, later on, more modern Harvards. 601 had been equipped with Hurricanes earlier that year, ahead of schedule, a fact that had caused some displeasure among other squadrons, which suspected, rightly, that 601's pilots had used their political connections to pull a few strings. Max Aitken's father, Lord Beaverbrook, had just become Britain's first minister of aircraft production. In those early days of the summer, before the Battle of Britain, the RAF's biggest problem wasn't a shortage of pilots, but of planes. And while Beaverbrook had helped triple production in the space of six months between January and June, they were losing so many that the overall number available was lower on August 15 than it had been at any point that year.

The Hurricane wasn't the most glamorous aircraft in service. That was the Supermarine Spitfire, which was faster and more agile. But the Hurricane had the advantage of being simpler, sturdier, easier, and quicker to refuel, repair, and rearm. And, while it was a little slower than the Spitfire, it was still a sight faster than anything Billy had flown in before, half as quick again as a Harvard. The extra speed was one thing that didn't bother him, but, that said, he made a bad start. The very first time he went up in a Hurricane, a tire burst as he touched down again at the end of the flight. "One of the boys told me it was very bad luck," Rose said. "Which didn't faze me at all. It never entered my head that anything would happen to Billy." He seemed, she said, "like a knight in shining armor, fighting for a cause he believed in. And if that was true, how could any harm come to him?" He had spent his entire adult life learning the skills he needed now, from those very first runs behind the wheel of a bobsled, through his days racing the Bentley Blower around the narrow dirt roads in the south of France, to his races on the Cresta. He had honed his understanding of how to handle a vehicle under g-forces, sharpened his decision-making at speed until it had become instinctive, and had learned to do it all under the pressure of knowing that even a single mistake could cost him his life. A week's practice was more than he needed. "Of one thing I am sure," wrote Archie Hope. "Fiske was an outstandingly good pilot. He took to the Hurricane when he joined the squadron like a duck to water. He was a natural fighter pilot." Another 601 pilot, Jack Riddle, remembered that Billy's "flying reactions were extraordinary, it was as though he was part of the plane."

There was more to him than that, said Riddle. "He was aware and caring, sensitive to those who maybe seemed unhappy. And he was usually the fastest to the club at nearby Bosham, with its brilliant wine cellar, which we made the squadron's HQ." Deputy Chief of Air Staff Sholto Douglas described 601 as "flamboyant and gay and indeed reckless, as harum-scarum in some ways as the service has ever known. They were a happy band of playboys; but when the heat was on, they became in the most effortless fashion one of the most gallant and courageous of our fighter squadrons." Billy was a natural fit.

By July, the flying, and fighting, was all over the Channel. The pilots were up, sometimes, for five hours in the mornings alone. They were tired; "sometimes dizzy from lack of sleep, limbs aching from long hours in tiny cockpits, they took off, flew, fought and landed almost automatically," notes Tom Moulson in the official history of 601. And yet, "among the pilots there was an indigenous optimism, a light-hearted and natural love of life, an unspoken philosophy of death." Their high spirits were soon taxed. Hope led one formation of five planes out of Tangmere and returned alone, as the other four had been forced down. Another member, Peter Robinson, had been shot down and then strafed on the ground, and was seriously wounded. As that incident showed, the conflict was getting uglier, and the gentlemanly code of conduct 601's pilots had lived by was becoming increasingly obsolete. On July 14, just two days after Billy's arrival, orders were issued that fighters should now start shooting at German seaplanes even if they were marked with the Red Cross, unless they were "directly engaged in a rescue operation." Ostensibly, those same seaplanes worked search and rescue, but the British suspected they were also performing covert reconnaissance on shipping in the Channel.

On July 20, Billy finally made his first sortie. The squadron was up three times that day. The first two patrols were uneventful. On the third, 601's Green and Blue flights had to fly out over the Channel to escort a convoy. One of the pilots spotted a white seaplane, ten miles off from the convoy. It was a Heinkel 59, complete with Red Cross markings. The pilots radioed back to the ground controller at Tangmere and were told to shoot it down if it was hostile. They decided, instead, to try to shepherd it back to Britain and force it to land, figuring the Germans would prefer that to the prospect of being shot down. So they swooped down on it, making several menacing passes without actually firing on it. The German pilots saw sense and turned toward Britain. But as they approached the coast, the pilot changed his mind and switched course back out to sea. At which point one of Billy's squadron shot it down. It was flying so low that although all four members of the crew bailed out, none of them had time to open their parachutes. It was an ugly act, and an awful sight—an induction to combat that dispelled what few romantic notions Billy had left about the war. When the RAF started to target the Red Cross planes, Hitler announced that they were "cold blooded murderers." And the German pilots, outraged, responded by machine-gunning RAF pilots who had come down at sea. Both sides had begun to target parachutists, too, as they escaped from their burning planes.

These were long, exhausting days. "Beneath the blazing hot summer sky time ticked inexorably away," wrote RAF pilot Wilf Nicoll. "The atmosphere at dispersals became electric and the tension tangible . . . It only required the resonant click of the microphone switch through the 'Tannoy' loudspeakers or the jangling of the telephone bell to send someone hurrying behind a hut or tent or the tail of an aircraft to retch and heave helplessly until he was rendered breathless, even if only the most innocuous messages followed." Supposedly, the pilots worked two days on and had the third off, though in these weeks they were up so often that their rest days were far more infrequent than that. Billy got two, which he spent with Rose, one in the last week of July and another the first week of August. Otherwise they were tethered to their planes, and idling, always, in one of four gears. The first was "Released," which meant they were off duty. "Readiness" meant they were at dispersal, a short sprint away from the plane and five minutes from the air. "Standby" meant that they were strapped into their aircraft, two minutes from takeoff. It was an ordeal, being strapped into that metal box underneath a noontime sun while the engine temperature rose and its fumes streamed past the open cockpit. But it was the last gear that they hated the most: "Available." It meant that they had to be ready to be in the air in fifteen minutes—too little time to undress, relax, or stray far away from the plane. The pilots felt caught between being on duty and off duty, and would most likely end up spending hours on duty with nothing to do to dispel the tension, uncertainty, and fear. Sometimes they would sneak off. Archie Hope once went for a bath, having checked in with Station Operations to make sure there was "nothing brewing." He was waist-deep in water with a loofah in his hand when the "Scramble" call came through. He made it up in fourteen minutes and thirty seconds.

For Billy, they were frustrating days too. He was scrambled three, sometimes four times a day, yet he always seemed to miss out on the action. Which infuriated him. Willie Rhodes-Moorhouse, who was Billy's flight leader, joked that "you may talk of the dangers of war, but you can have small idea of what it means until you try coming back across the Channel in a tight formation with

Fisky—in a rage because the Germans haven't stayed to fight—close on your tail with his finger on the button." On August 8, after several weeks of skirmishing, a British convoy of twenty-five ships, code-named "Peewit," was attacked by a force of hundreds of German aircraft while sailing from Southend on the east coast of England through the Straits of Dover to Swanage on the south coast. The fighting was so intense that many of the pilots, including Billy, considered it the start of the Battle of Britain. "Blitz starts," he noted in his logbook. Billy was scrambled four times. And he didn't get to fire a single bullet. He filled his log with little notes recording that he had been "too early for the fun," then "too late," then "too early," then "too late" again. The biggest fight of the battle yet had taken place off the Isle of Wight, just a few miles away. Billy had spent five and a half hours in the air and had seen only one "bandit" all day. He always seemed to be in the right place at the wrong time. His third patrol had ended ten minutes before the first German attack, and his final one started just as the last was finishing. And while 601 was shuttling back and forth and scouring the skies, 43 Squadron, the "Fighting Cocks," who were also based at Tangmere, had been fighting for their lives and had lost two pilots. Billy had been itching to "do something," as he wrote in his diary, for so long that the urge was getting to be unbearable. He wouldn't have to wait much longer.

That Sunday, August 11, was the finest morning anyone had seen all week. It had been bad for the last two days, all thick cloud and heavy rain, but that morning the sun rose into a clear blue sky. Billy and the others had already eaten breakfast and were stretching out in their deck chairs, warming their bones in the first rays of the morning sun, when the call came through. The radar stations over toward Dover had detected a swarm of enemy aircraft assembling over Cherbourg.

"SCRAMBLE!"

They had two minutes, from start to finish—an age for a man accustomed to covering the Cresta Run in under sixty seconds. The pilots grabbed their kit, helmets, gauntlets, "Mae West" life jackets, and sprinted across the grass to their aircraft. Their parachutes were waiting for them, on the wing. The ground crew helped the pilots shove the packs on, then boosted them up onto the wing. Billy trod warily, careful not to slip, then flicked his legs up and over and plopped himself down in the cockpit. Even for a man of his build, there wasn't much room to move. He was surrounded by instruments, gears, cogs, pedals, and levers, each with its own purpose.

First, before he could fire her up, he had to run through his final checks, just as he had once done with his Bentley back on La Croisette. Check the pneumatic pressure for the brakes, slip the trim in neutral and the rudder over hard right to counter the torque on takeoff, tighten the throttle nut. Then flick the magnetos, and start the engine. The exhausts fired shotgun blasts of blue gas back past the fuselage, which were immediately whipped into the air as the propeller began to spin. Billy had to crank the seat up as high as it would go so he could peer around the long nose of the aircraft as he taxied over to his takeoff position; even then he had to swing the plane this way and that to get a clear view of the ground in front of him. At the end of the runway he held the plane on the brakes as he advanced the throttle. As the note of the engine rose higher and higher, the plane began to buck and shudder. He let the brakes slip, and it shot forward across the grass. Lurching, bounding, bobbing, till the tail rose into the air; lift, bounce, lift again, and then the up-and-away into the sky.

The first reports from the observation posts were in now. It wasn't a wing the Germans were sending, but an armada. The single largest force that had come across the Channel in one body yet, almost two hundred aircraft, half of them heavy bombers, the rest fighters. All bound for Portland Naval Base, one hundred miles down the coast. The squadron had twelve planes up, all now assembled and in formation above St. Catherine's Point, and they got their orders from Control. They were given a vector and an altitude, and told to fly on toward Portland. It was fifteen minutes' flying time, even at top speed.

They were over Swanage, about halfway there, when they saw them. "A very large number of enemy aircraft," wrote Willie Rhodes-Moorhouse, "milling around some miles to the south." They were about twenty miles off. Rhodes-Moorhouse led the squadron in a turn toward the enemy. And at that exact point, his engine cut out. He turned back to Tangmere and told the squadron to carry on. Billy took charge. He called, "Line astern" over the radio, ordering the ten remaining planes to follow his lead as he flew, full throttle, toward the enemy. They were utterly outnumbered. But the odds didn't figure. They flew, without hesitation, into a formation so vast they hardly knew where to start. "They seemed to be in countless tiers upward ad infinitum," remembered Mouse Cleaver. "They were so thick we almost had a permanent target." Billy didn't stop to look back. He took it on trust that the squadron was following him in. And then "we came into direct contact with the enemy aircraft—and broke up for individual attack."

The South African RAF ace Adolph "Sailor" Malan had said that there were ten rules for dogfighting. The pilots knew them inside out because they were posted up on the noticeboards in the mess halls around the country. Billy and 601 had broken two of them before they'd even opened fire. *Air discipline and team work are words that mean something in air fighting; when diving to attack, always leave a proportion of your formation above to act as a top guard.* But now it was each man for himself. Billy focused, as he flew in, on the first rule: *Wait until you see the whites of their eyes.* He was three hundred yards out when he first fired. A touch too far, but he thought he saw the bullets hit home. And in that moment, he broke a third rule: *While shooting think of nothing else.* A second aircraft passed across his sights, so he switched his aim. In the confusion, he nearly collided with the second plane. He swerved. And then he was through and out the other side of the swarm. *Never fly straight and level for more than thirty seconds in the combat area.* He carried on out of range, climbing all the time. *Height gives you the initiative.* He circled around and, looking down, saw another target. He fired again and saw smoke explode from its starboard motor. It dropped down out of sight. He picked out another, this one flying straight on, a way below him. "I dived straight at him and gave a good burst, narrowly missing him as he passed underneath. He went into a steep dive from about 16,000 feet." He watched it all the way down ten thousand feet, and in doing so broke another rule: *Always keep a sharp lookout.* There was a Messerschmitt on his tail. *Always turn and face the attack.* Instead, Billy whistled down into a steep, spiraling dive. *Make your decisions promptly. It is better to act quickly, even though your tactics are not of the best.* If he held the dive too long, the engine would cut out under the negative g-force. He dropped, one thousand, two thousand, three thousand feet. It was enough. He had lost the Messerschmitt. And by the time he climbed again, the skies were clear. The enemy had gone. Just like that. He cut out for Tangmere.

They called it the Battle of Portland. Four of 601's pilots died fighting it, among them Dick Demetriadi, who was Rhodes-Moorhouse's brother-in-law, and W. G. Dickie, a wingman of Billy's in Blue flight. But 601 had shot down twelve themselves. Rhodes-Moorhouse had gotten two of them. He'd been halfway back to Tangmere when he realized that his fuel switch was turned to "reserve." As soon as he flicked it back the right way, the plane burst into life again, and he returned to the fight. Billy claimed three planes as "badly damaged": the truth was that the Browning .303 machine guns used by the Hurricanes were so small-caliber that the German planes were often able to absorb any damage inflicted and flee the fight, heading back to their bases in France. "Terrific fight," Billy wrote in his log. "Had to lead squadron in, Willie's engine failed! Terrified but fun." That night, when once he had come off duty, he drove over to the house at Chidham. He was in a great hurry to tell Rose all about it. "I'd never seen him so excited," she said. Her mother had come to visit. The two of them sat up, enthralled, as he talked them through the fight, blow-by-blow. "His description of that day was terrific," recalled his mother-in-law. "They found what looked like a spiral swarm of bees & Bill then went slap into them and out the other side 3 or 4 times—until the whole thing broke up and eventually disappeared under our fighters' onslaught. Bill himself got four. Said far the most difficult was not avoiding the bullets that day, but the other planes!"

Billy was high on excitement. Later, when the adrenaline surge had seeped away, he felt spent. All the pilots did. They slumped. Some started to shake. The stress was just too much. They drank cocoa to keep their blood sugar up, but that was all the relief they had. There was no respite. Tuesday, August 13, was the fiercest day of fighting yet. The Germans named it Adlertag—Eagle Day. They launched an all-out aerial assault on the RAF's airfields across the south. They meant it to be the beginning of the end for the RAF. Waves of enemy aircraft came in, as many as ten an hour, over Essex, Kent, Sussex, and Hampshire. The RAF would be stretched so tight across so many fronts that they would surely snap. And the Germans were right: the RAF was reaching its breaking point. At Tangmere, 145 Squadron had been withdrawn from action because it had lost ten pilots—half its strength—in just three days of fighting.

"The thing that all of us in the RAF were aware of, ground staff and pilots, was that we were running desperately short of pilots, aircraft [(A/C)], and A/C spares," wrote Bill Littlemore, a flight mechanic with 43 Squadron. "The problem of delay in waiting for spares and new A/C was minimized by the initiative of the maintenance crews bringing in the idea of cannibalization of just one A/C, to strip from it urgently awaited spare parts, rather than have a number of A/C unserviceable because they were all awaiting the arrival of spare parts before they could be got into the air . . . With regard to the losses of pilots which we could ill afford, and the rate at which we were losing them, [that brought] us to a position where but for the arrival of chaps like Billy Fiske and all those other wonderful guys who came from distant lands, we should have been the losers, of that there is no doubt."

At Tangmere, the first "scramble" call on Eagle Day came in at 6:30 a.m. "Too early," Billy grumbled. Flying north, they saw the enemy five miles distant, toward Midhurst. Bombers. They formed into Vs, ready to attack. Billy picked out one enemy, fired on it until he saw white smoke burst from its motors. "A good burst," four seconds long, as he closed from three hundred yards to within just one hundred. It broke off, and Billy watched as another Hurricane came down on its tail. He turned away, toward the rear of the enemy formation. He picked out another plane, toward the back of the pack. This one looked to be making a bombing run. Billy took a quick glance around. He couldn't see a target other than the Midhurst-Pulborough railway line. The plane must have been in trouble and looking to jettison its load before turning back. He fired again. He was so close to it that he saw the starboard engine stop turning. It broke into a dive, straight down from eight thousand feet into the low cloud below. He followed it, firing all the way. Each of the Hurricane's eight guns carried around 330 rounds, and they fired them at a rate of 1,100 per minute. Which meant, in all, Billy had only about eighteen seconds of firing time before he was out of ammunition. That was why it was so important to use short, sharp bursts. It was too easy to get carried away—which is what Billy did. By the time he had pulled out of the dive, his guns were empty. He could still see the enemy, smoke trailing from one engine. It was too damaged to climb. "At least," Billy thought, "I won't let him escape." He tailed it out toward the coast, calling out on his radio for someone to come and finish it off. He followed it, in fact, right over the top of his house at Chidham, and broke off the pursuit only once he saw the puffs of brown and black smoke start to explode as they came within range of the anti-aircraft guns on the Isle of Wight.

As soon as he got a chance, he called Rose. He was so excited, like a child who wants to show off to his mother. "Did you see me?" he asked her. He was sure she must have seen him chasing the enemy out to sea. But Rose had been tucked up in bed. And nothing, not even a dogfight over the rooftops, was going to drag her up at 7 a.m. All she wanted was for him to be happy. The reason she lived so near Tangmere, she said, was that he got "a day's rest at home, if that home was near. The only thought of all the women, myself included, was to make our man happy. We lived for them." But that day, worn down by stress and fatigue, "he was furious with me," she remembered. "He had got on the tail of a plane, and herded it right across our house so I could watch him. He was all in a rage because I wouldn't get out of bed to look."

"Well," Rose said, hoping to placate him, "if I'd known it was you of course I would have gone to watch." But it was no good. "He couldn't understand why I couldn't tell his Hurricane from all the others just by the sound of it."

Rose might not have been watching, but plenty of other people were. The fighting went on all day, and the skies above Britain were filled with webs of white vapor trails, sinuous plumes of smoke, bright sparks of metal in the sun, and occasional flashes of explosions. From the ground, it all looked so graceful, balletic even. For the pilots in the cockpits high above, it was hell. An unceasing assault on the senses. The sounds: the engine screaming three feet away, guns roaring, a constant crackle of static, shouts and cries in the earphones, and the dry rasp of their own breath in the microphone. The smells: hot rubber and metal, high-octane fuel, cordite, and, often enough, vomit. The stresses: stomachs heaving and revolting as the pilots threw their planes through the most violent maneuvers; eyes watering in the brilliant, blinding sun; necks wet with sweat chafing always against the collar, bowed down by g-forces then thrust back straight against the seat. As they dived and climbed, the sudden changes in air pressure would twist their guts and make them break wind and belch into their face masks. All the while they had to think coolly and clearly enough to survive the combat. Make a mistake up there and you'd had it.

"Death when it came was not always clean and swift," wrote Wilf Nicoll. "Many died trapped in the narrow confines of the cockpit while the fighter plunged thousands of feet before burying itself in the earth; conscious every second of the fall, struggling to release a trapped limb or jammed hood, coolly and clinically at first until realization came that there was no release and that time and height had slipped away: then, before the final impact with the earth, the final indignity of befouling themselves." The lucky ones, Nicoll thought, were those who were killed outright in combat by enemy gunfire. Through the Battle of Britain, the average life expectancy, in flying time, of the RAF's fighter pilots was down to eighty-seven hours. To put that in perspective, back when he was training, Billy had to clock ninety hours in the air before they even granted him a license to fly solo. The hard truth was that for many of them it had become a question of "when," not "if."

Billy's plane was hit for the first time later on Eagle Day. The squadron had been in a dogfight with forty German fighters over the sea past Portland. He had hit four of them, and claimed two probable kills and two more badly damaged. A cannon shell caught his wing and did such damage that he had to turn and run back to Tangmere. Archie Hope and some of the other members of 601 stayed out, circling around pilots who had come down at sea so the search and rescue teams would know where to look for them. Once the boat had picked up the RAF pilots, Hope made a point of circling the downed German fliers, so that they, too, would be rescued and brought ashore.

The morning of Wednesday, August 14, brought relief. The weather was too rough for anyone to fly. 601 was released, and Billy had his second day off that month. He spent it at Chidmere with Rose, fast asleep. Hundreds of miles away, in the Schorfheide forest north of Berlin, Hermann Goering, commander in chief of the Luftwaffe, called his top officers together for a conference at his country estate, Carinhall. Goering had decided to change tactics. They had tried to draw the RAF into committing all its aircraft into dogfights over the Channel, but it hadn't worked. They had tried, too, to destroy the radar stations upon which the RAF depended, but the British seemed to repair them even quicker than the Germans could knock them out. Instead, they would target the airfields themselves.

And so, on the 15th, the Germans came in greater strength than ever. They sent almost two thousand airplanes, so many that the British radar operators found it impossible to distinguish between the different formations on their screens. The front stretched from the River Tyne, right up in the northeast, around to the River Exe, down in the southwest. 601 joined up with eight squadrons in the largest wing the RAF had assembled yet. They fought out over the sea, against a formation of bombers. It was in this action that, according to 601 Squadron lore—and the official history—Billy, all his bullets gone, managed to maneuver a straggling enemy aircraft into a collision with a barrage balloon over Portsmouth and destroy it that way. It was one of seventy-two aircraft the Germans lost that day, which they came to call "Black Thursday." But the RAF's success came at a cost, as ever. Little Bill Clyde was hit. He managed to coax his plane back to Tangmere, though it was only the control cables that kept it hanging together. Mouse Cleaver got it too. An explosive shell hit his cockpit, and the hood exploded in his face. His eyes were punctured with shreds of Perspex. He did manage to bail out of the plane before it hit the earth, but he never fought again. That night, Billy was too tired even to write in his log. He left it all blank, thinking he would fill it in when he next had the chance.

They came for Tangmere at noon on the 16th. The radar stations on the Isle of Wight had picked up a group of around a hundred aircraft at Cherbourg, heading toward Portsmouth. They were Junkers 87s. Stukas. Dive-bombers. The Germans used them for the scalpel work of precision bombing. They had been the scourge of Allied Europe since the start of the war, the shrill wail of their sirens ("Jericho trumpets") a chilling herald of death and destruction. But for the RAF's pilots, they were easy meat. "Rats in a barrel!" 601's pilots called them. Compared with the Hurricanes and Spitfires, Stukas were slow, and poorly armed. If anything, the British pilots had almost come to admire the bravery of the men who flew them, since they were such soft targets.

The first call came through to Tangmere from Group HQ at Uxbridge just after midday. 601 was scrambled at 12:25. When the Stukas reached the Isle of Wight, the force split into three wings. One made for Ventor, another for Portsmouth, and the last for Tangmere. The RAF fighters split too. 43 Squadron met one flight of Stukas head-on, and routed them. But 601, led that day by Archie Hope, was told to sit tight at twenty thousand feet. In all the confusion, they had one clear order, which was to hold off attacking the Stukas and to go after the fighter escort. Hope could see the Stukas clear enough, flying in diamond formation down away to his left at twelve thousand feet. They were crossing the coast at Selsey. But there were no fighters that he could see. He asked for permission to attack and was told again, "You are only to engage the Little Boys. On no account must you attack the Big Boys." The Stukas were closing in on Tangmere now. Hope saw the first of them fall into a precipitous dive above the airfield. "To hell with it," he told himself. He ordered his squadron into the attack. "I think the fighters were a myth," he wrote later. "For we never saw them and neither did anyone from the other squadrons." He was wrong. There were fighters. The combat reports from the other pilots in 601 confirm it. But then, everyone involved in the mayhem of the raid, caught in the maelstrom of bombs, bullets, and screaming planes, lived those few traumatic minutes in their own way, and afterward those who survived could only try to piece it together as best they could.

There has always been confusion about what exactly happened on August 16, and why, but one thing's for certain: 601 was too late. By the time they started their attack, the Stukas were already turning for home, and on the ground, all hell had broken loose. 601 chased the enemy out south to sea. The pilots, furious that they had been held back while their base, and their people, were bombed, wreaked terrible vengeance, each man chasing his own target. "The fighting was low, right over the airfield," recalled Billy Clyde. "Almost every Hurricane scored a 'kill' or a 'damaged,'" notes the official history. "The 87s were twisting and turning all over the place," Hope wrote, "trying to fire their front guns." There were seventeen Stukas above Tangmere. Some reports state that 601 got fifteen of them, eight shot down, seven more damaged—such a severe toll that the Germans withdrew the Stuka from the theater soon after. Certainly three came down in the countryside around Tangmere. At the same time, the airfield was erupting in flames. "It was a slaughter," remembered W. G. Green, then a flight cadet at the base.

Maurice Haffenden, a fitter, was there too. He wrote about it, soon after, in a letter to his family. "I went head first down a manhole as the first bomb landed on the cookhouse. For seven minutes their 1,000-pounders were scoring direct hits and everything was swept away by machine-gun bullets. I never believed such desolation and destruction to be possible. Everything is wrecked—the hangars, the stores, the hospital, the armory, the cookhouse, the canteen—well, everything." In the horror and panic, the minds of the men and women fixed on strange, almost incidental details. "By special permission a Lyon's ice cream fellow is allowed in the drome," recalled Haffenden. "He always stands just outside the cookhouse on the square. He was last seen standing there guarding his tricycle, but now at the same spot is a bomb crater thirty feet deep." One hangar had collapsed, two more were burning. The workshops, armory, and pump house were all just heaps of rubble, the central stores were a shambles, the messes were damaged, and the runway was littered with craters. Planes on the ground had exploded into twisted scrap metal. The car park had been hit, and some of the vehicles had been thrown so far by the blasts that they were entangled in the girders that supported the roof of the garage hangar. Thirteen people were dead, twenty more seriously wounded. "In the early evening," wrote Haffenden, "they were still sorting out the bloody remnants of flesh and bones and tied them in sheets."

In the confusion, one voice had come through loud over the radio. "MAYDAY! MAYDAY!" it shouted. "Aircraft on fire! I'm injured!"

It was Billy.

Little Bill Clyde remembered Billy calling out to him, "I'm hit, I've got to land." Clyde just replied, "OK."

When the Mayday call came in, Dr. Courtney Willey, the only medical officer at Station HQ that day, ordered two nursing orderlies, Corporal George Jones and Aircraftsman Second Class Cyril Faulkner, to take the ambulance out to the airfield to meet the wounded pilot when he landed. "Proceeding along the perimeter we suddenly saw a cloud of dust some 25 yards ahead of us," Faulkner recalled. "We stopped and realized we were being bombed, the first salvo on to the parked aircraft causing the dust." They drove on. Willey, meanwhile, was busy moving twelve patients out of the sick quarters into a nearby bomb shelter. He had only just done that when the sick quarters received a direct hit. The chimney breast collapsed in through the roof, and Willey was buried up to his waist in rubble. He pulled himself out and immediately went to work setting up an emergency sick bay so he could treat the wounded. While all that was going on, Jones and Faulkner were driving through the raid to the runway. And over to the east, on the far side of the field, Billy's Hurricane appeared, low down above the trees and hedgerows. The sight of his fighter, trailing white smoke, stuck in the minds of many of the men and women at Tangmere that day—a single image that would last through the years while many others, too horrific to recall, were blacked out.

Clyde saw it. He was in the air, but he glanced down just as Billy's plane came in. He saw it touch down near the control tower, roll on almost to the end of the runway, and stop. "In all the activity," he said later, "he didn't sound like he was in bad shape." Clyde didn't have time to spare another thought for his friend.

John Bushby, a cadet, was also at Tangmere that day. "The rest of the day is in my mind a series of snapshots, and the clearest snapshot in my mind is the one which registered within a few seconds of the first alarm while I was still sprinting for cover," he wrote. "Through the gap between the two hangars I saw, across the green of the airfield grass, a lone Hurricane just touching down gently but with the undercarriage still retracted, over the panoramic blue sky. It came to rest and lay there, a thin stream of smoke settling behind it."

"Get out! Get out for Christ's sake!" Bill Littlemore, the flight mechanic from 43 Squadron, had called out when he first saw that Hurricane trailing white smoke, knowing that the plane would soon burst into flames. But Billy didn't bail out. He just flew on, toward the runway, even as the flames were licking up around his feet, burning his flesh. The Hurricane fell into a steep approach, the wheels still up. Littlemore was sure that it would explode when it hit the runway, but instead he watched as it leveled up at the last possible second and flopped down, "leaving a trail of smoke, sparks and flame in its wake," until finally it came to a standstill, and the smoke started to billow upward. The last thing Littlemore saw before he was snapped back into the raid was "2 or 3 bods" running toward it—the nursing orderlies, Jones and Faulkner.

It wasn't long before the rest of 601 Squadron was coming in to land on the runway behind them. As Archie Hope coasted to a stop, he saw a damaged Hurricane off to one side of the runway. As squadron leader, his first thought was always for the safety of his pilots. "I taxied my aircraft across, and found two ambulance men who had lifted Fiske out of the cockpit and laid him on the grass alongside," he said. "The aircraft was smoldering rather than burning." He jumped down from his plane and shouted across to ask if he could give them any help. He saw they were fumbling with the straps across Billy's shoulders. "They didn't know how to undo his parachute harness, so I showed them." He looked down at Billy, saw that he had burns over his feet and ankles, and all the way up his legs to his knees; his hands and face, too, were blistered, black and bloody. Hope told the medic to put medicinal cream on the wounds.

Forty years later, Hope's memory of those moments had faded. He no longer trusted his own recollections. "When I saw him he was not fully conscious or making a lot of sense & I certainly didn't ask what happened," he wrote. "I don't suppose anyone else did later." But in another, much earlier account, only a decade after the battle, he remembered that he had spoken to Billy. "He was more or less conscious and told me that his aircraft had been damaged by return fire from the rear gunner of a Junkers 87 which he was attacking somewhere near Bognor Regis. I cannot remember whether he destroyed the aircraft or even whether he was able to lower his undercarriage before landing." The truth of it is lost now; the stories are scrambled. But the second version, which was accepted by Cleaver, Clyde, and the other pilots in 601, is the nearest we have to an account of exactly what happened to Billy in the minutes before he made his Mayday call.

Clyde caught a glimpse of Billy's body, laid out on the runway. "The ambulance and fire tender were alongside the aircraft in a matter of seconds," he said, "and he was lifted from the aircraft. I was some distance away and since everything necessary was being done I didn't become involved."

Hope stayed only long enough to satisfy himself that Billy was going to be OK. Once they had loaded him into the ambulance and set off back toward the sick bay, he walked across to dispersal. "I told the rest of the squadron what had happened, and I remember saying that Billy wasn't too badly injured."

On the other side of the airfield, Dr. Courtney Willey was working in his makeshift sick bay, now overflowing with the dead and dying. The ambulance carrying Billy had to wait until Willey could turn his attention to it. When he climbed in through the back doors, he found Billy was badly burned but still conscious. He dosed him up with morphine and told the driver to take him to the Royal West Sussex Hospital in Chichester. Before they could set off, they had to wait twenty minutes until the roads around the station were clear. Billy, doped and delirious now, began muttering to himself. He kept asking, over and over again, "Is my airplane OK? Is my airplane OK?"

It seems odd that this particular thought was so fixed in his mind as he faded in and out of consciousness, until you consider the question all his friends were asking themselves and each other that evening: Why didn't he bail out? Billy's mother-in-law was sure the fire "must have started too low, and his one chance was to try and land and get out the minute it touched the ground—but I'm afraid he must have been semi-conscious by then." But 601 pilots Mouse, Archie, and Little Bill disagreed, as did the ground crew. They felt, instinctively, that he had flown home through the flames because he was determined to save his aircraft. He knew that they were too precious to write off. "Just how Fiske managed to fly and land his plane in such atrocious pain it is impossible to say," records the official history. "But the Legion knew why he did it, and within days his Hurricane was back in the sky."

The only thought in Billy's head in those minutes was to get his Hurricane back to Tangmere in one piece. He had drawn on all his skill, courage, and experience to get that plane home, all the while enduring agony more extreme than most can know. His final act at the wheel, when he pulled the fighter out of a dive and brought it down into a crash landing, was perhaps the most astonishing of the many remarkable drives, rides, flights, and races he had made in his life.

And where was Rose? She wasn't at Chidmere. She'd decided to drive up to London that morning, to go shopping on Piccadilly. She had called Tangmere at noon to check in with Billy. "We weren't supposed to call the field," she said. But she always did. This time he wasn't free, so she called again, right after lunch. "I couldn't get any information, except that I could hear over the phone that the field had been bombed. Our husbands always warned us not to be dramatic if an air raid came, and not to phone the aerodrome. But I couldn't keep away from the phone." She called back again, fifteen minutes later, "even though I knew Billy would be angry." They told her that he had been taken to hospital. Her first thought was "Thank God, Billy's been hurt. He won't have to fight any more." Later, it pained her to think about how flippant she had been, even though she knew "every woman whose man is fighting wishes that, whether she admits it or not." She jumped into the Morris and drove out of London as fast as she could. It took her three hours to reach Chichester. "And all the time I told myself that this was so lucky because surely he had done no more than perhaps break an arm or a leg and that would keep him out of the war for a while, and maybe he would get through the whole war all right. Over and over I said that." The refrain ran through her head. If she said it often enough, it would be true. "I had told myself again and again that Billy could never die."

By the time Rose got to the hospital, Billy was out of the operating theater.

When she walked into his room, she saw him, his skin swathed in "black goo" to treat his burns. He looked up as the door opened and said, "What the hell are you doing here?"

"He was conscious for a little while," Rose remembered. "And when he was delirious, all he would talk about was his plane. He wanted me to go and see if it was all right." Rose's mother said, "It was so dreadful for her seeing him looking so different. And though the burns on his face were superficial compared to those on his legs, it wasn't, of course, the Bill she knew. I would have died to have saved her that memory. Tho' she knows he wasn't conscious or suffering."

As he slipped away into sleep, Rose stepped outside to talk to the doctors. It was going to be OK, they told her; he was going to pull through. While he slept, she drove down to the post office and sent a telegram to the Dillon, Read & Co. office in New York. It was the best way she could think of to reach his parents, who were now living at the Waldorf-Astoria, having come back from Lisbon by boat.

Bill had bad crash this morning his legs and hands severely burned doctor thinks very good chance pray to god stop will keep in constant communication love Rose Fiske.

Billy died the next morning, August 17, 1940. He was twenty-nine. The doctors said it was "post-operative shock." And so, later that day, a second telegram arrived at Nassau Street:

Darlings Bill died this morning early from severe shock and burns from crash never recovered consciousness after I first saw him suffered no pain am trying very hard to be brave you must be too for his sake I feel he should have military funeral and be buried here but will arrange anything you wish may I come and stay when able to get away you can be very proud of him he has been so very brave all through all my love I wish I had not got to send this cable.

The doctors told Rose that if he had lived, he would have been paralyzed from the waist down. She tried to find some succor in that. "I'm glad Billy died," she said, months later. "He loved speed, constant movement. If he'd lived he would never have walked again. That in itself would have killed him."

They buried him on the Tuesday, at Boxgrove Priory, a mile away from the northern boundary of Tangmere. None of Billy's friends from 601 made it. The day before, August 19, the squadron was withdrawn from the front line, moved to RAF Debden in Essex. They had suffered too much, and lost too many. Rose wore black, a fur hat, and a simple necklace, a gift he had given her for her birthday. She had been so busy the last few days she hadn't had time to stop, or think. She'd had to organize the flowers and a wreath from his family and to write notices for the papers. But more than that, she was "overwhelmed at the letters from all over the world, despite a war going on, and from people I'd never heard of, who wrote to me with so much feel of loss." There were telegrams from Hollywood, St. Moritz, New York, San Francisco, London, and even Lake Placid. Representatives from the Air Ministry were at the funeral and from the US embassy. Lord Beaverbrook sent a wreath. So, they say, did Winston Churchill.

Lord Brabazon of Tara, who knew Billy from St. Moritz, wrote an appreciation that was published in the *Times*. "A very gallant gentleman—Billy Fiske has given his life for us," "Brab" wrote. "As a racing motorist, as a bobsleigh rider, as a flier he was well known, but as a Cresta Rider he was supreme. Taking some years to become first class, his fame eventually was legendary. No record he did not break, no race he did not win, he was the supreme artist of the run; never did he have a fall, he was in a class by himself. As an American citizen, blessed with this world's goods, of a family beloved by all who knew them, with a personal charm that made all worship him, he elected to join up in the ranks of the Royal Air Force and fight our battles. We thank America for sending us the perfect sportsman. Many of us would have given our lives for Billy, instead he gave his for us. The memory of him will live long in the Alps where he had his great successes. In the hearts of his friends it will endure forever."

They draped his coffin in two flags, the Union Jack and the Stars and Stripes, then loaded it onto a trailer and drove it across to the church. The pallbearers walked beside the coffin, a marching band came after. And once they had lowered his casket into the ground, they fired a final salute over his grave.

Later that very same day, the prime minister addressed Parliament, and the nation. "The gratitude of every home in our Island, in our Empire, and indeed throughout the world, except in the abodes of the guilty, goes out to the British airmen who, undaunted by odds, unwearied in their constant challenge and mortal danger, are turning the tide of the World War by their prowess and their devotion," he said. "Never in the field of human conflict was so much owed by so many to so few."

"I am at last beginning to realize I shall never see Bill again," Rose wrote that night. "I am so proud to have been his wife." She needed to get out. Away from Tangmere, away from Britain, away from the war. She booked a ticket on the *Scythia*, bound for New York, and put in an application for a travel permit. She wanted to go and visit Billy's family. But there was one thing she had to do before she left.

A fortnight later, on a warm weekday afternoon, she arrived at the Moorfields Eye Hospital in East London. She asked to see Mouse Cleaver. Of course he wasn't listed under that name, but they looked and found that they had him listed as Cleaver, G. N. Up she went. Mouse's eyes were bound entirely in bandages. They were picking the shards of Perspex out of his pupils piece by piece, one operation at a time. They talked for a while. "She was, by then, over the initial shock," he said, and though he couldn't see, from what he heard she sounded "comparatively cheerful, maybe for my benefit." She paused a while, then said, "We must keep on being brave." They both fell silent. And then he felt her tears fall on to the back of his hand.

EPILOGUE

London, July 4, 1941. Independence Day. It was a long walk to St. Paul's, especially in heels, but the sun was out, and besides, she thought the air would do
her good. How bleak and broken London looked. Was it really only a year and
a half ago that she'd walked these same streets and admired the pictures the
chichi shops had posted up in their blacked-out windows? Back then the only
thing she'd been worried about was stubbing her toe on a sandbag. She had
changed; it was obvious even from the look of her. Her dark hair was already
streaked gray. But there was tremendous strength in her face and determination
in her walk. The papers described her as "distinguished" these days, where they
had once called her "beautiful."

While she was in New York, she had given an interview to a friend from the
old days, when she'd first been in the city. "I've changed a lot," Rose told her. "My
sense of values is different. Things that used to be important don't matter any more.
The clothes and jewels I used to want—all that stuff makes no difference now. I
feel much softer and gentler toward people. I hope I have more sympathy and
understanding for them." It was a good piece. A little sentimental, perhaps, but
better by far than a lot of the bunk that had been written about Billy since the
previous August. The American press seemed so damn keen to make him out as
a hero. He would have hated that. Just as he had back at Lake Placid. What got her
was the way they exaggerated the details. As if what he had done wasn't enough in
itself. She'd heard of one that included the most preposterous account of his death,

which had him climbing out of the wreckage of his fighter, "the old grin still on his face," and calling for another plane so he could get back into the air. What rot.

She was on Ludgate Hill now. St. Paul's filled the horizon. It seemed a miracle that it was still standing, surrounded as it was by rubble and the shells of bombed-out buildings. Of course it was anything but. They had made extraordinary efforts to save it, on Churchill's orders. They'd installed tanks, baths, and pails of water around the roof and had special squads of firefighters patrol it with stirrup pumps. It had upset some, who felt that the services had let all the other buildings around burn just so long as they could save the cathedral. But it had been worth it, she thought. Churchill was right. He had always seemed to understand the value of things—speeches, ceremonies, symbols—and their effect on the public morale. Wasn't that what today was about, after all?

She could see a huddle of men on the steps running up to the great front doors. Journalists, radio broadcasters, even a couple of cameramen. She had been told NBC would be broadcasting the service back in the States. There were a lot of unfamiliar faces there. Officials. Young fighter pilots, from the new Eagle Squadrons, fresh-faced and wet behind the ears, as Billy and the others had once been. There weren't too many of the St. Moritz boys left now. Roger Bushell was in a prisoner-of-war camp. Mouse Cleaver was still in hospital, and still blind. Willie Rhodes-Moorhouse was dead. He had been shot down later in the Battle of Britain, finally paying for what his friend Max Aitken described as "his utter disregard for his own life."

Rose found herself making small talk with the US ambassador, a granite-faced man named John Winant, all square jaw and side-parting. They spoke about her trip to the United States, and he offered his condolences on the death of Billy's father, William Sr. He had died of a heart attack the previous October. It had been coming, but it arrived all the sooner because he was so distraught about his son's death. Billy's mother, Beulah, had gone off to the West Coast to live near Peggy. She had asked Rose to come too. But she wanted to get back to Britain. "Billy gave his life for my country," Rose said in the press. "I couldn't face myself if I didn't go back and do what I can to help. I've got to do it. Something inside me keeps saying that all the time." Winant introduced her to Brendan Bracken, too, though she didn't really take in who exactly he was. "An MP," she wrote. He was a little more than that—the minister for information, and one of Churchill's closer confidants. He was there representing the prime minister. And then Archibald Sinclair, the secretary of state for air.

The four of them led the procession down into the crypt beneath the cathedral. Billy's plaque was on the back wall, just off Nelson's tomb. They gathered around. Sinclair gave a short speech, sweet but perhaps just a little cynical. It was written for the benefit of an audience of millions across the Atlantic, as much as for the few men and women there that day.

Pilot Officer Fiske had no obligation to fight for this country. He was not an Englishman. He was a citizen of the United States of America. Yet a fortnight after war broke out, he joined the Royal Air Force. Having passed brilliantly through all the stages of his training, he was, on March 23, 1940, granted a commission in the RAF and was posted to No. 601 Squadron on July 13, a little more than a month before his death in action. He had left a promising career and a full and useful life to serve in the Royal Air Force. He was happily married; he was a member of a famous New York firm; he was renowned for his skill and daring at winter sports. Here was a young man—he was only twenty-nine when he was killed—for whom life held much. Under no kind of compulsion to come and fight for Britain, he came and he fought, and he died. The Latin Poet said that "it is sweet and decorous to die for one's country." In that decorum those British pilots who were killed that day with Pilot Officer Fiske were perfectly instructed. And these young men were Pilot Officer Fiske's friends. Billy Fiske was one of those people who made many friends. He had a great many friends of his own generation in this country. He played with them and when the stakes became highest he stayed with them and died with them and they, through me, thank him. So he gave his life for his friends, and for a great cause, the common cause of free men everywhere—the cause of liberty. That is why we honor his spirit today. That is why we have written the chronicle of his deed in letters of bronze in the shrine of our Empire's capital. He has joined the company of those who from Socrates to John Brown have died in freedom's name and freedom's cause. Of these men it was said more than 2,000 years ago that "Their virtues shall be testified not only by the inscription on stone at the time, but in all lands wheresoever in the unwritten record of the mind, which far beyond any monument will remain with all men everlasting."

They sang the Battle Hymn of the Republic, and the two national anthems, and then it was over. As the others shuffled out, Rose stepped in closer to the granite plaque. She saw Billy's pilot's wings, mounted on green felt in a small golden frame. And above them, the words

WILLIAM MEADE LINDSLEY FISKE III

AN AMERICAN CITIZEN WHO DIED THAT ENGLAND MIGHT LIVE.

She stayed there a moment, alone in the cool air of the crypt, and then walked out, up the steps, into the sunshine.

Rose Fiske spent the rest of the war living in London. In 1945 she married Colonel Sir John Lawson, another extraordinary man: Field Marshal Bernard Montgomery described him as "the best squadron leader in the 8th Army." They divorced in 1950. She married for a fourth time the very next year, to Ted Bassett. It was a stormy relationship. Bassett wasn't a popular man with her friends. Mouse Cleaver described him as "a professional gambler," and it is true that in the end she sold off many of Billy's assets, in the film company and in Aspen, to cover his gambling debts. The kindest thing Bill Taylor had to say about Bassett was that he was a "horny bastard, always hot for the hand that is nearest." They, too, eventually divorced. Taylor himself once asked Rose to marry him, only half in jest, but she turned him down, with a laugh, because he didn't have enough money. "I don't think," Taylor said, "that she ever really loved anybody except for Billy." Rose died just after Christmas in 1972, at the age of fifty-nine. Among the few treasured possessions she passed on to her granddaughter, Lady Charlotte Fraser, were a pair of earrings made out of the gold collar studs of Billy's RAF uniform. "Billy," says Lady Fraser, "was always the love of her life."

Beulah Fiske moved out to the West Coast to live near her daughter, Peggy. In December 1942 she received, to her great surprise, a letter from the First Lady.

> *Dear Mrs. Fiske,*
>
> *When I was going through St. Paul's they showed me with great pride the plaque which has been put up in memory of your son, the first American citizen who died "that England might live." Incidentally, I think that the United States might live also. I thought you would like to know with what reverence and admiration they show that plaque not*

*only to American visitors, but to a great many other people. If you have
not seen where it is placed, it is right near the pedestal on which stands the
statue of George Washington in peace time. This statue, of course, is now
put away. My deepest sympathy goes to you, but I must express also my
pride in your son,*

> *Very sincerely yours,*
> *Eleanor Roosevelt.*

Beulah died in 1949.

Peggy Fiske eventually divorced **Jennison Heaton** and remarried. She remained enormously fond, and proud, of her brother right through to the end
of her life in 1987. She told her daughters all about how, when they were very
little, their uncle Billy drove them in a horse and buggy to a park outside the
Fiske family home in Paris, cooked them baked potatoes in a campfire, and
scared them silly by telling them ghost stories.

Jack Heaton died in Paris in 1976, at the age of sixty-eight.

Eddie Eagan never did get back into the boxing ring, or into a bobsled. He was
busy enough at the bar. He spent the rest of the 1930s working as the assistant
district attorney for Southern New York. When the United States entered the
war, he joined up for a second time, in the Army Air Forces. He became the
chief of special service in the Air Transport Command. They even made him a
lieutenant colonel. After the war he became the New York State boxing commissioner. It was a hell of a job, too much even for a man like him. The boxing
business was lousy with racketeers, cheats, and gangsters. The great sportswriter
Red Smith summed it up: "Eddie Eagan is a genuinely sweet guy. He is profoundly honest and profoundly sincere, humble and considerate. The first two
qualities are indispensable in a boxing commissioner; probably the other three
are a handicap." Eddie vowed to "clean it up or quit," and he was as good as his
word: he stepped down in 1951. "Eddie brought with him honesty, sincerity, and
a passionate love of the sport," wrote Arthur J. Daley. "But he also brought what
amounted to naiveté into a sphere of hard-boiled pragmatism." In 1956, President Eisenhower asked him to head up the People-to-People Sports Committee,
and he spent the rest of his life working to encourage children to take up sport.
He ran the sports program at the New York World's Fair in 1964–65 and served

two years as the president of the Boys Athletic League of New York. He and Peggy were happily married right through. They had a house on Long Island Sound, which Eddie named Happy Harbor, one son and one daughter. Eddie died of a heart attack on June 15, 1967, at the age of sixty-nine. More than 250 people turned out for his funeral, among them Jack Dempsey. "He was a good boxer," Jack said, "and he meant a great deal to the youth of America." Gene Tunney couldn't make it because he was in hospital after a fall. Eddie remains the only man in the history of the Olympics to have won gold medals at both the Summer and Winter Games.

Clifford "Tippy" Gray spent the war living in Hollywood, working, as he put it, as a "self-employed writer." In the early 1950s he was living as a "permanent houseguest" of Edward Hillman Jr., a playboy who had inherited his money from his father's department store business. The two of them moved to Acapulco together in 1952, taking along another friend from the old days, the movie star Norman Kerry. Clifford never remarried. He settled back in Daytona Beach, Florida, where he became well known in local high-society circles for his immaculately accurate impressions of Winston Churchill. In his seventies he began to suffer from Parkinson's disease. He spent the final two years of his life in a care home in San Diego. He died in April 1968. Almost inevitably, the brief obituary notices he was given in the local papers confused him with his name-sake, announcing that "Clifford Gray, the composer of If You Were the Only Girl (in the World), has passed away at the age of 76."

The other Clifford Grey is still known in some quarters as a man who led an extraordinary double life as an English composer and an American Olympian, not least, of course, in the Old Cemetery in Ipswich, where his gravestone still marks him out as a two-time Olympic champion.

After Jay died, Dolly O'Brien spent two years in mourning. "A part of Dolly died with him," her friend Suzy Knickerbocker explained. Still, Dolly had a queue of suitors waiting. The most serious of them was Clark Gable, who was still in mourning himself, for his wife Carole Lombard. They had a long affair, and Dolly then dumped him for a Bulgarian count, Jose Dorelis, who was "suave, sophisticated, and always wore a monocle, even when playing golf." After a year's marriage, she divorced Dorelis on grounds of cruelty, explaining to the press, "It is a result of an accumulation of little things. Separately, they were so unimportant that I can't recall particulars. I think the underlying cause of our difficulties was that he seemed to resent, subconsciously perhaps, the fact that I knew so many people." After that, she decided not to marry again, declaring, "Four times is enough!" She died on January 10, 1965. "She may have been a siren," wrote Knickerbocker, "but she was nice to everyone, and she was never pompous or stuffy because she was never insecure."

I rene Fenwick remained married to Lionel Barrymore until her death from complications related to anorexia nervosa on Christmas Eve 1936. **Mae Murray** stayed married to the film director Bob Leonard for seven years. A year after their divorce, she got married again, this time to a dubious Georgian prince, David Mdivani, who also became her manager. She made the mistake of listening to him when he told her to quit her contract with MGM. Louis B. Mayer made sure she never worked in movies again. Her career stalled, and Mdivani burned through her earnings. They had a particularly ugly divorce. Still, she said, "once a star is always a star." She took a job as a dancer at Billy Rose's Diamond Horseshoe nightclub. In 1964 she was found, confused and destitute, wandering the streets of St. Louis. She told the police that she had forgotten the name of her hotel, and she refused to accept money for a ticket back to her hometown of LA because she insisted that she was trying to get to New York. After a spell in a Salvation Army home, she was eventually taken into the Motion Picture House in Woodland Hills, a retirement home for Hollywood professionals. She died there on March 23, 1965.

T he first "Wolf of Wall Street," **Clarence Dillon**, died in 1979. He was ninety-six. By then he was, in the words of his company's official history, "almost completely forgotten outside of the firm," although he remained involved in its running right up to the very end of his life. Whenever new partners or vice presidents joined the firm, they would be summoned for a dinner at his estate so they could meet him for the first—and in most cases, only—time. His son, Douglas Dillon, served as the US ambassador to France under President Eisenhower and as the secretary of the Treasury under President Kennedy. After his father's death, Douglas Dillon agreed to sell the controlling interest in the firm to the Bechtel Group.

G odfrey Dewey never did become the president of the Lake Placid Club Foundation, though he never stopped fighting other board members for the position. And the 1932 Winter Olympics didn't do much for the club. It floundered, and passed into receivership by the end of the decade. During the war, it was bought by the US Army, which turned it into a rest and recreation center for soldiers. Over the next three decades the club sold off most of its land, but stuck fast by its exclusionary practices, even in the face of an investigation by the state Commission Against Discrimination in 1958. Membership dwindled. Finally, in 1976, the clubhouse was made open, all year-round, to all members of the public, regardless of creed or class. It was a little too late to help: in 1977 it was converted to serve as a regular hotel. Dewey died in October of that year, at the age of ninety. Three years later, in 1980, Lake Placid became one of the few towns to be awarded the Olympics for a second time, a feat all the more astonishing when you consider just how small a community it is. The club finally closed in 2002.

rving Jaffee was elected to the United States' skating hall of fame in 1940 and to the International Jewish Sports Hall of Fame in 1979. He died two years later. Werner Zahn spent the Second World War running his manufacturing firm, which produced the leather liners for military helmets. In 1944 a photograph of Zahn, in full military fig standing next to Adolf Hitler, appeared in the American newspapers, prompting a gleeful retelling of his Olympic exploits in the pages of the *Lake Placid News*. "With typical German arrogance, the Berliners rejected Billy Fiske's offer to take them down the course to show them one bad turn. Zahn thereupon took his team down the run and at the curve which the Americans had indicated, the Heinies were hurtling through the air." Zahn died in 1971, apparently after crashing his Bugatti sports car. He was eighty-one at the time. Hank Homburger died in Sacramento in 1950. The bob run he helped build on Mount Van Hoevenberg remained one of the fastest and most dangerous courses in the world even after they closed the first half mile: Max Houben died at Shady in 1949, and Sergio Zardini at Zig-Zag in 1966. A new run was built in time for the 1980 Winter Olympics. Reto Capadrutt died in 1939, after crashing his bob on the track at St. Moritz. After the war, René Fonjallaz was imprisoned for two years by the Swiss government after he was found guilty of collaborating with the Nazis. Hans Kilian became a hotelier. Christian Fischbacher became the Honorary Life President of the St. Moritz Tobogganing Club. "Suicide Freddie" McEvoy was credited with, among other things, "launching the fashion for flowered shirts for men" when he sold his own, right off his back, to an Argentine millionaire for two thousand dollars. He became a great friend of Errol Flynn and gave evidence on his behalf when he was accused of statutory rape. He drowned off the coast of Morocco when his 104-ton schooner was wrecked on the rocks near Cape Cantrin during a storm. According to reports, McEvoy actually made it to the shore but went back into the water to rescue his wife.

Billy's friend from Cambridge, **Henry Longhurst,** became a golf writer for the *Times* and spent the Second World War serving as an anti-aircraft gunner. He didn't see much of Billy after university, but he thought of him every now and then. "A little incident at a Birmingham gun site will always stick in my memory," he wrote. "Twice a week, two kindly ladies used to appear in a YMCA van and hoot encouragingly at the foot of our tower—whereupon the monkeys would down tools and rush down for their bag of nuts. They sold us chocolate and cakes and razor blades and tea and lent out books, and were a cheerful and highly acceptable link with the outside world. One day, as I sipped my tea at the counter, I noticed the crossed Union Jack and Stars and Stripes on the side of the van. Underneath were the words 'Fiske memorial.' Billy Fiske! My mind raced back over the years to the time when we used to travel almost daily the 21 miles from Cambridge to Mildenhall in his monstrous supercharged green Bentley, and to the days when his father had helped send a team of us to play golf in the United States . . . Now he lies buried in a Sussex churchyard, and a plaque in St. Paul's commemorates our gratitude. I wondered what crisp comment this forthright little man would have come out with if he could have seen me drinking tea from the van that kept his memory alive."

Among the 601 pilots, **Max Aitken, Archie Hope, Little Bill Clyde, Paddy Green,** and **Mouse Cleaver** all survived the war. Cleaver regained some use of his eyes, after countless operations. **Willie Rhodes-Moorhouse** was shot down and killed during the Battle of Britain. **Roger Bushell** was executed by the Gestapo after orchestrating "the great escape" from the Stalag Luft III prisoner-of-war camp. He inspired the character of Big X, played by Richard Attenborough in the film about the escape. **Dr. Courtney Willey** was awarded the Military Cross for his conduct at Tangmere on the day of the raid, August 16, 1940. The two nursing orderlies **George Jones** and **Cyril Faulkner** were both awarded the Military Medal for retrieving Billy from his burning plane.

Billy Fiske received five posthumous decorations. The most notable of these was the oak leaf emblem he was awarded after he was mentioned in dispatches by Air Chief Marshal Sir Hugh Dowding on September 29, 1940, for "gallant and distinguished services." The Ashcroft Mountain resort project at Aspen was abandoned during the war, because, as T. J. Flynn explained, "frankly, after Billy was killed we had little heart for putting steel into ski lifts." But there is, to this day, a Fiske cross-country ski trail in Ashcroft, renowned as one of the hardest in the area. As Lord Brabazon of Tara predicted it would, the memory of Billy Fiske lives on in the mountains. The best bobsledders in the United States still compete for the beautiful Billy Fiske Memorial Trophy, which is awarded each year to the winners of the four-man national championship. And in St. Moritz, a Billy Fiske Trophy is still awarded every year to the rider who records the fastest time in the Grand National on the Cresta Run.

On September 23, 2002, the few surviving members of 601 Squadron gathered together at Boxgrove Priory with a group of friends, servicemen and servicewomen, and well-wishers, for a ceremony of thanksgiving for the life of Billy Fiske and to dedicate a new memorial headstone. The old, original stone is now kept in the memorial garden at RAF Tangmere. In 2008, sixty-eight years after Billy's death, the 601 Squadron Old Comrades Association paid for the construction and installation of a new stained-glass window at Boxgrove. It was designed and made by the artist Mel Howse. It shows Billy's Hurricane, with the Stars and Stripes trailing from one wing. When the sun catches it, the soft stone of this old English church is bathed in brilliant shades of red, white, and blue.

AUTHOR'S NOTE

*S*peed Kings is, to borrow a phrase, a nonfiction novel. The characters are real, and the events are true. There are, of course, certain limitations on how accurate you can be when you're telling a tale that took place so long ago and all the protagonists are dead. Still, it is as faithful and precise as I was able to make it. The weather, for instance, is taken from contemporary newspaper reports. Conversations, where quoted, are taken from primary sources. I've used a certain degree of license when relating the motivations and moods of the main characters, although in several instances I was fortunate enough to have access to private diaries and letters, which gave me a good steer as to how they were feeling.

I have made extensive use of previously unpublished material from a large archive of Billy Fiske's letters, diaries, photographs, and personal journals. These were drawn from four collections, the first of them owned by the family of Peggy Fiske: Charles, Setsuko, and Emi Zabalaga; the second of them belonging to Billy's cousin, Newell Fiske Wagoner; the third to Skip Grieser; and the fourth to Richard Perkins. I was lucky enough to have access to two unpublished biographies of Billy: *An American Original*, by Richard Perkins, and *Billy Fiske*, by Skip Grieser. Plenty of the additional material is drawn from the extensive interviews with members of the St. Moritz Tobogganing Club, 601 Squadron, and other friends of Billy's conducted by Perkins and Grieser. This book stands on their shoulders. I have also used previously unpublished material from the archives of Lake Placid Olympic Museum.

I've made extensive use, too, of innumerable newspaper and magazine articles, which are, in the main, cited in the text as and when they occur. Finally, I have drawn material and information from the following books:

Anger, Kenneth, *Hollywood Babylon* (Dell Publishing, 1998)

Ankerich, Michael G., *Mae Murray: The Girl with the Bee-stung Lips* (University Press of Kentucky, 2012)

Ardmore, Jane Kesner, *The Self-Enchanted: Mae Murray and the Image of an Era* (McGraw-Hill, 1959)

Barbee Lee, Mabel, *Back in Cripple Creek* (Doubleday & Co., 1968)

Bret, David, *Clark Gable: Tormented Star* (Da Capo Press, 2008)

Bushby, John, *Gunner's Moon: Memoir of the RAF Night Assault on Germany* (Futura, 1975)

Byron, Reginald, and David Coxon, *Tangmere: An Authorized History* (Grub Street, 2013)

Campbell, Christy, *Fenian Fire: The British Government Plot to Assassinate Queen Victoria* (HarperCollins, 2002)

Carter, Randolph, *The World of Flo Ziegfeld* (Praeger Publishers, 1974)

Cull, Nicholas John, *Selling War: The British Propaganda Campaign against American Neutrality* (Oxford University Press, 1996)

De Holguin, Beatrice, *Tales of Palm Beach* (Vantage Press, 1968)

DeArment, Robert K., *Bat Masterson: The Man and the Legend* (University of Oklahoma Press, 1995)

The Dictionary of American Biography (Charles Scribner's Sons, 2004)

DiGiacomo, Michael, *Apparently Unharmed: Riders of the Cresta Run* (Texere Publishing, 2000)

Douglas, Sholto, *Combat and Command: The Story of an Airman in Two World Wars* (Simon & Schuster, 1966)

Eagan, Eddie, *Fighting for Fun* (Lovat Dickson Ltd., 1934)

Fowler, Karin J., *David Niven: A Bio-bibliography* (Greenwood Publishing Group, 1995)

Henderson Clark, Donald, *In the Reign of Rothstein* (Vanguard Press, 1930)

Higham, Charles, and Roy Moseley, *Cary Grant: The Lonely Heart* (Harcourt, 1989)

Jasen, David A., *P. G. Wodehouse: Portrait of a Master* (Mason & Lipscomb, 1974)

———. *Tin Pan Alley: An Encyclopedia of the Golden Age of Song* (Routledge, 2003)

Kendall, Paul, *Aisne 1914: The Dawn of Trench Warfare* (History Press, 2012)

Kershaw, Alex, *The Few* (Penguin, 2008)

Klieger, P. Christiaan, *The Fleischmann Yeast Family* (Arcadia Publishing, 2004)

Knowles, Mark, *The Wicked Waltz and Other Scandalous Dances* (McFarland, 2009)

Kriendler, H. Peter, *"21": Memoirs of a Saloon-Keeper* (Rowman & Littlefield, 1999)

Large, Dorothy (ed.), *As We Were: Life in Early Longmont as Reflected in the Newspapers of the Day* (Sharer Books, 1977)

Longhurst, Henry, *My Life and Soft Times* (Littlehampton Book Services, 1971)

MacKenzie, Mary, *The Plains of Abraham: A History of North Elba and Lake Placid* (Nicholas K. Burns Publishing, 2007)

Marion, Frances, *Off with Their Heads* (Macmillan, 1972)

Martineau, Hubert, *My Life in Sport* (Water Martin Press, 1970)

Mason, Francis K., *Battle over Britain: A History of the German Air Assaults on Great Britain* (McWhirter Twins Ltd., 1969)

McCrary, John, *First of the Many* (Robson Books, 1981)

Mitgang, Herbert, *Once upon a Time in New York: Jimmy Walker, Franklin Roosevelt, and the Last Great Battle of the Jazz Age* (Cooper Square Press, 2003)

Mordden, Ethan, *Ziegfeld: The Man Who Invented Show Business* (St. Martin's Press, 2008)

Moulson, Tom, *The Flying Sword: The Story of 601 Squadron* (MacDonald, 1964)

Murray, Mae, *My Memories* (as published in the *Milwaukee Sentinel*, May 1942)

Nicholl, K. I., *The History of the St. Moritz Bobsleigh Club* (private press, 1975)

Olsen, Lynne, *Citizens of London: The Americans Who Stood with Britain in Its Darkest, Finest Hour* (Random House, 2011)

Ortloff, George Christian, and Stephen C. Ortloff, *Lake Placid: The Olympic Years* (Macromedia Inc., 1976)

Perez, Robert C., and Edward F. Willett, *Clarence Dillon: A Wall Street Enigma* (Madison Books, 1995)

Rider, Freemont, *Melvil Dewey* (American Library Association, 1944)

Rivadue, Barry, *Alice Faye: A Bio-bibliography* (Greenwood Publishing Group, 1990)

Schuessler, Michael Karl, *Elena Poniatowski: An Intimate Biography* (University of Arizona Press, 2007)

Seth-Smith, Michael, *The Cresta Run* (W. Foulsham & Co., 1976)

Small Town, Big Dreams: Lake Placid's Olympic Story (a Marc Nathanson– Scott F. Carroll Production in association with Sundial Pictures, 2010)

Smith, Amanda (ed.), *Hostage to Fortune: The Letters of Joseph Patrick Kennedy* (Viking, 2001)

Sobel, Robert, *The Life and Times of Dillon Read* (Truman Talley Books, 1991)

Stansfield, Dean S., *Images of America: Lake Placid* (Arcadia, 2002)

———. *Images of America: North Elba and Whiteface Mountain* (Arcadia, 2003)

Stewart Martin, James, *All Honorable Men* (Little, Brown, 1950)

St. Vrain Valley Historical Association, *They Came to Stay* (Longmont Printing Company, 1971)

Sutton, Antony C., *Wall Street and the Rise of Hitler* (Clairview Books, 2010)

Tangye, Derek (ed.), *Went the Day Well* (George Harrap & Co., 1942)

Tyrell Kelly, Barbara, *Growing Up in Lake Placid* (Graphics North, 2012)

Van Diggelen, Michael H. (ed.), *Billy Fiske: A Souvenir Brochure* (private press, 2002)

Wallechinsky, David, and Jaime Loucky, *The Complete Book of the Winter Olympics 2014* (Crossroad Press, 2014)

Wiegand, Wayne A., *Irrepressible Reformer: A Biography of Melvil Dewey* (American Library Association, 1996)

Wilkinson, Philip, *An American Citizen Who Died That England Might Live* (Lisek Publications, T J Kean, 1995)

Wood, Houston, *Displacing Natives: The Rhetorical Production of Hawai'i* (Rowman & Littlefield, 1995)

Woon, Basil Dillon, *From Deauville to Monte Carlo* (H. Liveright, 1929)

ACKNOWLEDGMENTS

I wouldn't have been able to write *Speed Kings* without the help and support of a lot of people. First, my agents, Rupert Heath, who had the perspicacity to spot that this was a tale worth telling, and Dan Conaway. Then my editors, Giles Elliott and Megan Newman, and the teams at both Transworld in the UK and Avery in the United States, especially Dan Balado, Brittney Ross, Gabrielle Campo, and Maureen Klier. Thanks, too, to my editors at the *Guardian* and the *Observer*, Ian Prior, Matthew Hancock, and Steve McMillan, for cutting me a little slack and showing a lot of patience while I was working on the book.

I owe Skip Grieser an enormous debt of thanks, for his hard work, his generosity with his time and research, and his lessons in how to shoot pool. He deserves the credit for unearthing many of the details about Billy Fiske's life that have never been published before. The book was hugely enriched by the kind cooperation of Billy's relatives, in particular Pat Zabalaga, Emi Zabalaga, and Charles and Setsuko Zabalaga, who gave up their time to help me look through his papers. Also, I spent an enchanting afternoon listening to Newell Fiske Wagoner's firsthand memories of '32, and I wish to thank Lady Charlotte Fraser for allowing me to see the heirlooms Rose passed on to her.

It would have been impossible to unravel the mystery of Clifford Gray without the help of John Cross and Brian Willey in particular, but also Bill Mallon, Hilary Evans, David Routh, Caroline Markham, Norman Carter, and Mel Allen. It was a pleasure talking to Tim Clark about the story he wrote back in

1980, and plenty of other things besides. Thanks to Vicki Barcus and the rest of Clifford Grey's family for the good grace with which they took the bad news that in fact their grandfather wasn't an Olympic champion after all.

Lake Placid is one of the friendliest little towns I've ever had the fortune to pass through. Thanks go to John Morgan, Jennifer Tufano, and Beverley Reid for their local expertise; Amanda Bird from the US Bobsled and Skeleton Federation for helping me arrange an absorbing hourlong interview with Steve Holcomb; and especially to the staff at the Lake Placid Olympic Museum, Alison Haas, Steve Vassar, and Susanna Fout, for giving me such a warm welcome and so much help. I'm grateful, too, to the bobsledding team out at Mount Van Hoevenberg for getting me down the run in one piece.

Thanks to Peter Hopsicker, associate professor of kinesiology at Penn State, for being generous enough to send me copies of his excellent series of articles on the 1932 Winter Olympics; Stephen Bartley, the archivist of the St. Moritz Tobogganing Club, for allowing me access to his library; William Morrison, the honorary archivist of the W. O. Bentley Memorial Foundation; Giles Richards, for helping me research the Le Mans 24; the museum staff at both RAF Hendon and RAF Tangmere; and Ewan Getley, for showing me around his wonderful workshop, and scaring me silly by taking me for a drive around Bicester in his Bentley.

Many thanks to all my friends for listening to me wax on about this book at such length for so long, particularly Paul Matthews, Will Small, Sarah Courtauld, and Jonathan Weil for their advice and guidance, and Maggie Asquith for her inspiration and encouragement. Finally, thanks most of all to my family, Tony, Sandra, Jon, Shoko, Keita, Arthur, and my partner, Hadley Freeman, for all her support, wisdom, and love.

INDEX

Page numbers in italics denote photographs.

Acton, Harold, 136
Aitken, Max, 219, 222, 245, 246, 266, 273
Alba, Duke of, 59
Albright, Hardie, 203
Amateur Athletic Union (AAU), 115–16, 151, 153, 156–57, 212
American Library Association (ALA), 101, 102, 105
Amundsen, Roald, 165
Ankerich, Michael, 40
Ardmore, Jane, 36
Argentina, 12, 57, 83, 86
Aspen, 206–8, 216, 218, 227, 274
Association for the Protection of the Adirondacks (AFPA), 110–12
Astor, John Jacob, 55
Australia, 12–13, 140–41
Austria, 163, 169, 174, 214, 221
Ayer, Nat, 67, 71

Badrutt family, 15–16, 18, 19, 25
Bailey, Roger, 217, 218, 222
Baillet-Latour, Count de, 96, 112, 184
Barcus, Vicki, 73
Barrymore, Lionel, 41, 42, 271
Bassett, Ted, 268
Bathurst, Ben, 230–31, 239
Beaverbrook, Lord, 219, 246, 262
Belfort, Jordan, 9
Belgium, 11, 55, 163, 164, 174, 178, 238
Bell, C. H., 29

Benchley, Robert, 207
Benjamin, Park, 48
Berlin, Irving, 34
Bickford, Jim, 211
Blane, Sally, 217
Blossom, George, 125–27
Boblet Grand Prix Cup, 23–24, 59
Bobsleigh Derby, 55, 82–84, 91
Bodrero, Jim, 202, 207
Bogart, Humphrey, 205
Boncompagni, Prince, 59
Boyd, William, 205
Bracken, Brendan, 266
Brancourt, J. D., 141
Brehme, Albert, 163, 189
Britain, 7, 10, 15, 20, 22–24, 30, 32, 47–49, 55, 70, 74, 76, 146, 215–16
    bobsledding in, 17, 18, 55
    boxing in, 137–40
    in Second World War, 226, 234, 236, 238–40, 246, 263 (see also Royal Air Force)
    Winter Olympics teams of, 86, 90–92, 145, 174
    See also London
Brown, John, 106
Brundage, Avery, 208, 212–13
Bryant, Percy, 150
Bullock, Hugh, 9
Burke, Jack, 132–33
Burke, Oscar, 26

Bushby, John, 258
Bushell, Roger, 219, 226, 227, 231, 244, 266, 273

Cambridge University, 5, 137–38, 146, 195, 205, 220
Canada, 7, 9–10, 15–17, 57, 65, 109, 151
    Winter Olympics teams of, 82, 89, 94, 174, 184
Capadrutt, Reto, 164, 171, 182–83, 186, 187, 189, 272
Carbery, Lord, 21
Carlsen, Armand, 87, 88
Carnegie, Andrew, 105
Carpentier, Georges, 139
Carter, Randolph, 68
Cassidy, John C. and Clara Louise Whelan, 78
Castle, Vernon and Irene, 34–35
Chaplin, Charlie, 203
Cherrill, Virginia, 203–4, 211
Churchill, Winston, 235, 238–39, 245, 262, 266, 270
Clark, Tim, 63–66, 72–74
Clary, Count, 90
Cleaver, Neil "Mouse," 203, 215–16, 219, 229, 239–40, 245, 250, 255, 259, 260, 263, 266, 268, 273
Clemenceau, Georges, 132
Clifton, Arthur, 138, 139
Clyde, Billy, 219, 222, 226–28, 230, 239, 245, 255–60, 273
Clyde, Rose, 227
Colledge, Cecilia, 174
Cook, B. J., 148–49
Corviglia ski club, 59
Corwin, Dean, 130
Coubertin, Baron Pierre de, 56–57
Cresta Run (St. Moritz), 16, 19, 55, 89, 90, 93, 214–15, 219, 230, 246, 249, 262, 274
Cross, John, 72–73
Curzon, Frank, 55

Daley, Arthur J., 169, 269
Davis, Al, 32–34
Davis, George, 66
Davis, Percival, see Grey, Clifford
Davos, 56
Dawes, Brigadier Charles, 10
Dawes Plan, 214
Demetriadi, Dick, 251
DeMille, Cecil B., 40, 203
Dempsey, Jack, 126–29, 131–33, 139–43, 148, 270
Denver, 120, 142
    Athletic Club, 119, 123–25, 127, 130
de Saulles, Blanca, 35, 38–39

de Saulles, Jack, 34–39
Devine, Charles, 166–68
Dewey, Annie (Godfrey's mother), 102–3, 107
Dewey, Emily (Godfrey's stepmother), 108, 158
Dewey, Godfrey, 96, 99–100, 105–16, 145–46, 149–58, 178, 195, 196, 207, 208
    antagonism toward O'Brien and Fiske of, 115–16, 149, 151–56, 170
    bigotry of, 113–14
    birth of, 103
    bobsled run built by, 110–13, 115, 149–50, 154, 171
    bobsleds designed by, 152–53, 165, 167
    death of, 272
    defeated to become president of Lake Placid Club Foundation, 157–58, 271–72
    education of, 106, 107
    family background of, 100–103
    Kirby's post-Olympics letter to, 191–92
    lobbying for Lake Placid as Olympics host city by, 99–100, 108–10
    local bobsled team preferred by, 150–51, 154–66
    at 1928 Winter Olympics, 86, 99, 149
    during 1932 Winter Olympics, 173–76, 183, 184, 186, 188
Dewey, Katharine (Godfrey's daughter), 169
Dewey, Marjorie (Godfrey's wife), 107
Dewey, Melvil (Godfrey's father), 100–109, 113–14, 158
Dickie, W. G., 251
Dillon, Clarence, 7–12, 197, 213–14, 231, 271
Dillon, Douglas, 271
Dillon, Read & Company, 8–12, 147, 213, 214, 218, 221, 227, 228, 261
Diop, Amadou, 141
Dix, Joan, 174
Doe, Tom, Jr., 85
Dolly sisters, 26
Dorelis, Jose, 270–71
Doubleday, Abner, 17
Douglas, Sholto, 247
Douglas-Hamilton, Douglas "Douglo," 137, 139, 140
Dowding, Hugh, 274
Duke, Angier, 33
Dupree, Paul, 181, 210

Eagan, Clara (Eddie's mother), 120, 125, 142
Eagan, Eddie, 118, 119–43, 185, 195, 215, 217, 227, 269–70
    amateur boxing championships of, 118, 119–25, 130–31, 133–35, 138, 180, 270
    in army, 129, 269
    at Billy's funeral, 238

death of, 270
Dempsey in exhibition fights against, 126–29, 139
Dewey's antagonism toward, 155–56
education of, 121, 123, 125, 129, 130, 132–33, 135–37, 139, 180, 185
legal career of, 143, 185, 269
marriage and family of, 143, 270
in 1932 Winter Olympics, 143, 148, 157, 178–80, 185, 187, 189–91, 245, 270
and 1936 Winter Olympics, 209–11
on world tour with Pirie boys, 139–42
Eagan, John (Eddie's father), 120
Eagan, Peggy Colgate (Eddie's wife), 143, 191, 270
Earhart, Amelia, 74
Eberstadt, Ferdinand, 11, 213
Edward, Prince of Wales, 47–49, 137
Eisenhower, Dwight D., 269, 271
Eisner, Mark, 113
Eliot, T. S., 18, 136
Elisabeth, Empress of Austria, 18
Elliott, William, 231
Ellis, William Webb, 17
Empson, John Howard, 122
Evanson, Bernt, 87–88, 90

Fairbanks, Douglas, Jr., 5, 201, 217
Fall, Louis Mbarick, 139
Faulkner, Cyril, 257–58, 273
Faye, Alice, 205, 245
Fenwick, Irene, 41–43, 75, 77, 271
Ferris, Daniel, 116, 151, 153, 156, 157
Finland, 56, 236
    Winter Olympics teams of, 87, 90, 94, 174
First World War, 129, 164
Fischbacher, Christian, 215, 219, 272
Fisher, Carl, 47
Fiske, Beulah Bexford (Billy's mother), 7, 26, 51, 236–38, 261, 266, 268–69
Fiske, Billy, 2, 3–7, 15, 26, 50, 79, 106, 146–49, 195–211, 213–22, 269
    adolescence of, 51–52
    Aspen resort project of, 206–208, 216, 218
    birth of, 7
    childhood of, 9–10
    in Cresta Run races, 54–56, 214–15
    death of, 257–63, 265–66
    Dewey's antagonism toward, 149, 151–56
    at Dillon, Read & Company, 218, 221
    education of, 12, 146–47, 195, 205, 273
    family background of, 6–7
    fast cars driven by, 3–6, 147, 246, 250, 273
    Hollywood production company of, 201–205, 218
    marriage of Rose and, 221
    memorial service for, 265–68
    in 1928 Winter Olympics, 14, 82–86, 89–94, 171, 195
    in 1932 Winter Olympics, 116, 148–49, 152–57, 164, 166, 171, 173–79, 182, 183, 185, 187–92, 211, 265, 272, 195
    and 1936 Winter Olympics, 208–11
    posthumous honors for, 273–74
    in RAF, 224, 225, 226, 228–40, 242, 243–55
    romances of, 198–99, 205, 215–19
    Satan bobsled of, 50, 52–53
    travels of, 12–13, 195–201
Fiske, Peggy (Billy's sister), 6, 84, 196, 201, 205, 218, 238, 266, 268
    and Billy's enlistment in RAF, 229–32, 236–37
    birth of, 7
    childhood of, 9–10
    in Nazi Berlin, 211
    romance, marriage and divorce of Jennison Heaton and, 55, 82, 148, 269
    in St. Moritz, 26, 51
Fiske, Phineas, 7
Fiske, Rose Bingham (Billy's wife), 240, 244, 246, 248, 252, 253, 255
    and Billy's death, 260–63
    and Billy's RAF enlistment and flight training, 229, 233–29
    death of, 268
    divorce of Greville and, 218, 221
    first marriage of, 216–17
    marriage of Billy and, 221
    at memorial service for Billy, 265–68
    in New York, 194, 217–18, 227, 230
    volunteer ambulance corps plan of, 231, 232
Fiske, W. L. M., I (Billy's grandfather), 6–7
Fiske, W. L. M., II (Billy's father), 6–13, 26, 51, 55, 82, 147, 197, 213, 236, 237, 261, 266, 273
Fitzgerald, F. Scott, 43, 71
Fleischmann, Julius, 42–48
Fleischmann, Lilly, 43–44
Fleming, Major Philip, 153
Floto, Otto, 127–29
Flynn, Errol, 217, 272–73
Flynn, "Fireman" Jim, 127
Flynn, T. J., 206, 216, 274
Fonjallaz, René, 170–71, 189, 220, 272
Forrestal, James, 9
Fox, John Donna, 208, 209
France, 7, 10, 11, 13, 45, 46, 90, 100, 146, 219
    resorts in, 100 (see also French Riviera)
    in Second World War, 226, 236, 238, 244, 251
    Winter Olympics team of, 87, 93, 163, 174

Francis, Owen, 219
Franks, Harry, 134, 138
Fraser, Lady Charlotte, 268
French Riviera, 3–6, 48, 49, 230, 246
Fuller, E. M., 33

Gable, Clark, 270
Garbo, Greta, 217
Garren, Jack, 208, 209
Germany, 10, 153
  Nazi, *see* Nazis
  1928 Winter Olympics team of, 57, 86
  1932 Winter Olympics team of, 157, 163,
    164, 166, 168, 170, 174, 183, 186–87, 220
  post–First World War economy of, 10–11,
    170
  in Second World War, 71, 226, 228, 234–36,
    238, 244, 247–48, 250–56
Gershwin, George, 70
Gestapo, 220, 273
Goering, Hermann, 255
Gold Cup, 26, 83
Gordon, Vivian, 177
Gould, Mrs. Frank J., 25
Grace, William Russell, 30, 31
Grainger, David, 84–85
Gramajo, Arturo, 24, 55, 86, 91, 93
Grant, Cary, 203–4
Grau, Fritz, 163, 183, 189, 1990
Gray, Clifford "Tippy," 72–79, 116, 148, 179,
    195, 215, 227, 238, 270
  birth of, 72, 74–75
  British songwriter Clifford Grey confused
    with, 63–66, 72–74, 79, 270
  Dewey's antagonism toward, 116, 149, 155–
    56
  in 1928 Winter Olympics, 64, 79, 82, 85, 86,
    92
  in 1932 Winter Olympics, 64, 148, 157, 178,
    179, 187, 189–91, 245
  and 1936 Winter Olympics, 208–11
  show business career of, 74–78
Great Crash of 1929, 9, 78, 111, 170
Great Depression, 98, 111, 145, 177
Great Neck (Long Island), 29, 71
Green, Paddy, 205, 206, 217, 219, 220, 273
Green, W. G., 257
Grey, Clifford, 61, 62, 63–74, 76, 79, 270
  Olympic bobsledder Clifford Gray confused
    with, 63–66, 72–74, 79, 270
Grey, Dorothy "Babs" (Clifford's step-
    daughter), 64–65, 73
Grey, Dorothy Gould (Clifford's wife), 67, 68,
    70
Grey, Jill (Clifford's daughter), 64–65

Grey, June (Clifford's daughter), 63–65, 73
Grossmith, George, Jr., 67
Grosvenor, Lord Edward, 220
Gudenus, Count Baptist, 169
Gyssling, Georg, 170, 220

Hachmann, Erwin, 187–88
Haffenden, Maurice, 257
Hanson brothers, 65
Harrow School, 17
Harvard University, 8, 106
  Law School, 135, 185
Hawks, Howard, 201
Healey, "Big" Tim, 120–21
Hearst, William Randolph, 71
Heaton, Jack, 26, 54–55, 59, 152, 153, 191, 214
  in Bobsleigh Derby, 82–84, 91
  death of, 269
  in 1928 Winter Olympics, 85–86, 90
  in 1932 Winter Olympics, 182–83
  world travels of Billy and, 195–200
Heaton, Jennison, 26, 54–55, 59, 206, 231, 238
  in 1928 Winter Olympics, 85–86, 90, 91, 93
  romance, marriage and divorce of Peggy
    Fiske and, 55, 82, 148, 269
Heaton, Trowbridge, 26, 54–55, 59
Hege, Louis van, 164, 178
Hemingway, Ernest, 74
Heminway, Laura Hylan, *see* O'Brien, Dolly
Henie, Sonja, 94, 174, 181
Hildebrand, Joel Henry, 210
Hillman, Edward, Jr., 270
Hine, Lyman, 84
Hitler, Adolf, 211, 213, 214, 225, 226, 234, 240,
    248, 272
Holcomb, Steve, 53–54, 166–67, 189
Holdstock, Tom, 134
Homburger, Hank, *144*, 165, 168, 171, 176, 195,
    208
  course record set by, 152, 155, 178, 184
  death of, 272
  Dewey's advocacy of, 150–52, 154–55
  in 1932 Winter Olympics, 155–57, 181, 183–
    84, 186, 187, 189–91
  at site of German crash, 162–63
  in Olympic trials, 154
Hood, Betty, 164
Hoover, Herbert, 171
Hope, Archie, 239–40, 244–46, 254, 256, 258–
    60, 273
Hope, Bob, 70
Hopmann, Helmut, 163
Hopsicker, Peter, 104, 112
Horlick, William, 8
Horton, Ed, 150

Horton, H. L., 32
Houben, Max, 178, 189, 272
Howard, Brian, 136–37
Howse, Mel, 274
Hulks, Henry, 138
Huxley, Aldous, 1

India, 140
Inter-Allied Games, 131–32
Interlaken, 56
International Bobsledding and Tobogganing
    Federation, 115–16, 151, 156, 170, 187–88
International Olympic Committee (IOC), 86,
    96, 112, 157, 212
    founding of, 56
    Olympic host cities chosen by, 108–9, 111,
        115, 174
    twenty-four-hour window after official
        close of games permitted by, 184, 188
    unpopular decisions of, 88, 90, 91
International Skating Federation, 88
International Society of Olympic Historians,
    66, 72
International Week of Winter Sports, 57
Irish Parliamentary Fund Association, 30
Italy, 11, 57, 140, 215–16
    1932 Winter Olympics team of, 163, 164,
        174, 186

Jaffee, Irving, 87–90, 176, 191, 211–12, 272
Janeway, Eliot, 9
Japan, 57, 201
    1932 Winter Olympics team of, 145, 174
Jenks, Jeremiah, 103
Jewish National Council, 113
Jews, 87, 211–14
    discrimination against, 8, 103–6, 113–14,
        149

Kearns, Jack, 127–28
Jones, George, 257–58, 273
Kaufman, G. B., 207
Kelly, Barbara Tyrell, 111, 164
Kelly, Eugenia, 33–34
Kelly, Helen, see Princess Vlora
Kennedy, John F., 271
Kennedy, Joseph, 230, 238
Kern, Jerome, 68, 69
Kerry, Norman, 270
Kieran, John, 83–84, 92
Kilian, Hans, 86, 91, 93, 183, 187–89, 191, 272
Kirby, Gustavus T., 58–59, 86, 88–89, 153–57,
    173, 191–92
Knickerbocker, Suzy, 48, 49, 270, 271
Krasnowski, Mademoiselle, 23–24, 55

Krotki, Rudolf, 163
Kristallnacht, 214
Kubes, Milton, 140

La Guardia, Fiorello, 212
Lake Placid, 103, 105–7, 207–11, 114
    National Championship competition in,
        153, 154, 156, 157, 166, 181, 190, 191
    1932 Winter Olympics in, 2, 63–64, 96,
        97–100, 108–16, 144, 145–46, 148–58, 162,
        164–66, 168–71, 172, 173–92, 219, 220,
        265, 272
    1980 Winter Olympics in, 63, 66, 99, 272
Lambert, Ernest "Henri," 55, 83–84, 86, 91–93
Langes, Gunther, 207–8
Lapowski, Clarence, see Dillon, Clarence
Lardner, Ring, 69, 71
Larisch, Count and Countess, 18
Larsen, Roald, 88
Lasky, Jesse, 75
Latvia, 57
Laughlin, James, 60, 103
Lausanne, 65, 71
Lawson, Colonel Sir John, 268
Le Mans 24-Hour endurance race, 6, 13
League of Nations, 201
Leipziger, Henry, 104
Leo X, Pope, 15
Leonard, Bob, 40, 41, 271
Littlemore, Bill, 252, 258
Lloyd George, David, 132
Lockhart, Ruby, 209
Logan, Colonel James A., 11
Lombard, Carole, 270
London, 11, 15, 49, 148, 219, 238, 260
    Cleaver in hospital in, 263
    Eagan in, 138
    Gray in, 76, 77
    Grey in, 67, 68
    Billy and Rose in, 221, 229, 232–33, 236, 239
    Billy's drives between Cambridge and, 5–6,
        147
    memorial for Billy in, 265–68
Longhurst, Henry, 4, 5, 147, 273
Loos, Anita, 38
Los Angeles, 142
    1932 Summer Olympics in, 98, 109
Luxembourg, 91

MacArthur, General Douglas, 58, 59
Mahoney, Jeremiah, 212–13
Malan, Adolph "Sailor," 250–51
Marion, Frances, 75–76
Maris, Mona, 203
Market National Bank, 43

Marshall, Louis, 104
Martin, George W., 154
Martin, James Stewart, 214
Martineau, Henry, 55, 86, 91, 92
Martineau, Hubert, 22–27, 53, 55, 56, 59, 93, 220–21
Martineau Trophy, 191
Marx brothers, 71
Mason, Geoffrey, 61, 72–73, 75, 81–83, 85, 86, 92–94, 99
Mathey, Dean, 9
McEvoy, Freddie, 219, 272–73
McIntyre, Odd, 26, 74, 76–79
McKinley, William, 43
McLemore, Henry, 181–82, 188, 191
McTigue, Mike, 139
Mdivani, David, 271
Melhorn, Hans, 167–68
Metro-Goldwyn-Mayer (MGM), 34, 217, 271
Mexico, 57
Miami, 42, 47
Mildenhall (England), 5, 147
Miller, Marilyn, 67, 69–70, 76
Miranda, Carmen, 227
Mistinguett, 77–78
Mitchell, Harry, 138
Monaco, 5
Monte Carlo, 6, 46
Montgomery, Field Marshal Bernard, 268
Moore, Owen, 75–76
Morgan, Harry Hays, 27, 148
Morgan, J. P., 11
Morrison, Walt, 179
Mosessohn, David, 113–14
Moulson, Tom, 220, 247
Mumm, Baron Walther von, 170, 186, 187
Munro, Jack, 141
Murray, Mae, 34–43, 71, 271
Music Corporation of America, 74
Mussolini, Benito, 215–16
Myberg, Lum, 119, 123–24

National Amateur Championship, 130
National League, 34
National Steeplechase and Hunt Association, 32
Nazis, 170, 211–14, 220, 236, 272
Neil, Edward J., 146, 156–57, 162–64, 167–69, 171, 183, 184, 188, 190
Neil, Herman, 103
Netherland Cup, 83
Netherlands, 57
Newburger, Deputy Police Commissioner, 33
Newell, Cyril, 231

Newell, David, 203
New York City, 30, 46, 58, 112, 114, 140, 146, 149, 191, 204
    Amateur Athletic Union in, 151, 212
    Dillon, Read & Company in, 8–9, 218, 221–22, 261
    Eagan in, 130–31, 133, 142, 211
    Gray in, 74–75, 77, 195, 208
    Grey in, 68, 70, 74
    Nazism of German consul in, 170
    O'Brien in, 32–42, 45, 84, 238
    Rose Fiske in, *194*, 217–18, 227, 230
    Walker as mayor of, 176–77
New York State Education Department, Board of Regents of, 103–5
New York State Legislature, 108, 110–12
New York Stock Exchange, 84
Nicholas I, King of Montenegro, 132
Nicoll, Wilf, 248, 254
Nieminen, Toni, 94
Niven, David, 205, 217
Nordic Games, 56, 87, 109
Norton, Al, 131
Norway, 56, 135, 236
    Winter Olympics teams of, 87–88, 94, 145, 174
Novello, Ivor, 67, 76
Nuremberg Laws, 212

O'Brien, Dolly (Jay's third wife), 43–49, 179, 191, 237–38, 270–71
O'Brien, Jay, 26–27, 29–49, 71, 143, 148, 176–77, 215, 227
    death of, 237–38, 270
    Dewey's antagonism toward, 115–16, 149, 151–53, 155–56, 170
    family background of, 30–31
    gambling of, 32–34, 42, 84
    horse racing by, 29–32
    in 1928 Winter Olympics, *28*, 59–61, *62*, 81–84, 86, 90–92, 99
    in 1932 Winter Olympics, 151–57, 164, 168, 170, 176, 178–79, 187–91, 245
    and 1936 U.S. Olympic bobsled team, 208, 209
    Palm Beach home of, 195, 227
    romances and marriages of, 35–49, 75, 77, 79
O'Brien, Mike, 135
O'Brien, Miles (Jay's father), 30–31
O'Brien, Thomas (Jay's brother), 30–31
O'Dowd, Mike, 133
O'Farrell, Val, 42
O'Hara, Ike, 125
Olavegoya Cup, 55, 83
Oxford University, 135–39, 179, 185, 220

Paige, Woody, 127
Papan, Lieutenant Alexei, 186, 187, 189
Papană, Alexandru, 164
Paramount Pictures, 37
Paris, 55, 60, 74, 81, 84, 148, 236
  Churchill's RAF escort in, 245
  1878 World's Fair in, 16
  Fiske family home in, 11, 12, 26, 148, 202,
    213, 226, 269
  Gray in, 74–78
  Inter-Allied Games, 131
  International Bobsledding and
    Tobogganing Federation congress in,
    115–16
  Jay and Dolly in, 45–47, 49
  1924 Summer Olympics in, 57, 139
Parke, Dick, 59, 85, 86, 92
Patten, Gilbert, 121
Pegler, Westbrook, 142, 156, 169–70, 178, 180,
    181, 185
Phillips, Mollie, 174
Pickford, Jack, 75–76
Pim, Cecil, 55, 86, 91, 92
Pirie, John, 139
Poland, 11–12, 226
  Winter Olympics teams of, 85, 174
Polignac, Marquis de, 57, 59
Poniatowski, Paulette, 215–16
Porter, Fred, 111
Potocki, Prince Alfred, 11
Pryor, Sam, 133, 135

Read, William, 7–9
Reid, Wallace, 39
Rhodes-Moorhouse, Willie, 219, 222, 244, 245,
    250–52, 266
Rice, Earl, 122
Rickard, Tex, 138–39
Riddle, Jack, 246–47
Robertson, Sparrow, 60–61, 79, 81, 82
Robinson, Peter, 247
Roch, Andre, 207–8, 218
Roche, Al, 130
Romania, 57
  1932 Winter Olympics team of, 163, 164,
    186
Roosevelt, Eleanor, 171, 268–69
Roosevelt, Franklin D., 98, 108, 111, 112, 114,
    149, 171, 173–76, 228, 237
Ross, Harold, 207
Rossi, Count, 164, 186, 187
Ross Moore, James, 66, 70–73
Rossner, Heinrich, 167
Rothstein, Arnold "Ace," 33, 34, 42, 84, 177
Rowan, Robert, 206

Royal Air Force (RAF), 219–22, 225, 226, 228–
    40, 242, 243–55, 262, 266
Rubien, Fred, 210
Runyon, Damon, 75, 121, 164, 179–80
Russia, 65, 233, 236
Ruth, Babe, 74
Ryan, Ted, 206, 207, 218

Sangro, Duke of, 59
Saranac Lake Red Devils, 144, 150, 152, 156,
    157, 181, 183, 187–90, 195
Sargent, John Singer, 133
Schatz, John, 179
Schroder, Werner, 165
Scorsese, Martin, 9
Seabury, Samuel, 177
Second World War, 25, 214, 225–40, 243–60,
    269, 272, 273
Selfridge, Harry Gordon, 26
Seth-Smith, Michael, 215
Shea, Jack, 176
Sherrill, General Charles Hitchcock, 116, 212
Sickle, J. Harrington "Pud," 40, 41
Silver, June Grey, 63–65
Sinclair, Archibald, 266–67
Smith, Red, 269
Smith, Wilson, 16
Sørsdal, Sverre, 134
Spears, Edward, 245
Spooner, William, 136
St. Leger Trophy, 55
St. Moritz, 13, 28, 49, 51–60, 80, 115, 207, 209–
    11, 218–20
  Badrutt family hotels in, 15–18
  Billy's English friends from, 219, 230–32,
    239, 245, 266
  Bobsled Club (SMBC) in, 18–27, 28, 53,
    55–57, 59, 83, 220
  bobsled runs in, 19, 272 (see also Cresta Run)
  Fiske family friends from, 201, 203
  1931 World Championship in, 154, 165, 191
  Winter Olympics in, 14, 28, 50, 57–58, 65,
    70–73, 79, 81–94, 99, 146, 149, 150–53,
    165, 174, 176, 178
Stevens, Curtis, 150, 156, 171, 181–83
Stevens, Hubert, 150, 155, 165, 168, 171, 181–
    83, 208, 209
Stevens, Paul, 150, 156, 181, 187–88
Stevens, Raymond, 150, 156
Sullivan, Sport, 34
Summer Olympics, 57, 98, 109, 133–35, 137–
    39, 143, 164, 270
Sweden, 56
  Winter Olympics teams of, 89, 174
Sweeny, Bobby and Charles, 6, 230

Swift, Otis Peabody, 114
Switzerland, 13, 16, 17, 20, 22, 57, 79, 100, 135, 221, 272
   Winter Olympics teams of, 89–90, 157, *160*, 163, 164, 170, 174, 186, 220
   See also St. Moritz
Swope, Herbert, 71

Tammany Hall, 30, 164, 177
Tammen, Harry, 127
Taylor, Bill, 217–18, 230, 268
Taylor, Megan, 174
Thalberg, Irving, 217
Thomas, Olive, 75–76
Thomas, Ralph Hill, 25
Thompson, Denman, 17
Thompson, Mace, 135
Thyssen, Fritz, 213–14
Tierson, Tommy, 125
Tobin, Abe, 120–22, 125, 133
Torrey, H.A.P., 103
Tracy, Spencer, 205
Tucker, Nion, 61, 82, 85, 86, 92
Tully, Jim, 130–31
Tunney, Gene, 59, 131, 142–43, 270
Tyler, Frank, 208

Unger, Donald, 186
United States, 10, 53, 146
   in Second World War, 236–37, 239, 269
   Winter Olympics teams of, 59–61, 81–94, 116, 150–57, 163, 164, 166, 171, 173–79, 183–85, 187–92, 219, 220
United States Olympic Committee, 58–59, 65, 72, 173, 208–14, 219
   and bid for Lake Placid as 1932 Winter Olympics site, 99, 108–9, 115
   selection of 1932 bobsled team by, 115–16, 151–53, 157
Ury, Ralph J., 156

Valentino, Rudolph, 38–39
Vallee, Rudy, 205
Vanderbilt, Virginia, 29–31
Vincent, Arthur "Bunker," 61
Vlora, Princess, 25–27, 34, 83

Walker, Jimmy, 176–79, 191
Wallechinsky, David, 66, 72

Ward, Hamilton, 111
Ward, Patsy, 203, 204, 219, 221
Warwick, Charles Greville, Earl of, 216–18, 233
Warwick, Rose Greville, Countess of, *see* Fiske, Rose Bingham
Waugh, Evelyn, 136
Webb, Spike, 131, 132, 134
Weber, Lois, 203, 204
Webster, Tom, 52
West, Kid, 123
Whelan, Charles and Frank, 78
Whitehead, T. North, 239
Wicks, Karl, 132
Wignall, Trevor, 138
Wilhelm, Crown Prince of Germany, 22, 59
Willard, Jess, 126, 129
Willey, Courtney, 257–59, 273
Wilson, Woodrow, 132
Winant, John, 266
Winter Olympics, 53, 56–57, 63, 73, 94, 166, 270
   1928 (St. Moritz), 59–60, 70, 81–94, 99
   1932, *see* Lake Placid, 1932 Winter Olympics in
   1936 (Garmisch-Partenkirchen), 208–12
   1980 (Lake Placid), 63, 66, 99, 272
   2010 (Vancouver), 53, 166
Wodehouse, P. G., 67–68
Wolfe, Tom, 95
Wong, Ronald, *242*
World War I, 10–11, 22–23, 129, 154, 164, 170, 191, 214, 219, 231
World War II, *see* Second World War

Yale University, 130–33, 135–37, 143, 185

Zahn, Werner, 152–54, 164–68, 171, 174, 180–81, 183, 189–91, 220, 272
Zanuck, Darryl F., 205
Zardini, Sergio, 272
Zentzytzki, Stanislaus, 110, 112, 113, 116, 150–52
Ziegfeld, Florenz, 36, 37, 68–69, 71, 74
Ziegfeld, Patricia, 69
Ziegfeld Follies, 37–39, 68, 71, 75, 205
Zimbalist, Efrem, 65
Zukor, Adolph, 37, 39